SOUTHERN LITERARY STUDIES
Louis D. Rubin, Jr., editor

*From the Sunken Garden*

# From the Sunken Garden The Fiction of Ellen Glasgow, 1916–1945

*Julius Rowan Raper*

**Louisiana State University Press**
BATON ROUGE AND LONDON

Design: Dwight Agner
Typeface: VIP Palatino
Composition: Graphic Composition, Inc.
Printing and Binding: Edwards Brothers

LIBRARY OF CONGRESS CATALOGING IN PUBLICATION DATA
Raper, Julius Rowan, 1938–
   From the sunken garden.

   (Southern literary studies)
   Bibliography: p.
Includes index.
   1. Glasgow, Ellen Anderson Gholson, 1873–1945—
Criticism and interpretation. I. Title
PS3513.L34Z748      813'.5.'2      79–16703
ISBN 0–8071–0653–4

The author gratefully acknowledges permission to reprint material that origi-
nally appeared in the following: "Glasgow's Psychology of Deceptions and
*The Sheltered Life*," *Southern Literary Journal*, VIII (Fall, 1975), 27–38; "Invisible
Things: The Short Stories of Ellen Glasgow," *Southern Literary Journal*, IX
(Spring, 1977), 66–90; "Ambivalence Toward Authority: A Look at Glasgow's
Library, 1890–1906," *Mississippi Quarterly*, XXXI (Winter, 1977–78), 5–16; "The
Landscape of Revenge: Glasgow's *Barren Ground*," *Southern Humanities Review*,
XIII (Winter, 1979), 63–71. Excerpts from novels of Ellen Glasgow are re-
printed by permission of Harcourt Brace Jovanovich, Inc.; copyright 1929,
1932, 1935, 1941 by Ellen Glasgow; copyright 1954, 1957, 1960, 1969 by First
and Merchants National Bank of Richmond; copyright 1926 by Doubleday
Page & Co. Excerpts from *Beyond Defeat* are reprinted by permission of University Press of Virginia, copyright © 1966.

*To F.R.R., K.A.R., and L.R.S.—*
*May you be masters of phantasy—*
*and in memory of J.R.R., Jr.*

# Contents

# A Personal Note

When I began the present study of the fiction Ellen Glasgow wrote after 1913, I fully intended to extend the critical approach previously applied to her earlier works in the book *Without Shelter* (Louisiana State University Press, 1971). There, using the novelist's early books, letters, and related materials, I demonstrated the depth of her original realistic impulse. Consequently, the focus fell upon her commitment to a positivistic concern for the objective surfaces of life in the milieus she knew best. The analysis followed certain dominant biological and cultural themes: conflicts between biology and civilization, problems of freedom and determinism, questions of environment and heredity, and Glasgow's critique of a form of artificial selection she called the sheltered life.

But as I approached the emotional center of the earliest novel considered in the present study, I discovered myself drawn in an opposite direction. I felt my attention passing through the mask of surface reality to the other hemisphere of human truth, the invisible core that seems to drive Glasgow's characters from Gabriella Carr through Roy Timberlake. In one sense, this discovery only recognizes that Glasgow no more escaped the influence of modern psychology than did her later confidant, James Branch Cabell. But that first novel, *Life and Gabriella*, also showed me that the technique Glasgow developed—or stumbled on—for exploring the invisible hemisphere of man's reality differs remarkably from the technique Cabell and other Freudian-minded Americans often employed. Her approach seems solidly rooted in a literary tradition as old as medieval romance, as old even as Homer. By and large, her method avoids the spears, triangles, pens, and pencils that once made Cabell's novels a delight for both censors and Menckenites. In place of the so-called Freudian symbols, Glasgow substitutes a technique combining devices as literary as the foil and the double with a process as psychological as projection—the act by which an individual externalizes or objectifies materials that are primarily subjective. Glasgow's combination permits her to create characters arguably more complex than the tripartite figures of the Freudians. The emergence, development, and perfection of this method provide the unifying thread of *From the Sunken Garden.*

In taking this technique as a focus, I am, I find, looking at one of three dimensions of a process that has long seemed to me the essence of the literary experience: the mystery of how a book can use words in such a way that, in Faulkner's sensitive image, the words themselves eventually, without ceasing, just vanish, and first ghosts, then men and women, living, breathing, take the place of the voice they haunted. I did not become a serious reader until, at sixteen, I met with this mystery in novels by Tolstoy, Dostoevsky, and Wolfe. And for a long while, as I listened to and learned about textures and tensions from the New Critics, I forgot that irrational, unstructured, seemingly indescribable power—even though I sensed it was central to what Aristotle had in mind when he talked about catharsis.

The essay that follows is not, however, a descent into impressionistic or subjective criticism. For Glasgow's later books suggest that the mystery I have in mind may assume three forms. It occurs every time we find ourselves, as readers, swept off our feet and transported into a world of fiction. As we might expect, it may also occur when a novelist sits down to write a story. But, most importantly for this study, the mystery may also exist within the world of the novel; for major characters in Glasgow's fictions are unendingly contaminating people they meet—and care enough about either to hate or to love—with the darkest secrets of their own psyche. Indeed, the secret lives of Glasgow's later characters reveal themselves minute by minute through the phantasies who are the people they think they know. By focusing upon the process as found not in the creator or in the reader but in the creation itself, I have sought to avoid both the Scylla of biographical criticism and the Charybdis of impressionistic analysis, and yet I have left readers who do not fear those two bugaboos a place to stand if they choose to extrapolate.

I wish to thank Louis D. Rubin, Jr., for applying the test of reality to the whole of this study; C. Hugh Holman for his helpful comments on Chapters IV, VII, and VIII; and Edgar E. MacDonald for his seemingly indefatigable interest in Glasgow studies. The secretaries in the Department of English, University of North Carolina, have been indispensable—especially Joyce Bradshaw, Susan de Francesca, Jo Gibson, and Elaine Johnson. JoAnn Rubin typed the final manuscript. The Research Council of the University of North Carolina provided funds for both research and manuscript preparation, for which I am grateful. And, finally, I must express my immense gratitude to my wife, Anne, to Jean Hume Browning, and to numerous other women among my relatives, students, and friends, both here and in Greece, who have contributed—occasionally, without knowing they did so but, more often, by speaking out boldly like Ellen Glasgow before them—to my initiation into what continues to be the greatest of all mysteries.

*From the Sunken Garden*

# Chapter I

# Whose Reality? Problems with Authority (1893–1916)

In "Whispering Leaves," one of Ellen Glasgow's ghost stories, a young girl named Miss Effie comes from the North to her mother's old home on the Rappahannock in Virginia. At one point in the story, after she has been left alone before a mirror that reflects her features as in a fog, she is drawn by a "provocative fragrance, the aroma of vanished springs," out of the house and along a "flagged walk to the sunken garden" beyond the summer kitchen. There she discovers a few old fruit trees, a mist that seems to release "the scent of a hundred springs," and a "starry profusion" of narcissi: "the garden looked as if the Milky Way had fallen over it and been caught in the high grass." Standing thus bewitched, she hears a bell ring, sees a light flash, and turns to find the figure of an old Negro woman "standing motionless under the boughs of a pear-tree." Then, Miss Effie tells us, "in the twilight I saw her eyes fixed upon me . . . with a look of entreaty. . . . While I returned her gaze I felt . . . that she was speaking to me in some inaudible language which I did not yet understand, that she bore a message to me which, sooner or later, she would find a way to deliver." By the time the story ends, the old woman has delivered her message, and Miss Effie has understood it perfectly—despite the fact that the woman has been dead for two years!

On the surface, this is a strange performance, even as a minor work, from the novelist who has been, time and again, called—for lack of a better label—the first realistic novelist of the modern South. But it is not alone among her fictions. She wrote three other ghost stories. Furthermore, two of her novels deal at length with equally abstruse modes of reality. Each novel owes a greater debt to Eastern mysticism or another mode of transcendental idealism than it owes to the pragmatic, commonplace reality that the authority of the material sciences led novelists in the mainstream of modern fiction from Honoré de Balzac through early Norman Mailer to accept.

Both in the ghost stories and in the two novels, a process of contamination has occurred. For Glasgow has proven unfaithful to the intent of that early realist, George Eliot. In Chapter XVII of *Adam Bede*, Eliot promised to make the strongest effort "to give a faithful account of men and things as they have mirrored themselves in my mind" and "to tell you as precisely as I can what that reflection is, as if I were in a witnessbox, narrating my experience on oath." By contrast, Glasgow has allowed her own report to be contaminated by the supernatural in the stories, by transcendental metaphysics in one novel, and by unattached emotion in the other. Although in the novels the distortion may constitute a serious flaw, in the stories contamination by the supernatural becomes itself the foundation for a new fictional technique. This new method eventually afforded the author a way to overcome problems that plagued her life and fiction from about 1904 until 1925. The essence of the struggle lies in shifts in the attitudes she held during those two decades toward authorities of reality, writers ancient and modern who sought to impose their vision, especially their ontology, upon persons who read their words. For Glasgow's early life had created in her an ambivalence toward the most powerful controllers of the Western world picture.

Indeed, her intellect had developed in concert with her rebellion against her family and the traditions of that part of southern society, the upper strata of Richmond, Virginia, to which she belonged.[1] Born April 22, 1873, she was the eighth

1 The biographical account that follows summarizes materials covered in more detail by my *Without Shelter: The Early Career of Ellen Glasgow* (Baton Rouge, 1971), and in my "Ambivalence Toward Authority: A

of ten children (eight of whom lived to maturity) of Francis Thomas Glasgow, a managing director of the Tredegar Iron Works in Richmond, which had a decade earlier been the chief supplier of munitions for Robert E. Lee's Army of Northern Virginia. Francis Glasgow's roots ran back to the Scotch Presbyterians of the Shenandoah Valley. Her mother, born Anne Jane Gholson, was the orphaned daughter of an orphaned mother; but the mother's ties were to many of the oldest families of Tidewater Virginia, including one of the so-called Virginia dynasties, the Randolphs of Turkey Island plantation. During her first fifteen years, Ellen Glasgow, who sometimes called herself Eleanor Anderson Gholson Glasgow, often roamed about the state capitol sector of Richmond or about Jerdone Castle, the family's seven-hundred-acre property located about thirty miles northwest of Richmond. She received almost no formal education, but relatives and tutors taught her to read and write. Her chief childhood activities included storytelling, reading, caring for animals, and listening to quarrels between her temperamentally opposed parents—conflicts often centered, it seems, on her father's interest in women of mixed blood. As late as 1892, evidence suggests that Glasgow's development still remained orthodox for her region; for in August of that year, she scribbled the plea, "Be merciful unto me, O God, be merciful unto me! " in a copy of J. R. MacDuff's *Morning Watches and Night Watches*, which she had been given by an older sister two years before. We do not, of course, know the tone of her comment nor whether it was stimulated by events in her life rather than by the sentiments expressed in MacDuff's book of vigils. It may have been sarcasm, for about this time, still in her late teens, she started a novel and shortly thereafter fell under the guidance of Walter McCormack of Charleston, her sister Cary's

---

Look at Glasgow's Library, 1890–1906," *Mississippi Quarterly*, XXXI (Winter, 1977–78), 5–16. The books marked by Glasgow are in the Glasgow Collection of the Rare Book Room, Alderman Library, University of Virginia.

husband-to-be. McCormack directed her attention to Charles Darwin and other thinkers who would shape her views of man and society. By July, 1893, she had read several of the major works of John Stuart Mill, had acquired Herbert Spencer's *Data of Ethics*, and had begun to revolt against the hard-shell Presbyterianism of her father.

Her interest in modern critical thought hardened quickly to pessimism when, within the period of a few years, she not only endured the pressure of her father's religion but began to experience difficulty hearing, watched her mother die (1893), failed to conclude satisfactorily either of the two novels she had begun, and finally in 1894 learned that Walter Mc-Cormack, for whom she had developed a deep respect and affection, had committed suicide under sordid circumstances while on a business trip to New York. These adversities helped to confirm her commitment to the more strenuous aspects of Darwinian thought. Between 1893 and 1900, she read most of the major works not only of John Stuart Mill and Charles Darwin, but of Herbert Spencer, William K. Clifford, Alexander J. Bain, G. Romanes, Thomas Huxley, and W. E. H. Lecky as well, to mention only the more familiar names. We can sample the flavor of her reading from a few of the scorching passages she marked in *The History of the Rise and Influence of the Spirit of Rationalism in Europe*, a book in which Lecky attacks religions of terror to defend the free intellect. Glasgow's notes show a special interest in Lecky's claims that the greatest human callousness arises when a certain class of men are regarded as "doomed by the Almighty to eternal and excruciating agonies," that Protestantism has made no advance in rationalism over Catholicism, and that the most Protestant nations, Scotland and Sweden, are both below the average morality of European nations as measured by the number of illegitimate births, whereas Switzerland is eminently moral and irreligious. When Lecky describes the fondness of the Church for torture, both here and in the hereafter, Glasgow reveals a special concern for the punishment by unceasing fire of "little children" who die in the mother's womb, infants who, though they had committed no sin, have drawn original sin to them "by their carnal conception and nativity." Indeed, when Lecky leans over backward to list a series of "Christian" virtues, Glasgow takes issue by scribbling the labels "Stoic" or "humanity" in the margin to replace "Christian."[2] Although Lecky saw himself in the tradition of Michel de Montaigne and Edward Gibbon, defending skepticism as the only foundation for toleration, Glasgow's drift is less detached: modern sciences and skepticism afforded the weapons she needed to defend her mind against her father's insistence that she conform to traditional theological authorities.

By the end of 1894, still more than two years before her first novel appeared, she had begun to balance her scientific outlook with an ethic grounded more and more in the Stoicism of Marcus Aurelius and Epictetus. She especially admired Stoic coolness, its detachment from the instability of pleasure, from the vanity of the world's treasures, and from the pernicious nature of passions. This combination of Stoicism with the body of thought called the Darwinian sciences provided the basic intellectual framework of mechanistic determinism, surface realism, and original cultural analysis that marks her first five novels. In her first book, *The Descendant* (1897), where she was obviously working out her own bitterness, the protagonist finds himself in a Darwinian conflict between cultural environment and personal heredity because his egoism or instinct of self-preservation limits him to behavior of a half-savage kind unacceptable to society. In *Phases of an Inferior Planet* (1898), which is, like her first novel, a study of New York's bohemia, her protagonist falls into conflict with civilization at large because social conventions prevent his obeying his own highly developed social instincts. In *The Voice of the People* (1900), her first book set chiefly in Virginia, Glasgow

2 W. E. H. Lecky, *The History of the Rise and Influence of the Spirit of Rationalism in Europe* (2 vols.; New York, 1892), I, 31–37, 150, 184–85, 200, 202, 257, 286, 322, 333, 362–63, 387, 391–92; II, 20, 46, 98, 173.

examined the ways in which rigid attitudes of social class can pervert human nature; and in her story of the Civil War, *The Battle-Ground* (1902), the career of her protagonist suggests that the destruction of hierarchal societies may liberate the finer possibilities of a man—especially if he can fall back upon the support of a stoical woman like the heroine of the book. By *The Deliverance* (1904), her fifth novel, Glasgow had found that in certain cases perversions of human nature by society can be remedied by milder measures than civil war: they can be overcome with human compassion.

Evolutionary theory also stimulated Glasgow's early interest in problems of strict determinism and in evasive idealism. In her first three novels, an irreversible determinism seems in effect: the exercise of individual will proves ultimately futile, though admirable for its stoicism. By *The Deliverance* she had decided that a radical change in environmental forces could significantly alter a character's patterns of conduct, if the original behavior was a result of class conditioning. In attending to the connection between two themes she called the sheltered life and evasive idealism, she developed the distinction that Darwin's chief advocate, Thomas Huxley, made between the savage state of nature and the artificial state of human civilization. Glasgow realized that the sheltering traditions and institutions of man's society often permit him to forget the abyss of savagery over which his civilization is suspended. Though understandable, this evasion is potentially dangerous. In *Phases of an Inferior Planet*, the protagonist withdraws from the savage struggle for life into the shelter of the church, where he carries on a completely hypocritical ministry. In her next three novels, the author was primarily concerned with the unreal world created by the sheltering tradition of the Virginia aristocracy; in *The Deliverance*, the false position of the protagonist's mother, Mrs. Blake, was the most powerful early representation of the pernicious aspects of the sheltered life. In her sixth novel, *The Wheel of Life* (1906), Glasgow used a spinster, Angela Wilde, to illustrate the way in which the

sheltered life may produce feminine invalidism and, consequently, the tyrannical female.

Two additional subjects that Glasgow's early novels extrapo-
lated from evolutionary theory were an understanding of the
pernicious effects a character's uncritical acceptance of hereditary determinism may have on his behavior and a concern for
the dangers of certain forms of sympathy, especially excessive
family feeling and compassion untempered by intelligence.
The latter shows one way in which stoicism reinforced her
scientific outlook.

Although three of these first six novels had New York settings and dealt critically with urban manners and social situa-
tions, all touched forcefully on problems closely associated
with the South: its rigid class attitudes, its often inflexible belief in hereditary determinism, its blind defense of traditional
order and feminine fragility, its uncritical elevation of sentiment and family feeling above reason. In addition, these
books dramatized the South's oppression of its poor whites,
the religious outlooks dominant in the region, the area's defense of slavery, the aristocratic obsession with revenge, the
vulgarity of the new rich after Reconstruction, the defeat of
reform politics by conservative forces, and the inability of the
protected "southern mind" to adjust effectively to the sensual
attraction of a great city.

In short, these early books were critical and realistic without
being slavishly mimetic: they did not merely report on life in
the upper South in the period between 1850 and 1905; they
considered such new possibilities as the reformers, revolu-
tionaries, and liberated women who often stand at the center
of these stories. Although the books thus dramatized social
roles unrepresentative of Glasgow's South, the new possibilities were generally imposed from without by the author as a
*donnée* without which the story could not exist. In other
words, the new possibilities usually did not arise spontaneously from the imagination of an evolving character; they
were not revelatory of a new phase in a growing character's

life; they were simply dimensions of a static character. In the one exception to these generalizations, Glasgow found it impossible to handle the emerging phase of her heroine's development because the character was too autobiographical: Glasgow did not fully understand the exigencies of her own personality at the time.

The problem began to develop in *The Wheel of Life*. The reasons for this are complex. During the fruitful six years (1899–1905) immediately prior to this book, Glasgow found herself involved in the most devastating of her three important affairs, a sometimes ecstatic romance with a married man she later called Gerald B. Gerald B. has been variously identified as a figment of her imagination; as another woman; as a middle-aged New York aurist, H. Holbrook Curtis (1856–1920); as an important New York neurologist, Pearce Bailey (1865–1922); and as the fiction editor of Bobbs-Merrill, Hewitt Hanson Howland. Although some of these possibilities need not exclude one another, recent evidence points to Howland (1863–1944), a more-or-less self-made man who took Glasgow's own publisher, Walter Hines Page, to be his model as man of letters. In 1903, in the middle of the period in which Glasgow may have been in love with Howland, his wife of fifteen years, the daughter of a wealthy wholesale coffee merchant from Indianapolis, sued for divorce on grounds that he had failed to provide economic support. By the end of 1905, according to Glasgow's account, the author had suffered the worst of her emotional pain (caused by whichever candidate might have been Gerald B.) and had begun to recover—with support from the sacred books of the East.

*The Wheel of Life* attempts to treat this experience in fictional form. In the novel we find a major character, probably the author's spokesman, who has, the narrator tells us, achieved the "ultimate essence of knowledge," a level of vision at which the personal self passes suddenly into the permanent universal consciousness. Moreover, in a period of profound stress brought on by the collapse of her engagement, the heroine finds herself staring at a small blue flower "until there

[is] revealed to her . . . the essence of the flower which [is] its
soul. And this essence of the flower [comes] suddenly in contact with the dead soul within her bosom, while she [feels]
again the energy which is life flowing through her body." The
exhaustive analysis devoted to this sort of experience distracts
from an otherwise good study of society and finally convinces
no reader who is not inclined toward mystical moments.[3] The
equally abstruse book that followed, *The Ancient Law* (1908),
also resorts to a force larger than life and seemingly outside
the characters to solve the chief problems of the novel. It
speaks of a strange illumination that surrounds and transfig-
ures the "ordinary daytime ugliness" of "each common fact"
to reveal "the secret of immortality." Through this "light of
love," the protagonist reaches a "new sense of security, of rec-
onciliation, that his life [has] again been taken out of his
hands and adjusted without his knowledge."[4] The novel attempts to use this aura of unattached light and love to sweep
the reader away in a mist of floating sentiment. Against both
of these novels, written at the start of the second decade of
Glasgow's career, one might bring the charge generally lev-
eled against works using any sort of deus ex machina to re-
solve the conflict: solutions must arise out of the characters
and by a process the work makes probable; they must not arrive from out of the sky or from off stage. Modern readers
generally are no more receptive to free-floating universal con-
sciousnesses and infinite immortal love than they would be to
Athena or Apollo—no matter how earnest the author in evok-
ing such powers.

Glasgow eventually saw the weakness of the two books and
omitted them from her collected editions, but in 1906 and
1908 she was altogether earnest in her attempts to found her
vision in one sort of transcendental reality or the other. This
effort led both to her abortive engagement, between 1906 and
1909, to Frank Ilsley Paradise, a roving Episcopal minister and

---

3 For a fuller discussion, see Raper, *Without Shelter*, 219–20.
4 Ellen Glasgow, *The Ancient Law* (New York, 1908), 135, 233, 483.

author, and to a fallow phase in her career, for she did not reach her full power again until *The Miller of Old Church* (1911) and *Virginia* (1913). The problem that surfaced in this way had roots we can trace through her readings back to the works of the Stoics. Her markings reveal an early interest in the dual reality implicit in Marcus Aurelius' concept of a *daemon*, an intelligence, a diety within us that keeps us uncontaminated by pleasure, pain, or insult. She noted his advice that we "live with the Gods" by doing all that our daemon, guardian, and guide from Zeus wishes; our daemon is our understanding and reason, our part in the divine whole.[5] In Epictetus, she remarked that all things in the Heraclitean flux dissolve into the primeval fire where Zeus is alone, and that our soul is immortal. These notations, some of them dated, reveal that by no later than 1901 she strongly desired to fit herself into the ordering of "the All," the "Universal," the "Whole"—the cosmic structure the Stoics called Zeus—although the urge did not begin to dominate her fiction for another five years.[6]

Further along the same line, her annotations dated 1903 in Annie Besant's translation of the *Bhagavad-Gita* show her eager to consider a philosophy that promises the peace of the eternal to those who will renounce all works of desire and relinquish the fruit of actions. This search indicated she had come a long way from her early apprenticeship to Spencer, Darwin, Lecky, and their group.

But there is a thread that runs through the decade from 1893 to 1903 and ties the extremes of her intellectual interests together. Her readings both in science and in wisdom literature reveal, even more than a disinterested pursuit of truth, a constant search for authority, a compelling need for a source of

5 Marcus Aurelius, *The Thoughts of the Emperor Marcus Aurelius Antoninus*, trans. George Long (Philadelphia, n.d.), Books II, 9, 17; III, 3, 4, 10, 12; V, 27; VI, 2; VII, 34, 61; VIII, 5; XII, 3, 30, 36.
6 Epictetus, *The Teaching of Epictetus*, trans. T. W. Rolleston (New York, 1889), pp. xxiv, xxvi, and Books I, i: 3–5; II, v: 4; III, ii: 4; V, xxvi.

knowledge to be used, first, against the canonical arguments
of her father and, later, to fill the void created when she rejected her father's traditions. In her quest for authority it was
inevitable that Spencer and Darwin would give way to works
like the *Bhagavad-Gita*, for the fiats of natural processes seem
shadowy indeed compared with the promise of an authority
that is before and behind nature. And Glasgow seems to have
been willing to obey when Krishna commanded total surrender: "On Me fix thy mind; be devoted to Me; sacrifice to Me;
prostrate thyself before Me; harmonized thus in the SELF,
thou shalt come unto Me, having Me as thy supreme goal."
Nor did her markings register any protest when Krishna offered himself as the source of pure knowledge, the "one indestructible Being . . . seen in all beings."[7]

During the first decade of the twentieth century, Glasgow's
heady pursuit of an absolute Being superior to all beings continued to pull her through the most esoteric mysteries of
Plato, Plotinus, Baruch Spinoza, Immanuel Kant, and Johann
Fichte, plus a number of contemporary heirs to these giants of
the spirit, including F. H. Bradley, Josiah Royce, and a lesser
light, Edward Carpenter. Throughout her texts by these men
we can trace her yearning for a state of mystic oneness, the
cosmic or universal consciousness in which, according to Carpenter, "the knower, the knowledge, and the thing known are
once more one."[8] But all her experiments to work her new vision of an absolute reality beyond this world into her fiction
led only to dead ends. For, having lost her moorings in the
concrete reality of her scientific masters, she continued to
have difficulty with dramatically unjustified metaphysics or
extraneous emotions through her second decade as a novelist.
Even the later chapters of the otherwise brilliant *Virginia*
(1913) suffer from a feeling of unattached pity for the title

7 *Bhagavad Gita; or, The Lord's Song*, trans. Annie Besant (London, 1896),
  IX, 34; XVIII, 20.
8 Edward Carpenter, *The Art of Creation: Essays on the Self and Its Powers*
  (New York, 1904), 51, 55, 79, 102, 105, 218; F. H. Bradley, *Appearance
  and Reality* (London, 1906), 3, 6, 136, 173, 298, 447–48.

character, who in the early sections was presented from a coolly satirical point of view. Much of the softness near the end of *Virginia* may arise from emotions released in Glasgow by the death in 1911 of her dearest sister, Cary McCormack. After Cary died, Glasgow took an apartment in New York. She still felt estranged from her father, and she lived in New York, for the most part, until he died in 1916; then she returned to the family home, One West Main Street, in Richmond.

*Life and Gabriella* grew out of her years in New York. In this novel and in the ghost stories of 1916, a solution began to emerge to the central problem—how, in fiction, to handle large powers and emotions that seem to come from outside the characters and take authority over their lives. To put it simply, Glasgow began to locate the source of such invisible powers no longer in the transcendental world, but in the human psyche. Like Miss Effie in "Whispering Leaves," her later characters see ghosts or experience cosmic powers or accept the peace of absolutes, not because such forces come from without to take over their lives, but because such forces mirror their fears or complement their needs. Her own pursuit of authority had taught her that ghosts, powers, and absolutes are simply the misunderstood yet essential phantasies people, in life and in fiction, create to satisfy their needs and to confess their fears. Between 1913 and 1923, she learned that even though *fantasies* are fanciful illusions, *phantasies*, in the root sense of their Greek name, are images that "show forth" the otherwise hidden motions of the soul.

Although the exposition of her solution constitutes much of the essay that follows, clues to the ultimate nature of the answer she reached can be found in two works she read and marked as early as 1905. In Edward Carpenter's discussion of Plato in *The Art of Creation*, she noted the following explanation of the irrational power some individuals have over others: "The strange psychology of passion" is "only explicable by the fact that we bear in our bodies the experience and memory of countless beings, who, having witnessed or embodied the same action from opposite sides, transmit to us" an intense magnetism or multiplied hatred of it. Love, for example, is a reminiscence, a vision opening up of the celestial world remembered from ages past. A face is familiar, and fascinating, because it recalls a "God seen long ago, or far down in the mirror of the mind."[9] In Plato's suggestion that we continually color the world outside us with subjective content lies an explanation, suitable for treatment in modern fiction, of the irrational forces that overpowered the books of her second decade as author.

But since Plato's archetypes are not without difficulties for the modern imagination, Carpenter should be supplemented with passages she marked about 1903 in Maurice Maeterlinck's *Wisdom and Destiny*. Maeterlinck writes: "Let us always remember that nothing befalls us that is not of the nature of ourselves. . . . Whether you journey to the end of the world or merely walk round your house, none but yourself shall you meet on the highway of fate." Judas meets Judas; Socrates, Socrates. Sometimes it is ourselves, sometimes our potential we find, according to Maeterlinck, projected upon the world without. In either case, the thrust of his position as a ground for fiction becomes most apparent from his (heavily marked) discussion of Emily Brontë—especially in the attention he pays to one uncanny assertion Cathy makes in *Wuthering Heights*: "I *am* Heathcliff."[10] If so, then it is theoretically possible to write a novel in which all the characters mirror needs and fears of a single person—possible to create a truly psychological novel, without the imposition of esoteric symbols and without the fuzziness of unjustified metaphysics or unattached emotion. But it took Glasgow twenty years to master the technique, as she did in *Barren Ground* (1925), and another year, until *The Romantic Comedians* (1926), to perfect it.

The study that follows recounts the struggle through which Glasgow developed the method of characterization that marks

9 Carpenter, *The Art of Creation*, 129, 164, 239.
10 Maurice Maeterlinck, *Wisdom and Destiny*, trans. Alfred Sutro (New York, 1903), 31, 81, 280, 302–13.

her major phase, 1925–1932; it also describes the rather rapid decline in her powers during the next decade. To appreciate fully the achievement of her best period, it is necessary to understand the difficulties that continued to plague her during the decade from 1913 to 1923. For her poorest work fell around 1918, when Howland remarried; Walter Hines Page, her early publisher, died; and rumors of her current fiancé's wartime flirtation with Queen Marie of Rumania caused the author to attempt suicide. In this period, Glasgow continued to reach out for new supports and authorities, an urge that eventually led her to seek help from modern psychology, where she seems to have confronted deeper levels of herself. Until the source of her unwitting need for authority was understood, it marred her fiction by diverting her stories from their true center in the inward needs, fears, and powers of her characters. Nowhere is Glasgow's thinly disguised need for external support more apparent than in *Life and Gabriella*, a book that, at the same time, demonstrates the limits of the sort of realistic novel she was still seeking to write in 1915.

# Chapter II

# The Limits of Realism: *Life and Gabriella* (1916)

*Life and Gabriella* is better read today, not for what it achieved, but for what it augured about Ellen Glasgow's subsequent career. Prior to *Gabriella* (1916), though basically a realist, Glasgow had constructed each of her ten novels either around a romantic plot, or with romantically vivid characters at the core, or by using both romantic plot and romantic characters. In *Virginia* (1913), the excellent novel immediately before *Gabriella*, she had gone beyond her earlier dependence upon love stories as vehicles for cultural criticism by writing as realistically as she could about a proper southern lady who believes, as her education prepared her to believe, that marriage is the solution to all the questions in a lady's life; a woman who lives, unfortunately, well beyond the marriage with which romantic melodramas often end to learn that marriage creates more problems than it solves. But Virginia herself remains romantic, and it is from the sentiment and humor inspired by her soft heart and benighted mind that the delight of the novel flows. In *Gabriella*, Glasgow took the inevitable next step toward a novel of pure realism down the zigzag road that she had been traveling for twenty years: she wrote as realistically as she could about a woman who generally lives as realistically as she can. But in doing so, Glasgow produced one of the dullest stories she would ever create. It proves the point Frank Norris made when he defended the excesses of his naturalism: some romantic element is essential to fiction. Still, the ways Glasgow and Gabriella react to the burden of reality are not without interest, especially as precursors of similar struggles in the books the novelist would publish between 1922 and 1941.

*Gabriella* comes from the decade when Glasgow was most wrapped up in the feminist movement, and its didactic portrait of a liberated woman seems to have been intended to satisfy the requirements of contemporary saint making rather than the criteria of literary judgment. Even so, Henry James, more than three decades earlier, had created in *The Portrait of a Lady* the literary model of a modern woman against which Glasgow's novel must be judged. If James's Isabel Archer seeks romance, freedom, and experience, in that order, while Gabriella Carr pursues reality, experience, and love, the two works still have the main focus in common: both use the resources of critical realism to create a full-length portrait of a liberated, self-realizing American woman. But the tedium of each book emerges from this commitment to an exhaustively realistic analysis of a single character. On the other hand, the power and the aesthetic distinction of each novel derives from the unique way each transcends the limits of the realistic method: James speaks of the hidden interior of his heroine; Glasgow turns her heroine inside out.

With this single nonrealistic exception, every essential element of *Gabriella* supports the thematic movement, which carries the title character, the table of contents makes clear, from "the age of faith" to "the age of knowledge." This process of development had served as the chief structural principle of American realistic fiction since Christopher Newman emerged from the chrysalis of innocence in James's *The American*. The time of Glasgow's novel is contemporary, from the middle 1890s to the early 1910s. The place consists for the most part of settings already made real in her earlier books: the gloomy Victorian parlors of Richmond, the bright new-money dining rooms of New York, a shabby apartment on the West Side, a more homelike house on Twenty-third Street. To these are added two establishments in which the resourceful heroine strives for financial independence: a respectable Rich-

mond dry goods store and Madame Dinard's, a fashionable
New York dress shop.

The action chronicles stages of feminine development also
familiar from Glasgow's previous books: the illusion of love
that leads to marriage and the disillusionment that comes
when the bride awakens to the husband's faithlessness and
general worthlessness. To these *Gabriella* adds two other
phases, which will become obligatory in many of Glasgow's
mature and woman-centered works. In the first, Gabriella
rises from her period of disenchantment through a Horatio
Alger–like commitment to hard work and success. ("It's over-
coming that really matters, nothing else," she asserts in a self-
justifying moment.[1]) In the second of the new phases, Gabriella at her thirty-seventh birthday passes through a
middle-life crisis in which she decides that, by devoting all
her energies to keeping her two children and herself finan-
cially independent, she has missed life and been defeated
(366–67). The focus falls upon this late-thirties crisis (a phase
through which the author had been and still was passing in
her life). In a chronicle covering eighteen years of Gabriella's
development (from age twenty to thirty-eight), about two-
fifths of the book explores the year that starts with the self-
doubt of her thirty-seventh birthday and ends with the adjustment she makes a week after her thirty-eighth birthday.
For reasons that have nothing to do with realistic fiction, this
is by far the most intriguing section of the novel, as we shall
see.

The point of view, style, and characters, however, are—
given Glasgow's commitment to realism—more predictable.
Despite the focus on Gabriella's mind, Glasgow stretches the
point of view to penetrate any character's mind that might
add to our understanding of the central character's situation;
in this way, mystery is sacrificed to instruct the reader. The

1 Ellen Glasgow, *Life and Gabriella: The Story of a Woman's Courage* (New
York, 1916), 474. This novel will be cited hereafter in the text by page
number only.

various styles seem equally informative and unintriguing. The levels of diction in the dialogue are dictated as much by class as by character, so that the speech of Gabriella's well-bred children is often over-Anglicized. Because there is not much action to narrate, many of the descriptions turn into social commentary or into abstract character analysis. Abstract values and principles may seem, on first thought, strange elements to find in a novel so imbued with the colors of realism, given the movement's positivistic roots; but the abstractions invoked generally belong to a small body of virtues and vices that Glasgow apparently had decided were pragmatically (if not scientifically) verifiable either in her own experience or as mainstays of the American reality. A good deal of the talk has to do with Gabriella's values, which progress as she matures from a longing for love to the pursuit of culture and finally to an interest in character (427). At the center of her conscious picture of herself stands the familiar vein of iron. At first this is an inflexible, even militant ancestral voice, "the Berkeley conscience," but during her marital and economic struggles, it develops into a moralized mode of endurance and resistance: "Thanks to the vein of iron in her soul she would never—no, not if she died fighting—become one of the victims of life" (30, 188, 242). As Gabriella contemplates her eventual success, the moral abstractions flow as thickly as in an Alger novel or in *Robinson Crusoe* itself: "By patience, by hard work, by self control, by ceaseless thought, and by innumerable sacrifices, she had made herself indispensable" (355). For the most part, abstract vices are reserved for the males, especially George Fowler. The man she marries, Fowler is over and over again utterly selfish, a spendthrift governed by "the trivial and commonplace quality of his soul" (87). Such rationalized vices and virtues serve too often as the springs of action and could, if pressed hard enough, turn the book, for all its realistic surface, into melodrama.

An element of irony saves *Gabriella*, however, from the simplemindedness of sexist melodrama; for the vices and virtues, the successes and failures, and the sexes get scrambled as the book moves along. In a fashion predictable from Glasgow's earlier work, the women arrange themselves at familiar poles: those who point righteously to their lifelong faithfulness have to acknowledge that their goodness has made them victims of the husbands for whom they sacrificed themselves; those who triumph over life and males, like Madame Dinard and Gabriella's rival, voluptuous Florrie Spencer, do so by exploiting their sensuality and by refusing to think in moral categories (492–93). Men provide parallel cases: the good ones either remain mother- and tradition-bound and cease to develop, like Gabriella's first love, Arthur Peyton, or grow repulsively fat, bald, and "empurpled" through their success, like the forceful Judge Crowborough (359–60, 515). The men who inspire romantic passion, like George Fowler, are themselves eventually destroyed by their passion for women and alcohol—a fate Glasgow deals out with less irony than righteousness.

When not contaminated by moralizing, the doublethinking of irony represents a significant advance over the one-dimensionality of melodrama. But no matter how appropriate for the rationalizing tendencies of realism, thinking in paradox, or through dichotomies and polarities, does not escape the shortcoming that besets all reductive thought: neither the two dimensions of a dichotomy nor the continuum posited by polarities can adequately deal with the spherical and changing nature of truth, which—if it exists at all—has become for the modern mind "that which most contradicts itself in time."[2] Indeed, it was the pursuit of the multiple and nonrational dimensions of human truth that ultimately caused the obsolescence of the surface realism codified by William Dean Howells and practiced by the young Glasgow.

The struggle to get beyond the rational surfaces of realism, with its commitment to the "natural phenomena or properties of knowable things," has led novelists since Henry James (including Marcel Proust, D. H. Lawrence, James Joyce, Virginia

2 One of Balthazar's axioms in Lawrence Durrell's *Balthazar*.

Woolf, William Faulkner, Samuel Beckett, Alain Robbe-Grillet, Michel Butor) through a fascinating chain of technical experiments. Many of these have been fruitful, some merely interesting, and others incredibly dull. To appreciate James's contribution without going into problems of the central intelligence or the internal monologue, let us simply acknowledge that as early as *The Portrait of a Lady* James was aware of a realm beneath the conscious mind of Isabel Archer, between which hidden core and her surface life little or no intercourse existed; and let us further note that to suggest the contents of this hidden world James invented a chain of symbolic images, including closed edifices, keys, flashing lights, chariots, horses, and wings, which pass through the character's mind and which he carefully structures to create a dramatic landscape *within* the portrait of his lady. Since James, Freudian psychology has, of course, provided ample support for the verbal and imagistic tricks he used to explore the reality within. And yet the symbolic method still fails to convince the common sense of many readers.[3] Perhaps the skepticism of the uninitiated should be given some consideration. Endowing mere verbal objects with so much significance—often greater meaning than the actions of the characters themselves—does, on reflection, smack of fetishism, not to mention an artifice more appropriate to literature than to the life we know outside novels and psychology books. Without denying the usefulness and beauty of the symbolic method, we may nevertheless admit that a more convincing (because less embarrassingly artificial) method for exploring the hidden reality may exist.

The alternative is to turn characters inside out, so that the needs and fears which drive them reveal themselves to the

3 I refer to the eternal sophomore who refuses to be either cajoled or intimidated into the literary way of thinking. James writes as follows about Isabel's hidden dimension: "Isabel had in the depths of her nature an even more unquenchable desire to please than Edith; but the depths of this young lady's nature were a very out-of-the-way place, between which and the surface communication was interrupted by a dozen capricious forces." *The Portrait of a Lady* (Cambridge, Mass., 1956), 40.

light of day. In this way the author avoids the awkwardness of probing with symbols beneath opaque surfaces. This projection outward of inner reality is a process so natural to life that it may escape the notice of critics when it occurs in literature. For example, according to E. R. Dodds, non-Mediterranean readers may have often been naive not to recognize that Homer intended his deities and spirits, among other things, as a device for dramatizing the psychological drives of his human characters. Along the same line, the medieval quest tales have apparently preserved through centuries of monotheism the major pattern of personality development once celebrated in polytheism, a pattern preserved even in our century by Jungian dreamwork.[4] In both cases, the forces working within the character have been projected outward upon archetypal figures. And if myth and romance were thus the verbal cinema of the prerational mind, the cinema and television of our own age of disbelief have created, from Rudolph Valentino and Theda Bara, through Babe Ruth, Frank Sinatra, and Franklin D. Roosevelt, Elvis Presley and Marilyn Monroe, to John F. Kennedy and the Beatles, the mythologies of the postrational mind. To understand the deep needs and anxieties of the age, we often study popular culture as the clearest externalization of those drives.

And, as *Gabriella* shows, even in the short-lived age of real-

---

4 E. R. Dodds, building on the work of the German scholar, M. P. Nilsson, argues as follows: "Ought we not perhaps to say . . . that the divine machinery 'duplicates' a psychic intervention—that is, presents it in a concrete pictorial form? This was not superfluous; for only in this way could it be made vivid to the imagination of the hearers. The Homeric poets were without the refinements of language which would have been needed to 'put across' adequately a purely psychological miracle. . . . I suggest that in general the inward monition, or the sudden unaccountable feeling of power, or the sudden unaccountable loss of judgment, is the germ out of which the divine machinery developed." Or again: "If character is knowledge, what is not knowledge is not part of the character, but comes to a man from outside. . . . Unsystematised, nonrational impulses, and the acts resulting from them, tend to be excluded from the self and ascribed to an alien origin." E. R. Dodds, *The Greeks and the Irrational* (Berkeley, 1968), 14, 17. For further suggestions, see David L. Miller, *The New Polytheism* (New York, 1974), 51–63.

istic fiction, reality was not enough—at least, one reality alone was not. For Glasgow treats the male characters in this book in a manner which suggests that, if the world beneath the skies and that behind the eyes are the two hemispheres of spherical truth, a mirror relationship nonetheless exists between the two; this mirror effect not only contaminates the facts of life with subjective content but also exposes the impotence of facts to satisfy human needs. And Glasgow employs both this inadequacy and this contamination of external reality to turn her heroine inside out. Because Gabriella is too skeptical for myth or romance and too provincial for contact with mass culture, she projects her needs and anxieties upon the only creatures she knows who seem to possess magical powers—men.

Early in the novel, Glasgow suggests, through the use of mirrors, the complicated sexual relationships she will explore. Gabriella is preparing for an evening with her fiancé Arthur Peyton, a comfortable male fixture of tradition-bound Richmond society. She has made up her mind to break the engagement, for she has convinced herself she must go to work to support her sister, whose husband has just been discovered making love to his wife's French dressmaker. But Gabriella has other, less altruistic motives, we learn during the scene that follows. As she brushes her hair, she sees a self with two dimensions in the mirror: "Beneath the charm of the face . . . [and] the fine, clear lines of her head and limbs . . . there was a strength and vigour which suggested *a gallant boy rather than the slighter and softer frame of a girl*" (31, italics added). Like her mother and sister, she might enjoy a sheltered and wholly ladylike existence, but none of them can afford it. Like the others, she possesses a nonfeminine dimension beneath the softness and will to incompetence: the Berkeley conscience, the vein of iron that keeps her resolute (30). And it is the mask of this male ancestor her face wears when she decides to break her engagement (32). This first look in the mirror establishes that the sexes are to be joined here in a fashion less sexual than psychological, that the heroine will prove capable of forms of behavior generally reserved for males.

As the scene continues, she gazes in the mirror a second time, but the face she sees now is neither her own nor Arthur Peyton's. Instead, "she saw it take form there as one sees a face grow gradually into life from the dimness of dreams. It was, she told herself to-night, the very face of her dream that she saw" (32). Gabriella's imagination thus turns her inside out: by revealing her secret desire, it shows that her present situation does not satisfy her. Gradually this imagined face will be rejoined with the man who originally inspired her dream, George Fowler; and the novel will proceed, not as an analysis of dreams through symbols, but as a straightforward story—one dramatizing why the new reality (into which she pursues the image of her desire) cannot satisfy all her dreams, or her needs, any more than committing herself to Arthur's world would have.

When Gabriella tears herself away from the mirror and crosses to the parlor to talk with Arthur, we discover he also has been mirror gazing. She surprises him just as he instinctively lifts his hand to smooth down an imaginary lock of his carefully brushed hair and frowns slightly at himself (33). This is vanity, to be sure, but the use of so many mirrors in rapid succession underscores the point that both parties are given to vanity of a complicated and significant sort. They may be engaged to one another, but each is more profoundly engaged to him- or herself: they may stare into one another's eyes, but the image each sees, as in the mirror, is likely to be that of his or her own face, or rather the reflection of a personal need. Arthur, for his part, is seeking in Gabriella a substitute for his first love, his mother, whom he cannot abandon even to marry. He thus idealizes Gabriella into someone like his mother, a "lady," "something essentially starlike and remote": "His mind was so constructed that he was able, without difficulty, to think of [Gabriella] as corresponding to this exalted type of her sex. By the simple act of falling in love with her he had endowed her with every virtue except the ones that she

actually possessed" (36–37). Gabriella's dissatisfaction with
Arthur indicates clearly that she has outgrown her childhood
dream of becoming a lady and the companion of an aristocratic, sensitive, pliable, but tradition-bound man like Arthur.
In short, her imagination is driving her beyond Richmond,
her childhood world (32–34).

Her subsequent relationships with men will elaborate the
pattern established in these early mirror passages: her sexual
encounters will trigger dreams of new possibilities, of a new
reality, a new life to live; she will pursue or be pursued by the
new possibilities until she has either reclaimed the longed-for
qualities as her own or exhausted them; then she will either
become disillusioned with the man or simply outgrow him. In
either case, she will discover that her present reality is not
enough and will, by dreaming new dreams, transcend it. Gabriella thus develops by taking into her own repertoire traits
she only notices after she has projected them out of herself
and onto another person. It is a complex process in which
phantasy becomes as compelling a test of reality as reality
was a test of phantasy in the earlier books. For phantasy
shows her the way she must grow.

In contrast to the reasonable, safe, static world offered by
Arthur Peyton, the face in the mirror—that of George
Fowler—promises Gabriella passion and change and an element of forbidden risk, irrational qualities she needs to derail
her life from the predictable track it appears set to follow. The
crisis in her sister's marriage provides the catalyst, the alibi
(self-sacrifice), and just enough disorder to leave Gabriella
free to change tracks. But the job she takes as saleswoman to
support her sister and mother can only be, given the forces
sleeping within her, a transitional solution. It simply opens
Cinderella to the prince's inevitable return. For both Gabriella
and George have been enchanted by their brief encounters:
George because he is easily charmed and Gabriella because
she needs someone different. That Gabriella can neither justify nor resist her passion may indicate that passion is a dimension of her spirit she has previously repressed (41).

When Fowler, a transplanted Virginian living in New York, hears of her situation and returns to Richmond, she responds more to forces at work in herself than to his person: "She hardly [hears] his words because of the divine tumult in her brain." She is "suddenly alive with ecstasy." She compares his face with that in her dreams but finds them different: his is "younger, gayer, more intensely vivid." Indeed, in the language of a romantic love story, "he [is] adventure, he [is] the radiant miracle of youth! " But Glasgow is never so at ease with love talk that she uses it without an ulterior motive. Here the heightened language indicates that what Gabriella sees and feels comes more from needs within herself than from Fowler; to her, "he [is] not only a man, he [is] romance." The heroine's desire for romance, Glasgow didactically warns us, has blinded her to "the trivial and commonplace quality of his soul" (87). The remainder of the novel supports the validity of her yearning for an alternative to Arthur Peyton, Richmond, and lady-dom; but it also shows the error of projecting that need upon an unworthy object like Fowler.

Gabriella enters the realm into which Fowler carries her with "a sense of lightness and wonder, as if she were driving in a world of magic toward ineffable happiness" (125). The plutocratic regions of New York City embody the values she willfully embraced when she went into business. But on Fifth Avenue she soon discovers the monotony and ugliness of those "depressing examples in brownstone of an architecture which, like George, was trying rather vaguely to express nothing" (126). Although many of the people inhabiting this strange land are pleasant enough, the milieu appears most perfectly embodied in the very wealthy Judge Crowborough, a tall, florid, turkey gobbler of a man with an "immense paunch flattened by artificial devices," "a hooked nose, where the red was thickly veined with purple, and protruding lips over square yellow teeth that gripped like the teeth of a bulldog" (144, 154).

This distaste for the judge Gabriella comes shortly to feel for Fowler himself. After four months of marriage, her love grows

"less passionate and more maternal," a response George plays
for with his charm and weakness, as he was encouraged to do
in his childhood relation with his mother (174, 182). Then, on
the night Gabriella has prepared herself to break the news of
her first pregnancy, George stumbles into her room drunk and
collapses there like some stranger. Her response now is to reject, with hysteria, the "very core of her nature," the longing
to be loved, as well as the man in whose eyes she first saw
mirrored that hidden self (120). She reverts to the righteous
hardness of the familiar Berkeley conscience, a change more
moral than wise: "How could she possibly have tenderness for
a man who had . . . become so lost to common decency that
he could let her see him revoltingly drunk?" (180). It would
appear that George's real character has proved as firm a check
upon Gabriella's phantasy of love as that phantasy had once
proved to Arthur Peyton's reality. But because Gabriella never
convinces the reader that George is as worthless as she makes
him out to be (she herself later has second thoughts), the
reader concludes that the severity of her judgment may provide a measure of the degree to which she senses her own
responsibility for her unfortunate marriage (284). Her con-
demnation of George forestalls the necessity of acknowledging her earlier blindness. She still sees George through a
veil of passion—only now it is her self-disgust rather than affection that colors his reality. Under this new illusion, she decides, after a few months of marriage, that love is over forever
(208). Even though during the next seven years she gives
George a second child before he finally runs off with one of
her blonder and plumper friends, her righteousness dominates their relationship. Ultimately, George becomes as
worthless in fact as he was in her fancy.

Abandoned with two children to support, Gabriella moves
from the cautionary to the exemplary phase of her life. Here
the masculine side of her personality reigns supreme: qualities associated with her Berkeley vein of iron are transformed
first into a resistance to resignation and to weakness and later
into economic self-reliance (242). Working hand-in-glove with

both her southern aristocratic appearance and principles and with the yearning after commercial values she had once projected upon George and his milieu, this hardness assures her economic survival and commercial ascent in Madame Dinard's dress shop. But if the story of a female Alger was ever very interesting, it is today less dull only than the legends of her male prototype. In this middle part of the novel, her struggle is against social and economic traditions rather than with herself; and such struggles, as William Butler Yeats said, are what produce rhetoric rather than poetry (in this case, rather than psychological drama). Even so, there are brief moments of weakness or doubt. For example, the visit of Dr. French, a young man with a pale, ascetic face and "the flame-like enthusiasm of the visionary in his eyes," puts Gabriella on the defensive against her more passionate self (309–10). But usually she sees her romantic drives and her feeling for people outside the family reflected in the frivolity of her daughter and in the social concern of her son, respectively. In each case she is able to control the force threatening her through her offspring, because it is external rather than hidden within a recess of her own personality.

The strange interest she begins to take after her thirty-seventh birthday in the once repulsive Judge Crowborough provides a more remarkable case of weakness, one that marks the beginning of her severe middle-age crisis of self-doubt. After ten years of working for Madame Dinard, she feels she should buy the shop and run it herself, but she needs an investor. She hesitates for three months, however, before calling on the judge. He is still hideous to look at, but because her needs are different, she chooses to look beneath the man's surface. There she sees the complement of her frustrated ambition: she feels "the tremendous power of his personality," which triumphs "over the corporeal mass of his body" (358–60). His force leads her to project upon him masculine qualities she misses from her dead father and from the husband who behaved like a son. For her, the judge is someone "bigger and stronger" from whom she can ask advice, someone "to adjust her perplexities": "She felt again that absolute reliance on the masculine ability to control events, to ease burdens, to remove difficulties, which had visited her in her childhood. . . . 'It's wonderful how men manage things,' she thought. 'It's wonderful being a man. Everything is so simple for men'" (361). Behind his paternal smile she senses "the acuteness and activity of his mental processes," which contrast delightfully with "the loose reasoning and the muddled thinking of all the women she met in the course of her work." Her will to feminine weakness remains so strong that she finds "a positive pleasure in following the exactness and inflexibility of his logic." She would submit her will without hesitation to this man who is "efficiency incarnate" (362). Although Gabriella is eager to accept psychological aspects of woman submitting to male authority, she finds herself unprepared for the physical concomitants, perhaps because they remind her of her previous defeat by sex; and the judge ruins the relationship by sealing their agreement with an affectionate embrace rather than a manly shake. That her awe before his power so easily reconverts into disgust at the vanity of men in general suggests how largely her brief admiration of the tycoon was an illusion bred out of personal need. She expected the judge to treat her as he would a gentleman, but she has acted in his presence like a helpless woman longing to depend on a male.

Having failed to find herself as either a gentleman or a woman, Gabriella is "overcome by a sudden cloud of despondency," which turns her courage into "a sodden sense of loss, of emptiness, of defeat" (365). She feels that her life has been a mean one and that, even so, the best of it is over. As she looks back over the years of work and blankness, she decides she has missed life altogether, by which she seems to mean "romance, enchantment, adventure" (367). But within four months she achieves a partial recovery from defeat. Rejecting her feminine weakness, she refuses the judge's help and integrates within her own personality the strong qualities she had imagined him to possess (380). Her resistance and self-reliance triumph once more as she devises a plan for buying the shop from Madame Dinard through her own work as manager. The Berkeley or masculine part of her personality ultimately makes her a success (430).

Her emotional core, still unappeased, however, begins to create phantasies around Ben O'Hara, who lives downstairs in her new house. The excitement of the novel increases each time O'Hara enters the story, for he brings into this world of moralistic and economic realism the romance of the West, the romance of democracy, the romance of money. Like many Glasgow protagonists before him, he is a self-made man; but his wealth turns out to be the sudden wealth of the West, taken from the Colorado mines, rather than the slow commercial success of the East. He possesses a magnetic character, as attractive to Gabriella as George Fowler once was; but he has far more substance, it seems. It is difficult to be sure about his substance, however, because we are told a good deal more about him than we see, and told it by Gabriella in her special need.

The qualities she sees in him are, in part, those she had sought in the earlier men. He first appears during her depressed revery over the life she has missed, a moment when her "young illusions and her young longings" call her persuasively again. She hears his voice before she sees him, and it comes "out of the wild, sweet spirit of spring." His person combines the ruddy good looks of George with "a vivid impression of height, breadth, bigness" and (sop to the Berkeley conscience?) "the cleanness of the winds and sea" (367–69). Like George before him, he comes from outside her commonplace reality bringing the sanguine glow of life—an exuberant, even redundant vitality. His energy expresses the western man, not the New Yorker: "he is cyclonic," and his eyes carry the gray of a sea storm (383, 388–89, 395). Like the judge, O'Hara gives her the sense of a man of action and achievement; she likes the way his aggressive masculinity revives in her "the almost forgotten feeling of having 'a man in the house'" (385, 394). She responds positively to his abstract power and to the almost fatherly protection his male experience and money enable him to lavish on her. Indeed, when George Fowler, near dead of alcoholism, returns unexpectedly, his intrusion creates a situation in which O'Hara can show his most forceful and considerate qualities (444, 472). Power and protection prove to be the traits she is consciously prepared to accept from a man.

But in descriptions of the way Gabriella reacts to O'Hara's account of his early life of poverty, his education, his various jobs, his days in the mining towns, the language makes it clear that O'Hara's presence affects levels deeper than the heroine's conscious mind. Gabriella feels excited, alive, more filled with energy than she has since her childhood, "as if a closed door into the world had been suddenly flung open and . . . she had passed beyond the narrower paths of convention into the sunny roads and broad fields of vision." It is the same "sudden quickening of life" and "magical sense of the unexplored mystery and beauty of the world" she had felt the evening George returned to Richmond. She convinces herself, however, that there is "no touch of personal romance," nothing of perfidious love in her present response. Since it is easier for her to accept a more abstract form of affection, she deceives herself into believing her strong feeling reflects the awakening of love, not for a single person, but for "the whole of humanity." She has experienced, she tells herself, "a conversion" from the intolerance, arrogance, and narrowness of her former life into a more democratic outlook (419–20). No one would deny that this is progress, but the remainder of the novel shows that the road ahead remains as long as that behind: to one with Gabriella's scarred affections, the collective emotions prelude the reawakening of sexual love.

Although, to Gabriella's hardened psyche, "brotherhood" for an Irishman proves a less forbidden emotion than sexual attraction, the former too presents some difficulty for her conscience in her first encounters with O'Hara; for, at the start, "vulgarities" she ascribes to his lower-class origins allow her to evade the sexual nature of her fascination. Her unexplained but recurring moments of class snobbishness sometimes amount to overt hatred of O'Hara and of his influence on her son and herself (369, 384, 391–92, 397). The narrator ultimately describes this hostility as a defensive reaction: "Her first antagonism, her injustice, her unreasonable resentments and suspicions, she recognized now, in the piercing light of this discovery, as the inexplicable disguises of love" (521). Although Glasgow had dealt with mental evasions, especially evasive idealism, almost from the start of her career, the irrationality of these scenes provides one of her subtlest and truest cases. The reader finds himself taken in by the early class arrogance and yet senses, even before Gabriella, that hatred may be the face love wears when it presents itself to a psyche as scarred and confused as Gabriella's. But the reader becomes aware of the irony in her snobbishness only when it gives way to its opposite.

Abstract love of humanity is merely the second mask (after snobbery) that her fear throws over sexual love as her emotions begin to regenerate after long atrophy (there is in this, perhaps, a loose parable of twentieth-century developments in southern class relations, if that is the way one prefers to take novels). The connection between the two modes of love shows itself when, after a good deal of ambiguous enticement, O'Hara moves in for the first kiss. Here Glasgow gives us that obligatory scene that runs like a string of bright beads through modern American fiction about serious women, from Isabel Archer through Kate Swift to Joanna Burden and Blanche DuBois: the feminine nervousness, the kiss, the initial melting to the male heat (repressed female desire), and then the outrage and indignation (482–86). It is, of course, the way our writers have always shown the schizophrenia of women who must somehow live with their own animal desires, with an inadequate self-image that nevertheless dictates freedom, and with a conscience created for them, like Gabriella's Berkeley voice, by an oppressive male tradition. Not only does Gabriella reject O'Hara and the sexual force she has projected upon him; she turns as well from the collective feeling, "that mental correspondence with the mood of the crowd,

with the life of the city," the "new faculty in her soul," under
which disguise she had begun to accept her deeper need. She
reverts to her class snobbery, which this time reveals its ugly
Anglo-Saxon racial nature: "The very faces of the men and
women around her—those lethargic faces which crowded out
the finer American type—awoke in her the sensation of hopeless revolt which one feels before the impending destruction
of higher forms by masses of inert and conscienceless matter."
She has, she feels, lost the vision and all hope for the future of
America—all this because O'Hara wanted a kiss rather than
brotherhood (490). Universalizing her disgust into the jargon
of class bigotry is simply the mechanism she uses to throw the
blame on O'Hara and his origins for her own deep-rooted inability to live with passion.

The third and most desperate disguise she uses to hide the
face of romance and sex turns out to be the ideal of her first
love, Arthur Peyton, from whose restricting reality she ran
when the doors of change first opened for her. She rejects
O'Hara with the lie, "I have loved another man all my life."
However, as Glasgow tells us, "it was as if she hoped by convincing him [O'Hara] to persuade her own rebellious heart of
the truth she proclaimed" (485). Shocked by the prospect of
profound growth, she rejects every degree of development she
has achieved in the story and flees for safety to the world of
her childhood. But the return to innocence is the oldest and
deepest of all illusions, as she learns when she takes the train
back to Richmond. The home she wishes to go back to has, of
course, changed: Richmond, for good or ill, has come down
with a case of progress. Worse disappointment still, Arthur
has done nothing. Mother-bound before, he has remained
tied to the past; he is even more handsome, but old, acquiescent, and ineffectual (515). Gabriella realizes she has used
the dream of an ideal man to evade her desire for a real one
(523–24).

The O'Hara to whom she then scurries back (just in time to
catch him at the station!) barely reappears in the novel, but he
is very alive in her imagination. This shadow of the real man

must bear a heavy weight of abstractions, for all Gabriella's needs she now projects upon him. In the final seven pages, she thinks of him as her destiny, her symbol of life, the mirror of her own "will to live, to strive, and to conquer"; his bigness she calls the source of her peace, security, and protection. He is her "choice between action and inaction, between endeavour and relinquishment, between affirmation and denial, between adventure and deliberation, between youth and age" (529). He is the future. Compelling abstractions like these, however, are actually phantasies that remain imperfectly embodied; they prove the imagination has failed to become flesh.

The novel ends thus, not with the kiss of romance, but with a string of abstractions—concessions, no doubt, to the heroine's image of herself as a serious and liberated woman and to her Berkeley streak. But the crisis arose from O'Hara's kiss. Is the ending another of Gabriella's evasions? Even if we concede that her acceptance of O'Hara as he is implies she has come to terms with the physical side of their complex man-woman connection (which is by no means certain), and even if we acknowledge that her need to strive, to affirm, to find a fatherlike pillar of security and all of the rest is as strong as her need for sexual romance (though it is not the core of her being), there remains a final possibility for self-deception. She has, in effect, turned O'Hara into her new symbol of reality, as though he could now and always bear with ease the weight of all her changing needs. Although this is a mistake often made, no doubt, by those facing marriage, isn't Gabriella in a position of superior self-knowledge? Hasn't her past taught her that, for her, one reality is not enough? That in time she will either reclaim as her own the positive qualities she now sees in O'Hara or discover that beneath the abstractions there exists a mere man? Perhaps Glasgow intends us to see that Gabriella's needs remain, as they always were, greater than her self-knowledge. This would be an appropriate irony with which to end.

But I do not think dramatic irony is what Glasgow has in

mind at the very end. The final portrait of O'Hara is every inch Gabriella's glowing invention. The narrator leaves it unqualified by ambiguities of character, which could have reached the reader even if the heroine refused to see them. No, Glasgow apparently meant her heroine's ultimate affirmation to be exemplary, not ironic; for this inflated estimate of a man was the point to which Glasgow's own personal need had brought her by 1916. It is as though, around her encounter with an Irishman named Mulhern, who owned the apartment house where she was living in New York City,[5] Glasgow had woven a pattern of imaginary traits that she would shortly attempt to embody in Henry Anderson, her future fiancé; she had invented a man very much like Anderson even before she knew him well. Gabriella's final blindness is that of her creator. The ending is didactic and unconvincing by the critical standards the novel itself establishes.

Although we have discovered a process of deep psychological growth structuring *Gabriella*, we have done so only by ignoring both the bulk and the surface of the story; for we have neglected the heroine's exemplary struggle to succeed on her own. Her success story is part of social history and holds limited interest for the contemporary reader. The pattern her psychological development follows, however, possesses great significance for Glasgow's future development as a novelist. Here, probably unwittingly, Glasgow had hit upon a method of portraying fictional persons by turning their psyches inside out. Although distortions caused by the mind that mirrors the facts of life had been a curse to George Eliot at the start of realism, the portrait of Gabriella suggests that such distortions might become the heart of a psychological method.[6] There is probably no way to determine whether Glasgow was fully aware that she had discovered an alternative to Jamesian

---

5  E. Stanly Godbold, Jr., *Ellen Glasgow and the Woman Within* (Baton Rouge, 1972), 104.
6  See Eliot's *Adam Bede*, Chapter XVII, and George Levine, "Realism Reconsidered," in John Halperin (ed.), *The Theory of the Novel* (New York, 1974), 251.

symbolism as an approach to psychological fiction. She had already approached the technique once in her career and abandoned it. The seed of the method was present in her work at least as early as *The Wheel of Life* (1906); there her cloistered heroine projected the mask of romance upon a pleasure seeker (much like George Fowler) and pursued her illusion until it led her very near suicide. But in 1906 Glasgow's attitude toward phantasy remained too moralistic for her to realize the potential of the method. In *The Wheel of Life* reality was used to test phantasy, but phantasy lacked equal authority to test reality. Clearly, in 1906 she still associated phantasies with dangerous lies. She had not yet learned that phantasy is more than illusion: it is the other hemisphere of human truth, that which makes fiction often truer than history. In *Life and Gabriella*, however, she freed herself, perhaps without knowing it, from the strictures—moral and otherwise—of realism. This freedom would eventually enable her to make the transition from the surface realism of her early career to the psychological realism of her major phase, which begins with *Barren Ground* (1925). But before she gained firm control over her new technique, she would write *The Builders*, a desperate novel more flawed by unembodied abstractions than *Gabriella*, more flawed even than *The Wheel of Life*.

# Chapter III

# The Hole in Reality:
# *The Builders* (1919)
# and *One Man in*
# *His Time* (1922)

In *The Builders* (1919), Ellen Glasgow's first novel to reflect the impact of World War I on her life and fiction, the primary male character sums up the meaning of the international disaster this way: "I can't explain how it is, but this war has knocked a big hole in reality. We can look deeper into things than any generation before us, and the deeper we look, the more we become aware of the outer darkness in which we have been groping. I am groping now, I confess it, but I am groping for light."[1] This was precisely Glasgow's own predicament in 1919, and *The Builders* is a total failure, in large part, because this uncertainty and hesitancy marred its conception and execution. Although her next novel, *One Man in His Time* (1922), is also weakened by an uncertain focus, its groping for light seems earnest and at times profound; it possesses a depth all of Glasgow's novels since the early chapters of *Virginia* (1913) had lacked.

Since her earliest novels, Glasgow had earnestly pursued emotional truth. To this end, she initially used evolutionary thought as the cornerstone of the vision she substituted for that of her region and her father. She needed the Darwinian world picture, in part because the Civil War and the changes following it had "knocked a big hole" in the traditional order of the South. More recently, in *Life and Gabriella* she had portrayed the crisis of values that accompanied the onset of

---

1 Ellen Glasgow, *The Builders* (Garden City, N.Y., 1919), 279. This novel will be cited hereafter in the text by page number only.

middle age; through Gabriella Carr, she recognized that a life devoted to struggle, work, and financial independence had robbed her of her youth, of romance, of adventure—of life itself. Like Gabriella and many others in mid-life, she had tried to salvage the forgotten side of herself by embracing a new life, by falling in love again with all the fervor of an adolescent. Gabriella chose the vigorous Irishman, Ben O'Hara; Glasgow considered an Irishman named Mulhern but settled upon Henry W. Anderson, an eligible Richmond bachelor in whom she became interested about Easter of 1916. On July 19, 1917, Anderson and she became engaged. The next day Anderson left Richmond to start one of the great adventures of World War I. President Woodrow Wilson had charged him with the rescue of Rumania from starvation. It was his responsibility to transport Red Cross doctors, nurses, food, and medical supplies by train across Siberia, then through Russia on the brink of revolution, and by truck over frozen waters to the small Balkan kingdom otherwise cut off from the Allied powers. Anderson was chairman of the mission and Glasgow's brother Arthur, the vice-chairman. The rescue proved so important to Rumania that Queen Marie began conversing with Anderson in private and accompanying him on inspection tours. Eventually, the agreement Anderson and Glasgow had reached under the pressure of war proved too weak to survive the gnawing jealousy that grew each time she received a report, by letter or rumor, of his adventures in the Balkans. They remained engaged, but the trust had gone out of it.[2]

*The Builders* is not so much the story of their love affair as the fruit of their stormy collaboration. Anderson's letters show that he actually wrote the first draft of many of the chapters

2 See Henry W. Anderson to Ellen Glasgow, July 31, August 20, August 25, August 29, September 11, September 19, September 26, 1917, in the Ellen Glasgow Collection, Alderman Library, University of Virginia. Also "Henry Anderson Tells of Work in Roumania," Richmond *Times-Dispatch*, July 12, 1918, p. 4; and Godbold, *Ellen Glasgow and the Woman Within*, 110, 119–22.

(those with long political statements, we would imagine) and would have done more except that his long-promised "letter from Russia" was either lost in the mail or destroyed by the censor.[3] Written before the rift in their relationship and before Glasgow's attempt at suicide (July 3, 1918, with sleeping pills), the early chapters set forth a situation with good potential: the plot is to record the education and psychological development of Caroline Meade. A private nurse from southside Virginia, where she is oppressed by the boredom of her commonplace existence, Caroline has waited, full of hope, expectancy, and dreams, for "something different" to "come up [the] long empty road" that leads to her home. Her natural development thwarted by a love affair recently ended, she is especially excited when a letter arrives calling her to assist with the invalid daughter of delicate and lovely Angelica Blackburn and David Blackburn. She remains excited even though she knows the rumors that say Blackburn treats his wife badly and votes Republican. Caroline projects all her dreams and needs upon the melodramatic situation of the good wife, brutal husband, and delicate child. She thereby turns her call to service into the start of a romantic quest.

From the beginning she identifies her own inner loveliness and male-abused self with Angelica. In her imagination she sees the unknown woman, "fair, graceful, suffering . . . against the background of the unhappy home, in an atmosphere of mystery and darkness. . . . By a miracle of imagination" she transfers "this single character into actual experience. The sense of mystery was still there, but the unreality had vanished. It was incredible the way a woman whose face she had never seen had entered into her life." Glasgow here is using the technique of character portrayal she had developed in *Life and Gabriella* to explore the unconscious mind: the character turns herself inside out by projecting the unrecognized part of herself upon another person. If, for Caro-

3 Anderson to Glasgow, June 10, 1917, November 3, 1918, January 24, 1919, in Ellen Glasgow Collection, Alderman Library.

line, Angelica is "more real than anything . . . more real even than the war," it is because she personifies the frustrated dreams of Caroline's thirty-two years (6, 9–11, 17–18).

Glasgow structures the novel around Caroline's progressive disillusionment with Angelica and her slow shift in loyalty to David, with whom she of course falls in love. (There is, I fear, a political allegory intended here with Angelica standing for the feminine, helpless, self-pitying traditions of Virginia and the South; Caroline [Carolina?] for the plainer but more vigorous parts of the South; little Letty Blackburn for the present sickness of the region under the dominance of the Angelica ideal; and David for a new, more energetic, and intelligent male leadership. But once we have recognized the symbols, there is little else to do with the allegory.) Although Angelica plays upon that part of everyone which needs some lovely and abused ideal to believe in, she loses Caroline's affection when she neglects her daughter during a pneumonia crisis to attend a charity benefit, becomes romantically entangled with the fiancé of her husband's sister, and then spreads the rumor that her husband has beat her.

As the darkness and mystery surrounding Angelica lose their hold on her, Caroline is seduced by David Blackburn—but at first only in an intellectual manner. Like Gabriella Carr, Caroline can respond to a compelling male with her mind long before her heart becomes involved. This is in part because she has already been wounded in her affections and in part because Blackburn's way of thinking and speaking reminds her of her now dead father and of household political chats he encouraged. Time and again Blackburn brings back her warm feeling for her father, so often that we cannot fail to notice that his chief fascination for her is as an authority figure rather than lover (61–62, 196, 243). He is variously described as a man of ideas, of theory, of thought, and of idealism. In short, he is a carrier of the word; and she responds to his intellectual dominance, in association with his immense wealth, power, and energy. Within her he creates a sense of peace and order. As the novel progresses, Caroline fails to test these abstractions against Blackburn's reality. Instead, she views him more and more as a symbol—of the future, of the South becoming, of southern individualism. Eventually, her idea turns into an even more general emotion: "Something within her soul, which had been frozen for years, thawed suddenly and grew warm again. . . . Now, in an instant, she was born anew, and entered afresh into her lost heritage of joy and pain" (300). Or so the author claims.

Shortly after this, Blackburn, like almost everyone else, sails for France. There he seems to metamorphose into a voice hidden behind a cloud of words, going on and on about the need for individuality within democracy while at the same time sacrificing himself and everyone else to the half-dozen or so abstractions that are his current favorites. This is a fine irony, but one wasted on all the characters and on the novel itself, which ends didactically with Caroline and Blackburn staring together at a light "shining on the far horizon." With so much idealism, so much light, it is difficult to remember the hole the war knocked in reality. Perhaps Caroline's need to grasp at abstractions provides the measure of the size of that hole. It does, of course, for the abstractions are symptoms, not solutions. But this is not the sort of message Glasgow meant to communicate in the only novel she ever agreed to have serialized in a popular magazine. Although not her dullest book, it is her worst executed. Even the minor characters, with whom her touch almost always seems sure, come across here as types without life or individuality.

*One Man in His Time* (1922) is an improvement, despite two glaring flaws. First, the plot has a triple focus, a confusion that suggests the author changed her conception of the story while writing the book (the unity of time, perhaps the most effective since the early chapters of *Virginia*, only partially offsets this sprawl). Second, the book is overwritten, as Frederick P. W. McDowell has pointed out.[4] Glasgow's novels since *Virginia* re-

---

4 Frederick P. W. McDowell, *Ellen Glasgow and the Ironic Art of Fiction* (Madison, 1963), 144.

veal an intermittent tendency to overwrite; indeed, the romantic struggle to pin down the ineffable with words has
replaced her previous realistic manner of undercutting earnest
struggle with irony. Although a weakness of the book, the
strained language is nonetheless revealing; as Glasgow tells
us, *One Man* was created "in the midst of a nervous breakdown . . . in the effort to escape from too much living"[5] —an
apparent reference to the painful relationship with Anderson.
Without violating the integrity of the book, we may wish to
remember during the following discussion that the novel almost certainly contains clues to the nature of Glasgow's illness and to her manner of treating it.

Two additional assumptions will assist our approaching
*One Man* in the most fruitful manner possible. First, we may
conclude from her work after *Virginia* and from her affair with
Anderson that she had ceased to consider romantic love as an
adequate subject on which to build a serious novel. And second, from *The Builders* and her whole relationship with Anderson, we can infer that she had exorcised whatever faith she
possessed in public men and political theories as solutions to
the problems that beset herself and mankind. Henceforth, romantic love and public men might serve as the raw materials
for a novel, but they will never again be more than means to
an end. The end her subsequent novels will explore is the
ageless ethical and metaphysical one: how is an individual to
live best in a world that is not the best of all possible worlds?
Love and social concerns will become increasingly insignifi-
cant aspects of solutions that are more and more psychological. If we agree on these points, we can resist the temptation
to regard Gideon Vetch, the novel's most magnetic character,
as the center of the plot; his sensational career simply provides the story, the raw material out of which Glasgow con-
structs the plot—a psychological one.

With Vetch placed in a proper perspective, it is still necessary to come to terms with an awkward double focus. If Glas-

5 Glasgow to Allen Tate, September 22, 1932, in Blair Rouse (ed.), *Letters
of Ellen Glasgow* (New York, 1958), 125.

gow was striving for a parallax view of the way World War I
affected individuals, she went about it badly. Almost every
shift the narrator makes from Stephen Culpeper's point of
view to Corinna Page's weakens the novel. For Culpeper's
story holds the true appeal.

There exists for Stephen Culpeper, unlike David Blackburn,
Caroline Meade, or Corinna Page, a palpable hole in reality,
one that abstractions can never fill nor good manners hide.
But it seems as much the emptiness felt by Matthew Arnold,

> Wandering between two worlds, one dead
> The other powerless to be born,
> ("Stanzas from the Grande Chartreuse")

or Prufrock, or the Hollow Men, as it does a void created by
the war. Culpeper suffers chiefly from the gap that divides the
conventional surface of his life, dominated by old-fashioned
family traditions and a pity-collecting mother, from the core
of his being, where uncontrollable impulses and "rich veins
of feeling" long for the "heroic and splendid deeds" of his
Virginia ancestors who made the Revolution.[6] The war has
"left him with a nervous malady" and "increased both his romantic dissatisfaction with his life and his inability to make a
sustained effort to change it" (2–3). In the process, the war has
made him hypersensitive both to the suffocating conventions
of the world in which his fathers lived and to the vulgarity of
the democratic forces he feels the war unleashed. In seeing the
world about him divided between convention and democracy,
he has simply projected his inner split between tradition and
raw impulse upon his environment. He further imagines taking place, both within him and without, a struggle between
two spirits: "the realistic spirit which saw things as they
were" (that is, the skeptical view of the conservative) and "the
romantic spirit which saw things as they ought to be," an outlook elsewhere called the progressive view (2, 69–70). He links

---

6 Ellen Glasgow, *One Man in His Time* (Garden City, N.Y., 1922), 2. This
   novel will be cited hereafter in the text by page number only.

the realistic spirit with his race, his aristocratic tradition, philosophy, and age, and associates the romantic forces with the individual, adventure, experience, and youth. The war has destroyed his surface reality and has called the core of his being to begin its adventure in a world larger, wider, and deeper than the small city that sits beside James River. But tradition, which speaks most poignantly with his mother's voice, has kept him impotent to break completely with the past and to plunge into the future. With "neither the fortitude to endure the old nor the energy to embrace the new," his present life appears a pernicious nothing, to which he is at best apathetic when not moved by it to profound revulsion. The medical specialist his mother calls in tries "first to probe into the secrets of his infancy" and "analyse his symptoms away." But the Freudian approach seems so ludicrous to him that his laughter drives the doctor off (69–70).

Stephen's own intuitions prove acute enough for him to know that what he needs most—like Caroline Meade before him—is not analysis but that magical "something different," the intervention of a new force that might enable him to express the uncontrollable impulse and rich veins of feeling he keeps buried beneath his conventional surface (2, 70). Only in this way might he develop the "exotic flower," which sprang up within him in response to the challenge of war (69). To smother that flower, on the other hand, by marrying Margaret Blair, the "gentle, lovely and unselfish" girl his mother has picked for him, would mean the end of his inner being and, we may infer, would bring worse apathy and lead to further withdrawal (71).

Because Stephen lacks the energy to embrace change or his buried self directly, they must present themselves in disguise. Even so, he initially rejects what he wants most. Glasgow had already dealt in *Life and Gabriella* with the sort of evasion in which an inhibited individual experiences a strong attraction forbidden by commonplace values not as pleasure but as revulsion. This is precisely what happens to Stephen in his dealings with Virginia's Governor Gideon Vetch and with

Vetch's daughter Patty. The Vetches are difficult for him to accept because they freely express the impulses he has bottled up
within himself. Although, before they meet, Stephen hates
Vetch with "all his heart" and sees him as a demagogic outlet
for political tendencies produced by international violence, the
young man cannot, standing in the governor's presence, deny
that he is fascinated by the man's qualities of natural freedom:
his freshness, health, and sanguine vitality, his human eyes,
magic handshake, strange power, and charm. Vetch seems to
project arrested energy and zest for life (5, 22–24, 27, 82).
Raised on reticence, Stephen finds himself simultaneously put
off and drawn by Vetch's violent candor; for the truth Vetch
offers proves often to be the dangerous one—self-knowledge
(23, 45–46). Stephen feels safer when he can base his opinion
of Vetch on rumors that circulate about the questionable
means the governor uses to pursue his high social goals; or,
safer still, when he can judge the politician by his flashy
clothes—a green tie with red spots, a shirt striped with blue
or purple, a suit of fuzzy brown stuff (31–32, 173). But these
are largely defensive reactions, and the attraction of the man
who is different proves much stronger than Stephen's
defense.

Glasgow has thus created a compelling modern situation:
the seduction of a southern Prufrock. Because it is his own
unrecognized core tempting him through Vetch, the seduction will prove so powerful that either his rebirth or his guilty
self-destruction must follow. Vetch mirrors the part of Stephen that claims kin with Virginians who made the Revolution. Vetch echoes the past as it was when it was still new—
vigorous, violent, healthily vulgar—not yet corseted in polite
traditions by the Daughters of the American Revolution or in
legal ones by the American Bar Association. Stephen's seduction should proceed very much along the pattern of self-devel-
opment Glasgow established for Gabriella Carr: first the
character discovers unacknowledged aspects of the self projected upon another person; next he or she experiences some
combination of enchantment by and rejection of the mirroring

other; then he or she accepts, even reclaims, the qualities hitherto suppressed; and finally he or she passes through a period either of disgust and disillusionment or, if fortunate, of realistic adjustment.

Although Vetch provides a truer mirror of Stephen's hidden self, Stephen proves better able to embrace his buried impulses when he finds them projected upon the governor's daughter. Patty's attributes parallel those of her father. Stephen thinks her wild, candid, crude as life, courageous, colorful, unusual, unexpected, vivacious, inspiriting, glowing with romance, power, and brave adventure, but full of questionable tricks and possibilities. Her vulgarity reminds him of cover girls; like her father, she dresses garishly. In addition to her father's qualities, he finds her young, pretty, alluring, elusive, enchanting, full of spring sweetness (8–9, 12–15, 17, 19, 23, 35, 77, 95–96). Patty first leads Stephen to Vetch, and she ultimately becomes his reward for accepting the governor and coming to terms with himself.

Along the way, however, Stephen looks deeper into the hole in reality than any Glasgow character had for a decade. Patty only forces him to recognize his class priggishness. Her father goes further when he introduces Stephen to a carpenter named Darrow, a natural aristocrat. In the surest scene Glasgow had written since the "White Magic" chapter of *Virginia*, Darrow shows him his guilty tie with humanity. What Stephen sees in a basement in the workers' slum of Richmond proves a self-portrait in a double sense: he is both a victim and an abuser of others. The man he meets there, named Canning, is out of work, living with a soiled haggard wife, three noisy children, and a badly nourished baby tied in a high chair. But, like Stephen, Canning is suffering from a nervous breakdown brought on by the war. When Canning says he is tired even before he begins, Stephen understands exactly what he means (185–90). The deep shock of self-knowledge comes when Darrow tells him that this tenement row and those on the next block or two are part of the Culpeper estate; they are Stephen's heritage, his "noble past"—as Canning is the per-

fected image of his fatalistic present (192). This blow carries
Stephen through the darkness in which he has been groping
to a new reality; for Vetch has, he feels, "knocked a hole in
the wall" behind which he was suffocating and "shown him
the way out" (196). Vetch has spoken to the democratic and
collective impulse in Stephen, and some barrier in his soul
"between himself and humanity" has broken down. He responds with new energy. He takes his father to task about the
tenements and prepares to mutiny against his mother's evasive idealism (197). At this point, however, the voice of his
conscience, his "ancestral custom of good breeding," closes
"over him like the lid of a coffin." Even so, he holds to the
image of Patty Vetch (200–201).

Whether from lack of imagination or of nerve, Glasgow fails
to keep her focus upon Stephen. This is unfortunate, because
in him she has found a strong and objective representation of
nervous disorders that the war and the pull between past and
future, between reality and romance, had created in her own
life. (She has left this story for Robert Penn Warren to develop
in *All the King's Men*.) Instead, she avoids deeper exploration
of Stephen and his fate by shifting with increasing frequency
to Corinna Page's point of view. Although Corinna's problems parallel Stephen's, they are neither as severe nor as objectively presented—nor as compelling. The temptation of Diana
cannot be as intriguing to a modern reader as the seduction of
Prufrock. Worse still, Corinna is too much the author's
spokesman. We can accept the richness and mystery of her
autumnal beauty because it represents a gain in objectivity
achieved through mythicizing Corinna's mature femininity
(39, 103). But Corinna's struggle to decide whether any man is
worth the marrying seems imbued with sentimentality and
with her creator's self-pity. Still, there is a poignancy to her
feeling that, despite her wealth and the glamour of being the
daughter of the former ambassador to Great Britain, her life
has been futile and mean. It was wasted, she decides, on a
passionless marriage to a first cousin, and he is now dead (37,
103, 110, 286, 294).

Corinna's sense of frustration finds initial expression when she meets Patty. Enchanted by the girl's rebellious vital spirit, she comes to see the wild unformed beauty as the image of "the suppressed audacities of [her own] past" (101). If Patty mirrors Corinna's feminine self, Vetch himself seems to her, as he does to Stephen, "the very fountain of life—no, of humanity" (115). He speaks with the voice of collective mankind "to some buried self beneath the self that she and the world knew, to some ancient instinct which was as deep as the oldest forests of earth . . . a buried forest within her soul which she had never discovered" (282). He enables her to look through the hole in reality into "another mental world beyond the one she had always inhabited," a world "filled, like her own, with obscure moral and spiritual images" (284). Under the spell of Patty and Gideon, she recognizes that she has been cut off from this larger world by the "beliefs and sentiments with which life had obscured and muffled her nature"; she has "been ruled not by passion but by law, by some clear moral discernment of things as they ought to be" (282, 294).

Because she has the moral strictures of the romantic vision but lacks its emotional force, Corinna proves even less willing than Stephen to embrace this new life of the Vetches without reservation. One of the weaknesses in the conception of the novel arises from the fact that Stephen, a self-styled prig and objectively presented as such, comes across as less a prig than Corinna, whom the author attempts to represent as generous and open to life. Glasgow obviously intends her as a spokesman for philosophic moderation and balance. But one must entertain both extremes of a dialectic before he can balance them; and Corinna is, and remains, much more adept at raising others than at stooping herself, even toward the life sources. Instead, she undertakes the traditional role of a sophisticated older woman when she educates Patty Virginia-style by helping select her clothes, then teaching her good manners and the rudiments of culture. When she cautions Patty about Stephen's tie to his family and warns her to love cautiously, she is not only meddling in the affairs of others

but diverting the natural momentum of the book; she thereby
creates complications that keep Stephen from his mirror self
for over a quarter of the novel (238). To correct for her interference, this "fixer of destinies" later advises Stephen that "feeling [*i.e.*, Patty] is everything" (she has just hectored a minor
character on the danger of sentiment) and thus restores the
movement of the (by now) halting plot (315, 324). At this
point it is difficult to distinguish the middle way she is meant
to embody from stagnation and inconsistent characterization.

In addition, Corinna attempts to stand between Patty and
her moment of self-discovery (the most sensational in the
book) when the latter hurries to the deathbed of a drug-ad-
dicted woman she does not know, a former circus rider, who
as she was being carried off to jail for murder fifteen years
before, gave her only child, a daughter, to a sympathetic
stranger named Gideon Vetch (351). This descent into the
darkness surrounding Patty's mother's death Corinna manages to transmute from a scene of terrifying poverty into a
moment of discovery—not of self (even though a gnarled destiny figure and a child seem meant to mirror Corinna's old
and new selves), but of abstract beauty and even more abstract life (358–60). Corinna's perceptions here do not con-
vince because they are stimulated by events that affect her less
directly than they do other characters; they are observations
rather than existential discoveries. But her grasping at abstractions does provide a measure of the need her empty life has
created for a meaning and a purpose she has never felt in her
bones, and only now knows in her head. Her notion that she
has never faced life before may explain why she habitually in-
terferes in the affairs of Patty and Stephen.

But Corinna is most trying when she gets between the
reader and other characters, as she does with Gideon Vetch.
Seen at the start from Stephen's point of view, Vetch comes
across as a compelling though obliquely developed character
of mixed moral nature—a Richmond trial run for the Huey
Long scenario; in other words, the sort of self-styled reformer

whom others cast as demagogue.[7] His vitality comes from his circus roots (his mother ran away from her very good Virginia family to marry a half-Irish circus performer). Introduced into the enervated upper circles of Richmond, his energy seems as exotic and potentially revivifying as the wild ponies Flem Snopes will later bring to Faulkner's sleeping hamlet. A man of realities, Vetch wants to confront the people, not with words and ideas, but with facts and actions relevant to his progressive programs (174–78). The people, the old labor politician Darrow points out, had rather be fooled, however, than helped; they want something—party labels or other "conjure stuff"—that works magic (184). Vetch's strange past and nonpolitical manner fill this need in much the same way the sensational story of his life creates the necessary suspense of the novel (why *should* voters be more immune to romance than readers?). Even apathetic Stephen leaves their first encounter aroused to an "intense, a devouring curiosity" by "the mystery of his birth, of his upbringing, of his privations and denials" (32–33). Initially, these details ring the familiar (and already mythic) Lincoln-as-rail-splitter bell in Corinna's mind, and thus in the reader's mind; but by the time she has finished with Vetch, she has managed to turn Stephen's once intriguing mountebank into a DAR draft of a founding father.

In light of Corinna's repressed past, it is not surprising that the look of abstract humanity in Vetch's eyes attracts her in-

7 Henry Anderson's letters to Glasgow concerning Woodrow Wilson, especially the way Wilson was handling a rail strike in August, 1916, contain vituperations similar to those Richmond conservatives in the novel direct against Vetch and suggest Wilson as a model for the progressive aspects of Vetch's character. Anderson to Glasgow, August 31, September 8, 13, 1916, in Ellen Glasgow Collection, Alderman Library. In this novel, Anderson obviously appears as the proper but enervated political figure John Benham, the suitor Corinna sends back to one of his earlier loves. Anderson is not Vetch. He tended, however, to identify himself with Corinna's accommodating father and to associate Miss Glasgow with helpless Alice Rokeby to whom Corinna "returns" Benham. See Anderson to Glasgow, "Tuesday [1922]," in Ellen Glasgow Collection, Alderman Library.

stantly, nor that she discerns "his point of view not by looking outside of herself, but by looking within. . . . All that had been alien or ambiguous" in the man becomes "as close and true and simple as the thoughts in her own mind. What she [sees] in Vetch" is his "resemblance to herself" (223). But there is a good deal more life buried inside this middle-aged woman than this commendable collective feeling. Even though she prepares her weapons and "goes to war" to keep Vetch from falling into the snares of the opulent, golden-haired Rose Stribling, who, gossip says, took Corinna's husband from her while he and Rose were stationed in France, she never comes out from behind her stockade of abstractions so that she and Gideon might meet on a field more open than the intellectual one (38, 52, 110). Unfortunately, "moral discernment" remains to the end the law of her nature, "stronger than any emotion" (294). Because hers is increasingly the point of view of the novel, Vetch becomes less and less flesh and blood and more and more an idea in Corinna's mind—a fate worse than turning into one more of the "imposing statues standing around" Richmond, monuments he once scoffed at (178). In the end, Corinna, with Stephen, turns Vetch into a personification of the golden mean between "the romantic and the realistic temperament, which divides in politics into the progressive and conservative forces" (321). Even alive, he has become a rock for her to lean on (365–66). After he gets caught between the human extremes, like every golden mean, and his death removes all the class and sexual problems his flesh-and-blood continuance would have posed for Corinna (or Glasgow), she promptly transforms him into an imposing and innocuous "symbol of a changing world," an abstraction with which she can comfortably face the future (376–79).

It might seem that *One Man* fails for the same reason as *The Builders*—that in both cases the author tries unconvincingly in the end to fill "the hole in reality" with abstractions (as Gabriella Carr had done even before the war). This shortcoming the two political novels have in common. But other less obvious faults set the two apart from one another and explain why *One Man* is a better, though seriously flawed, book. In *The Builders* the abstractions are doubly unembodied and depersonalized: neither Caroline's need (as suppliant) nor Blackburn's presence (as provider) proves strong enough to provoke such a flood of general values. In *One Man*, on the other hand, both Stephen's need and Vetch's presence seem strong enough (at least at the start). The difficulty emerges when Corinna takes over and the treatment goes to the opposite extreme: it becomes too personalized; the world is seen too much through the eyes of a character too close to the author. The objective interest of the story gets buried beneath an imperfectly fictionalized portrait of the spiritual needs and solutions of the author. Although propaganda dramatized in the mind of a character is better than the plain tracts that conclude *The Builders*, propaganda is still not one of the higher literary arts. A similar problem with a point of view sometimes too autobiographical awaits Glasgow in *Barren Ground*, the much finer novel she will write next.

The pattern of character development used in *The Builders* and *One Man* also anticipates *Barren Ground*. In *The Builders* and *One Man* the process of growth Glasgow hit upon in *Gabriella* takes the form of a romantic quest for a new self. The quest begins in each case with a clear indication that present reality is not enough: the heroine's longing for "something different" signals the coming of dangerous changes. After this signal, the heroine passes through the phases of projection, fascination, and introjection explored in *Gabriella*. But in neither *The Builders* nor *One Man* does Glasgow seem to know how to end the quest for self once it is underway. She apparently did not believe that the commercial and emotional success Gabriella sought could satisfy Caroline, Corinna, or Stephen. It is as though her intuition caused her to drop the quest midway through each of these two inferior novels, so that in *Barren Ground* she might pick it up, follow it to completion, and thereby transcend it. When she came to write the latter novel, the experiments she had been conducting since 1916 in her short stories helped her understand how she might carry a character's need for the self to unfold nearer fulfillment.

*Chapter IV*

# The Words for Invisible Things: The Short Stories (1916–1924)

The short stories of Ellen Glasgow have attracted little critical attention, aside from the introduction Richard K. Meeker wrote for *The Collected Stories of Ellen Glasgow* (Louisiana State University Press, 1963). This neglect exists in large part because the stories do not lend themselves to easy grouping. Glasgow scattered them through thirty years of her career. Some seem to be simple love stories while others are rather transparent ghost stories, and neither approach was typical of her career as a novelist. Nevertheless, there exists one group of stories that played a role in Glasgow's development of far greater significance than they have been accorded. Despite the popular magazine quality of several, this group constitutes a series of experiments in characterization—experiments that opened up essential new realms of behavior for the novelist's later exploration. From discoveries she made here emerged the psychological insight that distinguishes the novels she began to publish with *Barren Ground* in 1925 from those she wrote before 1916.

Of the thirteen short stories Glasgow wrote and preserved, all but three belong to the eight-year period (1916–1924) when her ability to create novels had reached its nadir. Although these ten stories are in general better executed than the novels of the period (*Life and Gabriella*, *The Builders*, and *One Man in His Time*), they reveal some of the same groping toward a new technique. Editor Meeker divides the ten into two large groups—the ghost stories and those that treat "the relationship between men and women."[1] But seen in relation to the three novels, all the stories are united by a single problem. The character who narrates "The Past," the central story in the group, seems to speak as much for Glasgow as for herself when she says, "My mind has dealt so long with external details that I have almost forgotten the words that express invisible things" (134). Like the three novels, these stories belong to Glasgow's search, during her decade of emotional and aesthetic crisis, for a language to express the invisible world that had very nearly wrecked her life and career. What is most surprising about the stories compared with the novels is the variety and clarity of the languages Glasgow discovered. Whereas the three novels attempt to fill the "hole in reality" with abstractions, the stories reveal a wide range of literary modes that enable a fictionist to grasp and communicate the invisible world inside a character. They thus provide a record of the ways one well-established American novelist came to terms with the psychological knowledge that began, after 1910 or so, to be more and more the central concern of fiction.

Appropriately then, the protagonist of what is probably the earliest of the stories happens to be an "analytical psychologist," a label applied to schools using mainly the introspective method and chosen by Carl Jung to distinguish his type of psychoanalysis from that of Sigmund Freud. Glasgow's Dr. John Estbridge in "The Professional Instinct" has, in the last few weeks before the story begins, treated "several cases of changed personalities," "men and women, not far from his own age [he is 'nearing fifty'], who [have] undergone curious psychological . . .crises that brought quite new personalities." Although Dr. Estbridge recognizes "that he [is] in something of the same mental state at this moment," the story shows him powerless to understand, much less to heal, himself (240). Because the "coveted chair of physiology at the Univer-

---

1 Richard K. Meeker (ed.), *The Collected Stories of Ellen Glasgow* (Baton Rouge, 1963), 12–16; citations throughout are to this edition and will be given parenthetically.

sity" for which he worked for twenty years has just been awarded to his assistant, he is toying with the thought that he "should cut it for good and begin over again"—by accepting a position in Shanghai. His inner struggle becomes very much tied up with his view of women. As the narrator tells us in the two versions of the text: "Like most men [and all *changed to* according to the] analytical psychologists, he had identified his own dreams with the shape of a woman" (240). This reference is to the anima theory of analytical psychology—according to which men may project the unacknowledged feminine side of their personality, especially the emotions, creativity, and intuition, upon women, who then possess inordinate powers over the men—and explains the dynamics of the story. There are three such women in Estbridge's life.

The first is his wife, Tilly Pratt. Twenty years ago when Estbridge was a youthful reformer, he saw Tilly dressed as the Florentine reformer Savonarola in her graduating play. Even without the theatrical robes and cowl, she "impersonated the militant idealism" of his youth: "For he had loved Tilly, not for herself, but because she had shown him his own image" (240). Although he has kept his own body compact and muscular while his career moved from idealism to prosperity, Tilly has grown "florid, robust, and bristling with activity." Woman as ideal has become the smothering mother figure who ruffles a man's contentment, devours his time, and triumphantly checkmates him. She has become the embodiment of his prosperous failure, even before she tells him that his hold on the chair was sabotaged by her rich uncle at her suggestion (240–43).

The second woman, and the seeming opposite of Tilly, is Judith Campbell, with whom he has previously had a warm friendship. Judith enters the story just after he decides that he will take the post in Shanghai, a solution that brings a "vision of freedom" in which he sees ahead of him ten vigorous years filled with "adventure, accomplishment, and reward" (245). Suddenly Judith seems the perfect complement, if not embodiment, of his new vision. She is the professor of philosophy in a college for women; but she is soft, graceful, gentle, and yielding, "as feminine in appearance as any early Victorian heroine of fiction." For Estbridge she is instantly "everything that his wife was not and could never become"—"the complete and absolute perfection of womanhood." She is what he has wanted since his youth (239, 245–46). In opposition to his judgment, his old ideals, his teaching, and his habits, she is the other pole of his "will to live," an "air of spring" bringing him "the miracle of renewed youth" (246–47). Most miraculous of all, she is, when he asks, willing to refuse an offer of the presidency of Hartwell College and meet him in one hour at Pennsylvania Station so that they may start cross-country for Shanghai—before they have time to compromise their futures. Estbridge sheds his past self like a husk; for once, destiny moves in obedience to his will (247–49).

Estbridge's third woman, his true mistress, is what he sees when he looks in the mirror: "*Science* had kept him young in return for the *passion he had lavished upon her*. In his bright blue eyes . . . still glistened the eternal enquiring spirit of youth" (242–43, italics added). Because young Tilly was, and Judith is, a mirror in which he sees himself, it is most likely the image of his science—Sophia, the ancients would have called her—he sees reflected in each. This possibility adds poignance to Estbridge's dilemma when, at the end, his assistant dies suddenly in a street accident and Estbridge himself feels "like a man who had died and been born anew"; in an instant he is "living with a different side of his nature—with other impulses." And yet he is a man torn asunder. If he embraces his true mistress (his science) directly, he must remain in New York with domineering Tilly, who will not divorce him (252). If he chooses Judith still waiting for him at the station, he will have only an indirect grasp of his deepest love—what he wants more than he wants any woman, as an old friend Jim Hoadly tells him (252). Speaking as though he were the voice of Estbridge's better judgment, Hoadly underlines the story's theme when he points out, "The only thing you ever loved in any woman was your own reflection" (251). The story ends with the clock ticking slowly on, while Estbridge stands "transfixed, bewildered, brooding," unable to decide between his two selves, between the "absolute perfection" of Judith and the fulfillment of his intellectual ambition. But while Estbridge stews, Glasgow steers the reader to a position of safety by giving us an ironist to identify with. Hoadly, with "the smile of some inscrutable image of wisdom," goads his friend: "It would be a pity to miss that train, wouldn't it?" (253).

Glasgow chose to withhold "The Professional Instinct" from publication, perhaps because the reversals, although appropriate to the psychology she sets up, are not appropriate to "realism of the probable and representative," which was the literary mode in which she worked prior to 1916. Or perhaps she withheld the story because it is too much a psychological essay; it too plainly sets forth the salient characteristics of the theory of behavior she was developing. When Hoadly says, "You aren't the first analytical psychologist who has identified the world with himself," he is giving too much away about the way individuals, according to Jungian psychology and more and more in Glasgow's fiction, impose masks of themselves upon the people they know best (251). Perhaps too she was not certain yet how she felt about the theory of psychological homeostasis the story hints she is moving toward: homeostasis, because Estbridge's psyche seems to possess a capacity for restoring its own equilibrium by creating phantasies to compensate for the prosperous failure he has become with Tilly Pratt. Glasgow seems of a divided mind, as she was with Gabriella Carr, whether such phantasies are illusions bred of male vanity or calls to renewed psychic health. Later short stories will throw more light upon these alternatives.

At any rate, the projection of unrecognized dimensions of the self and the spontaneity of compensatory phantasies are both central to analytical or Jungian psychology. Their concurrence in this early story provides a perspective we need to

understand Glasgow's later assessment of the effect Jung and
Freud had on the modern novel. In her autobiography she
wrote:

> It is true that the novel, as a *living force*, if not as a work of
> art, owes an *incalculable debt* to what we call, mistakenly, the
> new psychology, to Freud, in his earlier interpretations, and
> *more truly, I think, to Jung*. These men are to be judged by
> their own work, not by the excesses of a secondary influ-
> ence. For my part, though I was never a disciple, I was
> among the *first, in the South*, to perceive the invigorating ef-
> fect of this approach to experience. That the recoil went too
> far does not dishonor its leaders, for it is a law of our nature
> that every dynamic recoil should spring too far backward.
> Moderation has never yet engineered an explosion, and it
> requires an explosion to overturn a mountain of prejudice.[2]

Interestingly, she both stresses Jung and uses his theory of *en-
antiodromia*, by which things turn into their opposites, to describe the excesses of the movement, as though Jung
represented the moderation she preferred. Her claim, that she
was "among the first, in the South," to recognize their value,
is ambiguous; the books by Freud in her library were published in 1913 and 1914, but those by Jung go back no further
than 1936 and 1939.[3] Yet, there exists in *The Wheel of Life*
(1906) a very strong parallel to Jung's theory of masks and
personality change, though 1906 was probably too early for
anyone in America who did not read German to know Jung,
unless he or she had associates who kept up on new work in
the field. Because *The Wheel of Life* is heavily autobiographic,
it is likely that Glasgow's introspection (supported by passages in Carpenter's *Art of Creation* and Maeterlinck's *Wisdom
and Destiny*) had led her toward the Jungian position even before she knew of analytical psychology. But her understanding
lacked objectivity: in rejecting the phase of her own life de-

2 Ellen Glasgow, *The Woman Within* (New York, 1954), 269, italics added.
3 Carrington C. Tutwiler, Jr., *A Catalogue of the Library of Ellen Glasgow*
   (Charlottesville, 1969), 10–13.

scribed in *The Wheel of Life*, she failed in 1906 to appreciate what she had discovered about her own and, according to Jung, everyman's personality development.

By 1916, if not earlier, she did know someone who read German; had studied in Heidelberg, Vienna, and Munich; and probably kept up with work in the field. The nature and extent of her relationship with Dr. Pearce Bailey of New York are far from clear; he was definitely her suitor, probably her lover and doctor combined. He was also her literary collaborator, at least for the one story "The Professional Instinct." His letter to her written March 8, 1916, contains these suggestions: "It seems to me that Estbridge's review of his life should follow the scene with Tilly. Won't you write the scene right in & get it back to me before Wednesday. I think you might go right on from where I stop [illegible]. . . . Have given no thought to the other stories—want to keep the characters of this one clear in my mind. You will know [illegible] that what I send you is merely dictated & you are free to cut it up [?] or do away with it altogether as you please."[4] The possibilities this note raises are intriguing. Is the story so much the product of Bailey's mind that Glasgow did not feel she could publish it under her own name? Probably not—she did not follow his advice. Is the story part of their affair? Is it Glasgow's reply to the suit of a man who loved her and who, parallel to Estbridge, had been adjunct professor of neurology at Columbia from 1906 to 1910 and cofounder in 1909 of the Neurological Institute of New York? Perhaps—but Bailey's own wife had been dead since about 1912. Is it then Glasgow's view of what had happened in an earlier phase of their relationship? Was it too personal and transparent to publish? Possibly.

The note from Bailey gives clearer answers to another group of questions. It shows that the story of Estbridge was begun by March, 1916, and that this tale belongs with the earliest of the stories included in *The Shadowy Third and Other Stories*. It

4 Pearce Bailey to Glasgow, in Ellen Glasgow Collection, Alderman Library, University of Virginia; Raper, *Without Shelter*, 104–106, 115, 210–11.

implies that Bailey would eventually give some thought "to the other stories" Glasgow had underway in 1916—"The Shadowy Third," "Thinking Makes It So," and possibly "Dare's Gift," all three to be in print by March, 1917. It also proves that we should not be surprised if we discover elements of a sophisticated psychological structure beneath the comic or gothic surfaces of any of Glasgow's fictions written around or after March, 1916; for she had by then made solid contact with analytical psychology and, with Bailey's help, had begun to add professional, presumably objective, insight to her own more valuable introspections and intuitions.

All the short stories reflect this new direction. The ghost stories, which seem a little opaque but are probably simpler than the stories of "men and women," will become clearer if we look first at the latter group. Each of these adds subtlety to the psychological discoveries of the prototypic Estbridge pattern.

"Thinking Makes It So" has been dismissed as a childish "example of wishfulfillment" by editor Meeker because the protagonist of this Cinderella phantasy metamorphoses in her forty-third year from a tired, faded, old-fashioned librarian into a woman who is brave, strong, pure, and beautiful— changes apparently because a man she has never met, a railroad builder in far-off Colorado, thinks of her this new way. Meeker's interpretation overlooks the "fairy godmother" of the tale—the process of psychological homeostasis that seeks to balance Margaret French's personality. She is "worn and repressed and overworked" because she has allowed herself to be aged by a "habit of self-effacement": in a "family of commonplace beauties" someone had to be plain and work hard. Margaret, never pretty or young, *chose* the role of the female martyr-saint, suppressed her own drives in the interest of the female selfishness of her sister and nieces, dressed in "colorless and wan and monotonous" clothes, and gave up her poetry to support the others by writing "silly stories" (73–75). The beautiful woman in flaming rose whom the railroad builder John Brown, like Estbridge, dreams into being is partly the product of Brown's Colorado isolation—that is, his projected need for the feminine—but she is also the shadow side of Margaret's personality, the suppressed beauty and energy and youth Margaret distilled into her early poems. In the poems Brown has seen the unconscious half of her which she doesn't believe exists. Even after she chooses this new self and sees someone with "shining eyes," "strangely young and innocent," in her mirror, she remains too critical to accept her own revolt; she considers her choice a lie (78, 81, 82). The chorus figures chant that change is unnatural; the Bible claims, "You can't make yourself over by taking thought" (84). Only one philosophical niece insists that nature has a "way of equalizing things," of "trying not to let you be cheated." The niece thereby confirms Margaret in the contact she has made with "the wealth" of her own nature, "some inexhaustible source of hope and joy," "the very essence of life" she feels in her veins, the woman whom Brown's thought has created (83, 85). In the end Brown's phantasy is transformed into a reality, not because Glasgow has ceased to be critical of evasive idealism, but because she has begun to see that, if imagination is rooted in psychic need, surface reality has no right to tyrannize phantasy. Here there is no ironist for the reader to identify with. Consequently, we are asked to expand our view of reality to allow for abrupt personality changes in which shadow selves come suddenly to the surface.

Glasgow's interest in such dynamics of the personality in part explains why she does better when she deals with the doubleness of adultery than with the single-mindedness of young love, for her married characters generally have suppressed great parts of themselves. In "The Difference," the next of the nonghost stories although it was published six years after the account of Margaret French, Glasgow focuses upon the split within Margaret Fleming, whose conflict chiefly reflects the pull toward opposites in her husband, George. When, after twenty years of happy marriage, Margaret receives a letter from Rose Morrison announcing that she, Rose, is George's mistress, the shock brings with it the

strange power of repressed truth suddenly revealed. Margaret
feels that "on the surface of her life nothing had changed,"
but that in "the real Margaret, the vital part of her . . . hidden
far away in that deep place where the seeds of mysterious impulses and formless desires lie buried . . . there were unexpressed longings which had never taken shape even in her
imagination," "secrets . . . she had never acknowledged in her
own thoughts" (167). She begins to think that Rose does the
things with her husband that she herself has become too old
and "Victorian" to do.

Margaret sees Rose and herself as opposites in a disjunc-
tion, of questionable validity, which divides women into
those men admire and those men love, women of spirit—herself—and women of "raw flesh"—Rose—Victorian women
and modern women (169, 174, 176). When she meets her opposite, she is blinded by "beauty like a lamp." Even when she
decides it is no more than the blaze given off by the burning
of dead leaves—which she had previously associated with
parts of her own life—she is still struck by the security, com-
petence, candor, infallible self-esteem, and freedom from
shame that Rose's youth gives her (173). Rather than embrace
her opposite and thereby transform her own life, as well as
George's, she retreats to the serene spiritual haven of a role
she knows better, the martyred wife who sacrifices herself for
her husband's freedom and happiness (177). Even so, Rose
has penetrated Margaret's traditional and sternly moral mind
enough for the latter to gain some sense that George is
"larger, wilder, more adventurous in imagination, than she
had dreamed," possessed of "some secret garden of romance
where she had never entered" (178). She also recognizes that
behind "the marionette" George sees when he looks at her
there is her real self. Though silent, the latter longs to tell him
that she too is "a creature of romance, of adventure," capable
of giving him in marriage "all he sought elsewhere" (180).
Despite her timid silence about his longed-for union of opposites, she is irked with George when he rejects her own righteous self-sacrifice by characterizing Rose as a mere

"recreation," a girl young enough to be his daughter (181, 182). She finds her tie to Rose, not in the enriching union of opposite traits, but in shared, narrowing qualities: "the bond of woman's immemorial disillusionment" (183). Both women remain mere reflections of a Western man's neurotic split between love and desire. Margaret might have healed this neurosis (which Freud called "The Most Prevalent Form of Degradation in Erotic Life"[5]) if she had insisted upon her own wholeness. Because "The Difference" lacks the ironic perspective of "The Professional Instinct" and the comic vision of unity and health of "Thinking Makes It So," its tone is chiefly pathetic, if vaguely amusing; its perspective, that of flat realism.

Published in the same year, "The Artless Age" shows how a similar view of personalities that are only partially developed can be turned to satiric capital. The contrast here is between Mary Louise Littleton, a "nice girl" who wears the "Victorian aura" although she is just twenty, and Geraldine Plummer, a "modern young girl" who paints her face like a geisha and bobs her hair (185). The older characters have a sense that some sort of synthesis of the two would be desirable; they find each of the extremes as designing and selfish as all youth and figure it "would be good for Geraldine if they could be thrown together" (195, 199). The want of this synthesis produces much of the humor: one-sidedness turns even the virtue of Mary Louise into a vice. These one-dimensional personalities evoke the same response as the character called the "vice" in Roman comedy: we laugh at such divisions of the self to make ourselves whole. We also laugh, with relief, to learn that neither Mary Louise nor Geraldine is as one-sided as she appears: angelic Mary Louise has her duplicities and devilish Geraldine her Victorian female arts. The male characters reveal a similar split between surface and real selves. Richard Askew, a "nice boy" so flawlessly handsome

5 Sigmund Freud, *The Collected Papers of Sigmund Freud*, ed. Ernest Jones (New York, 1959), IV, 203–16.

he appears unreal, chooses Geraldine's element of surprise over Mary Louise's static perfection. And Geraldine's father, a "faithful widower" for twenty years, falls, like a dirty old man, for Mary Louise, who is literally young enough to be his daughter. In each of the four characters, the change in conduct brings laughter because it comes as a surprising sign of health.

All the stories discussed thus far share a shortcoming common to much psychological fiction: they are mere fragments. Each either rips the mask off a character or takes a core sample of a character's buried life. They give no hint how such moments of insight might be structured into a full-length novel. If Glasgow had been able to do no more than describe thwarted individuals or tell tales of characters who have brief but revealing adventures, she might have been forced to create catalogs of grotesques like Sherwood Anderson or books of fragments like the novels Thomas Wolfe wrote after *Look Homeward, Angel*. And she probably would have done so without the brilliance of these two and certainly without Faulkner's genius for collage and montage. But she was better trained than any of these in two traditions of the novel: the realist novel of James in which an innocent protagonist becomes lost in a thick web of self-deception only to have his illusions destroyed in a moment of tragic self-discovery and the "evolutionary" novel that traces "the process of cause and effect" and thereby explores the source of the innocence that traps the protagonist in Jamesian realism.[6]

"Romance and Sally Byrd," the last of the stories Glasgow published, provides a bridge from the story as personality exposure to the novel of personality evolution. It does so by combining the psychological theory of the earlier stories with the self-deception and disillusionment of such earlier novels as *Virginia*. But a change has occurred since *Virginia*, for Glasgow now has a different appreciation of the psychological origins of phantasies: she no longer regards them as "mis-

6 Quoted by Meeker, *Collected Stories*, 6.

takes" but as signs pointing the way to health. Because phantasies are necessary and compensatory, they continue to occur, even when "corrected" by reality, until the phantasy maker achieves a more viable compromise between inner and external reality—or resigns himself to defeat. This structure extends the psychological probe of the buried self as well as the Jamesian pattern.

The first quarter of "Romance and Sally Byrd" parallels "Thinking Makes It So." Sally Byrd's life has suddenly begun to repeat her imagination; there is a name singing "in her mind, as if a thrush were imprisoned there and could not get out" (217, 219). It is the name of Stanley Kenton, whom she met three weeks before by one of those strange chances that occur as though "a beneficent Providence" had intervened "in the chaos of circumstances" (217–18). She has begun to contrast the "fairy ring" of his name in her thought with the "dreary round" of her life before. His name adds the expectation of "something delightful" about to happen where only drabness and poverty and monotony—teaching, eating, caring for her joyless grandparents—had been (217). Bred out of this emptiness, her first phantasy leads her to a sense of community in the joy of living. But it also causes her to pity her family for not escaping, like her, into freedom (220). This illusion collapses when magical Stanley announces he is married—estranged from his wife, but still married. "I thought you knew," he adds, before offering an arrangement slightly different from that Sally had counted on. Although she grows hysterical—the situation suddenly strikes her as absurd—and longs to accept his alternate offer, her moral instinct survives the shock (222–24). Her second phantasy is that she will let him go but never forget him: she converts this "hopeless love" into a "secret garden" she enters simply by shutting her eyes (225–26). The third phantasy grows out of the second when she hears that Stanley has been injured in an accident and hurries to New York from Richmond because she feels he needs her desperately: a "picture of herself leading Stanley along a crowded street" flashes in her mind as though cast "on a blank white sheet by a magic lantern" (227–28). The light of illusions two and three goes out when Sally finds Stanley's wife already there to nurse him. The fourth phantasy occurs on the train home and takes the person of a "young man with blue eyes," who lives only a few blocks from her house and who happens to be much better looking and much younger than Stanley. He leaves her in the day coach with her fifth phantasy, that—like Stanley's wife, who gave her a lecture on the relief of having your heart break at last and thereby finishing with love—she has finished with romance forever. She sees her "future as a gray, deserted road strewn wth dead leaves." Still there is the "indestructible illusion" that she might any day meet the young man with blue eyes again. Although at the end she enters her house with "withered leaves on the front porch," dramatic irony offsets the imagery; for her final words ("Never again!") are the illusory ones that began the story (236–38). Written during the same period as *Barren Ground*, this story offers in Sally Byrd a preview of the psyche of young, romantic Dorinda Oakley. Perhaps both heroines are by-products of Glasgow's own excursion into triangular love.

After we have grown used to finding the unconscious content of one character projected upon another, in Glasgow's stories of men and women, we should have no difficulty understanding a similar process when we find it in the ghost stories; for the supernatural has been employed as a language for the invisible things of the psyche at least since Book I of *The Iliad*. There Athena, goddess of wisdom, descends to stay the hand of Achilles and thereby keep him from hacking Agamemnon to pieces. Editor Meeker says that Glasgow's ghosts "are only objective correlatives" for an idea, "the necessity and difficulty of believing in the intangible" (14). To put the problem differently, Freud used the mechanics of the nineteenth century for metaphor to reify the intangible needs and fears of man in the "compartments" of the psyche (id, ego, superego); he also described the "energy flow" between these inner "reservoirs."

Literature of the supernatural uses the figurative language of religion and superstition to reify the same intangible processes, but in an external form.

Two recent developments may have given ghost stories a type of validity they lacked in Glasgow's generation. Today we know enough about the effects chemical alterations have on consciousness to acknowledge that sane people may sometimes *see things that are not there*, and see them as substantially as though they were there—even when these phenomena exist *only* as chemical changes in the brain. We also know that strong emotions like fear, hatred, guilt, and desire involve significant chemical changes throughout the body—sufficient to color, perhaps even to alter, what we see. This is not to say that Glasgow's ghosts are to be dismissed immediately as figments of disturbed imaginations; to the contrary, the attitude toward the supernatural in these stories covers the full range from the belief of the truly *marvelous*, through the ambiguity of the *fantastic*, to the *uncanny* and merely *exceptional*.[7] Such variety is possible because the narrator in each of the stories is also a character, and the degree of reliability of each narrator determines the reader's response to the supernatural element.

The first-person narrator of "The Shadowy Third," a nurse from Richmond named Margaret Randolph, is—like Margaret French, Sally Byrd, and Caroline Meade (of *The Builders*)—extremely impressionable and receptive to calls to adventure beyond her normal reality. She thinks she is "too emotional." A critical reader might call her romantically hysterical: she accepts her call to care for Dr. Maradick's wife as though it were the "imperative summons" of her "destiny." She is also fey: she frequently knows her fate with a kind of foreknowledge she insists is "beyond any doubt." Endowed with the sympathy and imagination of a novelist, she cannot help putting herself into cases (52–54). Most important, she is telling the

---

7 Here I follow the terminology of Tzvetan Todorov, *The Fantastic: A Structural Approach to a Literary Genre*, trans. Richard Howard (Ithaca, N.Y., 1975), 25–33, 36, 46–48.

story in the past tense—*after* she has been somehow involved in the mysterious death of Dr. Maradick, a man she once hero-worshiped. But because she does not mention this involvement until the penultimate paragraph, we spend the story trying to outwit the narrator (and the author) concerning the motive and conditions for her seeing the ghost of Dr. Maradick's daughter Dorothea.

The first apparition follows a strong suggestion from a superstitious servant and, like the first three appearances, involves some tricky lighting (56, 58, 67). Even Margaret says that she eventually began to persuade herself "that the little figure had been an optical illusion," despite the fact that Mrs. Maradick also sees Dorothea (68). But then Mrs. Maradick seems even more unreliable than Margaret: she is suffering from the fear that Maradick killed Dorothea to get his hands on the large trust her first husband had set up for Dorothea, an arrangement bypassing Mrs. Maradick unless their daughter should die (55). Margaret's doubts about the ghost (after Mrs. Maradick dies in an asylum) tend to reestablish her credibility just before she reports the fourth appearance of the girl, this time skipping rope. Although this apparition is "as clear as day," it comes hard upon the news that Dr. Maradick, now in possession of all his wife's money, is soon to marry again—an announcement that leaves the narrator nervous, "shaken by the suddenness" of his plans. The reader also knows what she doesn't admit: that she now hates the doctor, as much for his choosing a woman other than herself as for whatever he did to Mrs. Maradick. The ghost of Dorothea, especially Margaret's insistence that she saw a child's jump rope on the stairs just before the doctor fell to his death, becomes the phantasy through which Margaret deals with her guilt. The implication is not necessarily that she planned and executed his death, but that she *feels she did* because she wanted revenge and she startled him, enough to cause him to stumble, by suddenly flipping on the light—to warn him, she tells herself and the reader (71). That Mrs. Maradick may also have had guilt to hide from herself is at least implied by the fact that her first husband chose to bypass her with the trust: was it simply to avoid inheritance tax? Otherwise, for Mrs. Maradick, Dorothea reflects the young goodness the former lost when she realized she had married the sort of doctor all the nurses and patients fall in love with (53–54, 57). In any case, Margaret insists on the ghost to the end, and the reader can choose either the psychological or the marvelous interpretation, an ambiguity that marks literature of the phantastic.[8]

"Dare's Gift," despite the narrator's heavy hints of the incredible and the supernatural, is really little more than uncanny or exceptional, and the choice depends upon how superstitious the reader may be about the effects of place. Dare's Gift is one of those James River plantations like Shirley or Berkeley or Westover but less well-known because it has mainly been associated with treacheries since its first owner betrayed Nathaniel Bacon to Governor Berkeley. Rather than a visible ghost, there is some "spirit of the place" associated with the "thought of the house" and with "the psychic force of its memories," a power that proves too strong for both the neurotic and phlegmatic temperaments of persons who inhabit the place. In the Civil War, Lucy Dare betrayed her Yankee fiancé to Confederate soldiers. More recently, the male private secretary of one owner ran off with embezzled funds, and a caretaker absconded with his own wife's sister (92, 94). The wife of the present owner goes to the opposition with some business secrets her husband, a corporation lawyer, has stumbled across, a scandal that involves the railroad line her husband is employed to defend against charges of illegal rebates (99–101).

Only the Lucy Dare and railroad episodes are developed. The lawyer is the narrator; he is told the tale of Lucy Dare by a long-winded local doctor who had his leg shot off in the Civil War. The relative morality of the two betrayals receives no attention. The emphasis falls instead upon the psychological origins. The Lucy Dare episode becomes an explanation for

8 Todorov, *Fantastic*, 31.

the southern "sense of place," especially the excessive loyalty
and evasive idealism of the region. The Dares, the old doctor
claims, had the extreme enthusiasm for the war cause of non-
combatants; with no outlet for passion except "thought," they
made the idea of the Confederacy into a dream or ideal that
ruled them. Lucy had always appeared cold to the men she
loved, but during the war her physically starved brain became
inflamed, obsessed with the southern cause. Faith in the Lost
Cause began as an illusion to compensate for defeat. It was a
dangerous illusion, for with Richmond ready to fall in any
case, Lucy sacrificed her fiancé to save the Cause (106–109).

Mrs. Beckwith, the lawyer's wife, presents several parallels
to Lucy. Her outspoken response to the railroad scandal is
compensatory: for ten harmonious years she has been a silent, acquiescent wife, used by her husband as a sounding
board for his ideas (95). Probably as a result of this repres-
sion, she had the nervous breakdown that led Beckwith to
purchase Dare's Gift for a retreat. Her neurosis makes her,
like Lucy, susceptible to the isolation of the place, especially
to the noises of the country at night. She grows bitter when
Beckwith leaves her there to pursue his work in Washington;
and after he tells her the details of the scandal, she likely hears
the same voices he heard urging him "to something—somewhere—" (99–101). Beckwith's insistence that his wife's behavior was caused by the "invincible spirit of darkness" that
hovers about Dare's Gift is simply his way of projecting the
guilt he feels for each of her breakdowns. He lacks the objectivity the old doctor brought to the case of Lucy Dare. Were
he to achieve that objectivity, he would be forced to reclaim
the responsibility he reads into the spirit of the place.

Published in 1920 and the central story in the group, "The
Past" runs the risk of turning into an allegory—one, as the
title implies, about the rather Bergsonian persistence of the
spirit of the past—for it is here that Glasgow spells out her
ideas about "words that express invisible things" (134).
Ghosts are part of the forgotten language. The ghost of the

first Mrs. Vanderbridge is simply (the second Mrs. V. tells us) the thought in her husband's mind of his first wife; it is, specifically, his guilt because he married her when she was too young and she died in the first year of the marriage, eight months pregnant (132–33). But beneath this seemingly transparent surface, there are several hidden and therefore intriguing currents. First, Mr. Vanderbridge's subjective reality has become visible without his knowing it: nearly everyone in the story sees the first Mrs. V. sitting with them as they eat. In other words, her ghost embodies a separate fear or other meaning for each person who sees her. She is Mr. V.'s guilt. But because his obsession is destroying not only his mind and health but his second marriage and the health of his new wife—they are all "drugged" by the past—the ghost, selfish and childish, is a visible sign that the new wife feels she may be inadequate to replace the first wife in her husband's affections. The narrator, Miss Wrenn, the present Mrs. V.'s secretary, sees the ghost simply because she is *sympatico*: she comes from Mrs. V.'s background, which gives her the power to step inside the phantastical scenario of the household. The letters Miss Wrenn discovers, written to the first Mrs. V. by her lover *after* her marriage, are suggestive in light of the first wife's early and troubled pregnancy. But they are an effective solution only because they lay the ghost for Mrs. V. by restoring her sense of adequacy compared with the idealized first wife. And her new superiority to the past will better enable her in the future to lay the spirit for her husband. The overt psychologizing reduces the marvelous in this story to the merely uncanny.

The same lack of ambiguity can be charged against the last of the ghost stories, "Whispering Leaves" (1923), for its ghost is obviously an embodiment of the maternal instinct. The story is interesting, however, on two counts. First, it is an unexpected story to come from the pen of a woman who insisted the maternal instinct had been left out of her—unless we recognize that the supernatural has traditionally been a mode by which the artist evades censorship, that of his (or her) own psyche as well as of society.[9] The ghost of the black woman is obviously a substitute mother created by seven-year-old Pell to fill the gap in his emotional life. Not only are his mother and the real Mammy Rhody dead, but Pell is also estranged from his stepmother. He has become a grotesque: birdlike, "ugly and pinched," a nervous, sensitive child with an excitable imagination, though a child not totally lacking in charm (144, 151). Meeker suggests that Pell is a fictional mask of Glasgow's own lonely childhood (10).

Rhody is also visible to Miss Effie, the narrator, *who never saw her alive.* Miss Effie finds "her serene leaf-brown face strangely attractive, almost, oddly enough," she thinks, "as if her mysterious black eyes . . . had penetrated to some secret chamber of my memory. . . . I felt as if I had known her all my life, particularly in some half-forgotten childhood which haunted me like a dream. . . . Stranger still, I felt not only that she recognized me, but that she possessed some secret which she wished to confide to me, that she was charged with a profoundly significant message which, sooner or later, she would find an opportunity to deliver" (147). This language is as close to that of dreams as to the rhetoric of the supernatural, especially since Effie seems to be describing an image from her racial memory—Rhody nursed her mother and grandmother—a figure of the sort that might appear in an especially moving dream.

The second element of special interest is the texture that the setting and the symbols create. Rhody, whose name means *rose* is consistently associated with trees, flowering shrubs, and underbrush in a way which suggests to the animistic mind that, like the birds she tames, she might be a fleeting spirit dwelling in trees (144, 150, 151, 157, 159). But Rhody has a special affinity for the "sunken garden," a flowery space of old fruit trees and shrubs walled off by banks of honeysuckle. Even in this story—where the setting is supposed to

9 Raper, *Without Shelter*, 60; Todorov, *Fantastic*, 158–62.

appear as though it were part "of a universe painted on air"—
the sunken garden seems exceedingly dreamlike (142, 150).
Just before the scene in this graden, Effie stands before a
"greenish mirror," which reflects her "features in a fog"; her
image floats there "like a leaf in a lily pond." Then a "provocative fragrance, the aroma of vanished springs," draws her
to the garden, where the moisture of the "low ground by the
river . . . released the scents of a hundred springs." "Never,"
she says, "until that moment had I known what the rapture of
smell could be. And the starry profusion of the narcissi! From
bank to bank of honeysuckle the garden looked as if the
Milky Way had fallen over it and been caught in the high
grass" (150). Here in the "enchanted silence" she hears a bell,
then sees a light flashing from the house, before she turns to
see "the old negress . . . standing motionless under the
boughs of a peartree," with the "inarticulate appeal" in her
eyes, speaking "in some inaudible language which I did not
yet understand" of a message "which, sooner or later, she
would find a way to deliver" (150). The mirror and the narcissi
offer strong evidence that Rhody's inaudible language is the
forgotten one, the word that, when we remember it, carries us
past the "primitive wooden stile" to the sunken garden of the
mind. In other words, Rhody's ghost here speaks for the deep
maternal and fertile and forbidden core of Effie's being. Just
how forbidden to Effie—even to her creator—may be suggested by Rhody's race. As the story progresses, Rhody turns
out to be a projection of Effie's maternal concern for Pell; and
Rhody's secret message, as Pell delivers it, happens to be,
"Mammy says you must take me with you when you go
away" (160, 163).

Thus far Rhody has been shown to express an obvious need
in Pell for maternal "sympathy and understanding" and a secret need in Effie to give him a mother's care (154). If we follow the image clusters of the story, they lead us to a parallel
interpenetration of the three identities—Rhody, Pell, and Effie.
As we saw, Effie's image in the mirror is like a leaf, but leaves
in turn are associated by Effie with birds: "Dreamlike, too,

were my own sensations. . . . Feathery branches edged with brighter green brushed my cheeks like the wings of a bird; and though I knew it must be only my fancy, I seemed to hear a hundred jubilant notes in the enchanted gloom of the trees" (147). Birds are compared to ghosts tamed by Rhody and thus seem an avatar or attribute of Rhody; at one point an apparition of Rhody actually dissolves into a scarlet tanager and an ancient crepe myrtle—spirit and body (146, 157). Pell's hand is said to be "like a bird's claw" (152). The three characters thus seem to come together in the leaf and bird imagery. In other stories by Glasgow, especially "The Difference," another of the 1923 stories, leaves represent the past phases of the central character's life (165). As an archetype of dreams and myth, the bird often is an image of spiritual transformation in its flight from the earth to the heavens.

With all these factors taken into account, especially the tightly knit identification of the three main characters, "Whispering Leaves" suggests an exceedingly creative and healthy dream by someone—presumably the narrator Effie, otherwise the author—who set out in her phantasy life to rescue the helpless and deprived child in herself from the indifferent stepmother and complacent father to unite that child with the eternally maternal potential of the self. The final image of Effie, now in Rhody's role, taking little Pell—who has just been rescued by a shadowy Rhody from an "old storeroom, which was never opened"—in her arms and holding him there "safe and unharmed" indicates that the integration of the parts of the self has succeeded (163). The fire that destroys "Whispering Leaves" suggests that the old self—if not the whole social order—has been left behind.

"Jordan's End" may be another story about setting the self free of its past. Although there is no ghost in the story, it is the most ghostly Glasgow wrote. It could be argued that in "Whispering Leaves" Glasgow discovered that the language of dreams provides a more exact tool for expressing invisible things than does the rhetoric of the supernatural, for "Jordan's End" is also the most dreamlike of the group. As in "Whispering Leaves," the landscape suggests a dream journey, this time through the twilight of a deep tunnel in the November woods to a decaying house—haunted, not by ghosts, but by figures from the past, fates and madmen. There seems to be even more condensation of identities than in "Leaves." This effect is achieved in part by the shadowy quality of the characterization (there is, for example, very little evidence that the narrator is male) and in part by a pairing of characters into sharp alternatives: the narrator is paired, as the new doctor, with Carstairs, the old one; his guide, old man Peterkin, is set off against Peterkin's son Tony; old Mr. Timothy Jordan is mentioned in contrast to his nine-year-old grandson (204–205). Most important, Judith and Alan Jordan are joined, not only by their marriage, but as antithetical parts of a whole. She is tall and thin, with flesh that seems luminous, "as if an inward light pierced the transparent substance"; her beauty is "not of earth, but of triumphant *spirit*"—"perfection" (207). Though "lost within the impenetrable wilderness of the insane," Alan still possesses "the dignity of mere *physical* perfection"; he is at least six feet three, with blue eyes and hair the "color of ripe wheat" (211, italics added). Already in "Whispering Leaves," Glasgow had assigned two sets of twins to little Pell's stepmother but then did not develop that dream motif as she does here (151). Although the logic of day-to-day reality can account for many of the elements in "Jordan's End," only dream logic can account for the meaning concentrated in these pairings of young and old, of spirit and body, and ultimately of the past and the future. In dreams such opposites are halves of a single whole.

Along the same line, all the archetypes of the classic story of the decay of southern culture, from "The Fall of the House of Usher" to *Absalom, Absalom!*, are compacted in this short piece: the big house, the incest, the madness, the burial of the "living dead" (here in padded cells). In addition, the focus falls upon euthanasia, a theme that runs like an unmentionable current through much important writing in the South. It is suggested, for example, by the ending of *Absalom* and by

Webber's view of the web of his Joyner past in *The Web and the Rock*; and it is the theme that ties Ike McCaslin's education, in helping to kill the beloved Ben, to his lifework, the dismantling of a cultural order his grandfather created. Since the dream logic of "Jordan's End" suggests that, as in "Whispering Leaves," all the characters are attributes of the narrator, it may well be that these stories of euthanasia or beneficent death—a death from which the narrator usually rides away—are actually tales of attempted rescue: the narrator dreams his or her way to the core of his psyche, identifies what is still vital there, rescues it, and allows the dead past to be finally dead. In this case, Judith and Alan are paired at the vital core, but Judith is the viable half that must be delivered. The body has grown unhealthy; it is tainted by its heritage. In addition, the power of the body has become an unspecified threat to the spirit: "Last night something happened. Something happened," Judith repeats. And later: "He is very strong." Again: "We keep two field hands in the room day and night." Finally, when the narrator sees one of the three old crones crocheting an infant's sacque, Judith says, "You know now?" (209–11). Although the narrator answers affirmatively, it is doubtful he knows *all* that Judith has implied. He passes her the opiate, but his ignorance separates him from guilt for the two—or is it three?—acts of euthanasia she will eventually perform.

The narrator has passed through a tunnel of dreams, made contact with his vital center, and delivered her from the impenetrable wilderness of the insane to a lawn where "leaves were piled in long mounds like double graves." He leaves her standing on that neutral ground, "nearer to the bleak sky and the deserted fields than . . . to her kind," her shawl slipping "from her shoulders to the dead leaves" like an old worry or an old self. The narrator then drives "across the field and into the woods" (215–16). Afterward, he "gives up medicine, you know, and [turns] to literature as a safer outlet for a suppressed imagination" (210). Does this not suggest that he senses there is a level of knowledge in the episode that he both fears and lacks the intellectual background to handle? Only the literary tradition preserves the forgotten language he needs to express these invisible things.

With this insight and these stories, Ellen Glasgow transcended the flat realism based on external details that had generally been her métier before 1916 and did so by assimilating many of the insights regarding the unconscious self we usually associate with Freud and, especially in her case, with Jung. Perhaps she preferred Jung because his approach was more literary. The introspection, the supernatural and mythic elements, the waking dreams, the mystic moments, the romantic quests, and the strange personality transformations we find in literature have, as Jung showed, preserved for millennia the forgotten language of man's invisible hemisphere.

Written during the low point of her life, the short stories record the path Glasgow followed from emotional bankruptcy to a level of art she had never before achieved. They are her experiments. In them she masters the technique for revealing a character's unconscious side by projecting it upon other characters, a technique she experimented with, but less successfully, in the three novels between *Virginia* (1913) and *Barren Ground* (1925). In the novels the major characters ultimately believe their needs can be satisfied by unembodied abstractions. In the stories, by contrast, the characters discover their deeply felt emotions—their fears and loves—embodied in one another. In the stories Glasgow also seems to accept something very much like a theory of psychological homeostasis, according to which the psyche tries to achieve inner equilibrium by creating phantasies to guide the individual toward a wholeness of the self. This process can produce abrupt personality changes when the buried self comes suddenly to the surface—an abruptness the realism of William Dean Howells and Henry James would have considered improbable and therefore would have discouraged. But Glasgow could find strong precedents for such strange exceptions in the romances of Edgar Allan Poe or, better because nonromantic, in the psychological realism of Feodor Dostoevsky.[10] All these techniques would be brought to bear when Glasgow sat down to write *Barren Ground*. In addition, the landscape of this important novel would prove to be even more subjective than the sunken garden of "Whispering Leaves." The brand of satire that emerges when characters get stuck in one-dimensional roles, as in "The Artless Age," would be brought to perfection when she came to write *The Romantic Comedians*. The combination of compensatory phantasies with the realistic structure of self-recognition and disillusionment that produced "Romance and Sally Byrd" would eventually lead to the tragedy of manners that is her finest work, *The Sheltered Life*.

One device she did not carry forward into her major phase was the use of the supernatural in either the phantastic or marvelous modes; even in three of the ghost stories, her ghosts are less ghosts than ideas. In *Barren Ground* her ghosts will further evolve into living people, for there is something exceedingly ghostly about the way, in the second half of that novel, wraithlike Geneva and mummified Jason seem to emerge from Dorinda's mind. Glasgow had obviously decided, by the time she wrote "Jordan's End," that the invisible things which interested her could be better expressed in the dreamlike mode of the merely exceptional than through either flat realism or any variety of the supernatural.

We may safely conclude that without the short stories we would never have known Glasgow's major phase, which begins with *Barren Ground*.

10 Todorov, *Fantastic*, 48.

# Chapter V

# The Landscape of Revenge:

## *Barren Ground* (1925)

Ellen Glasgow's *Barren Ground* (1925) stands squarely in the doorway through which the tradition of southern writing passes from the often barren past into its fruitful modern period. The novel appeared midway between the book publication of H. L. Mencken's scornful but inspiring essay, "The Sahara of the Bozart," and the *annus mirabilis* of southern literature, 1929–1930—the year that brought *They Stooped to Folly*; *Look Homeward, Angel*; *The Sound and the Fury*; and *I'll Take My Stand.* Along with the special interest Allen Tate, Stark Young, and Robert Penn Warren took in Glasgow's writing, the novel's position in time implies that the book must have cast a significant shadow across the southern imagination of the decade that followed. If so, Glasgow's remarkable use of the land ought to hold special interest for critics. In this work the landscape frequently turns out to be a manifestation of the psyche; it serves both as a screen upon which the protagonist projects the otherwise ineffable contents of her mind and as a mirror of her body through which she expresses otherwise forbidden feelings about the physical parts of her being. Through the land the protagonist seeks to complete her all-consuming project: liberation from, and revenge against, male abuse of her body and emotions.

In a recent essay, "Ellen Glasgow as Feminist," Monique Parent Frazee argues that Glasgow's environment prevented her from dealing with the underlying tenet of the contemporary women's movement, which asserts "that reform must begin with a revised appraisal of the female body"; Glasgow,

Frazee implies, is too squeamish about the body to investigate its potentialities. In a literal sense Frazee is probably correct. And yet, in an indirect way, *Barren Ground* reveals a great deal about the manner in which the female body affects female emotions. If we miss this dimension of the book, it may be because Glasgow explores the attitude Western woman has traditionally taken toward her body and her sex, not through a literal assault upon the body, but through the landscape. In few places has the Western pattern of sublimated thinking about the female body been stronger than in the defense of the body citadel that passes for courtship in regions of the American South dominated by the teachings of the puritan Protestants. *Barren Ground* tells the story of a daughter of such Protestants (Presbyterians here), a young woman who has been wounded in her sex. Her story passes through three phases: first, the siege and capture of her citadel; then her recovery and her long project of revenge; and finally the effort to accommodate her damaged emotions to the order of nature. But Glasgow disguises this tale of revenge—from the casual reader and usually from the heroine herself—as a female success story, an exemplum of survival, struggle, and triumph over circumstances.[1]

The disguise creates an interesting but not unique problem for the careful reader: how do we know anything about levels of meaning hidden from a heroine "through whose sensibilities the entire narrative takes its course"?[2] The answer, of course, turns out to be that we know things that the heroine, Dorinda Oakley, refuses to become fully aware of. To convey this added information, the author employs four fictive devices: (1) a narrator more sophisticated than the heroine, (2) symbols of the heroine's unconscious life, (3) projections of

1 Monique Parent Frazee, "Ellen Glasgow as Feminist," in M. Thomas Inge (ed.), *Ellen Glasgow: Centennial Essays* (Charlottesville, 1976), 171–72; Ellen Glasgow, *A Certain Measure* (New York, 1969), 160.
2 J. Donald Adams, "The Novels of Ellen Glasgow," *New York Times Book Review*, December 18, 1938, p. 1.

the heroine's deeper levels upon other characters, and (4) projections of similar levels upon the landscape.

Of Dorinda Oakley as the point of view, Glasgow wrote: "From the first page to the last, no scene or episode or human figure appears outside her field of vision or imagination."[3] This has led critics to assume that Glasgow intended every element of the novel to be seen from Dorinda's point of view. This is certainly not so. On the second page, a single temporal allusion setting the story "thirty years ago" firmly establishes the presence of a narrator outside the mind of the twenty-year-old heroine.[4] Although between this narrator and Dorinda a Siamese connection exists that allows the former to flow at will in and out of the latter's thoughts and feelings, the narrator persists as a separate personality, at least until the final three pages of the book. At the very end, the possibility arises that Dorinda has achieved full sophistication in the author's mind, thus closing the distance between character and narrator. If so, the ending loses the potential for irony implicit in all the earlier chapters. The ending thus presents problems with which the narrator can give us no help, and we must postpone consideration of them until later.[5]

The personality of the narrator is most often that of a knowing, objective, and ageless social historian who lays the material foundations of the story. There are other passages, however, where the narrator speaks as a psychologist; and these are important occasions if the book is truly, as Glasgow claimed, about "the universal chords beneath regional variations of character," rather than about the tenant system and scientific farming.[6]

---

3 *"The Sheltered Life,"* in Glasgow, *A Certain Measure*, 200.
4 Ellen Glasgow, *Barren Ground* (New York, 1925), 4. This book will hereafter be referred to by page number only.
5 For additional problems with the point of view, see Louis D. Rubin, Jr., *The Teller in the Tale* (Seattle, 1967), 12–13.
6 Glasgow, *A Certain Measure*, 152–54.

It is the narrator as psychologist who enables us to speak with authority about the hidden levels of Dorinda's personality. In the first quarter of the novel, the narrator talks of two dimensions—public behavior and hidden passion. For example, the narrator tells us: "To the girl, with her intelligence and independence, many of her mother's convictions had become merely habits of speech; yet, after all, was not habit rather than belief the ruling principle of conduct?" (84). Habitual conduct makes up the sum of Dorinda's life, both public and private, until her passion for Jason shows her another side of herself: the "golden light of sensation," a "flying rapture," "the piercing sweetness of surrender." Suddenly she knows that the existence her family and friends lead—of "milking and cooking, of sowing and reaping"—amounts to a "strange conspiracy of dissimulation," which has never, for a reason she does not yet understand, "betrayed to her" the "hidden knowledge . . . of life" (27). When her formerly repressed emotional and sexual self has, in turn, run its course and left her seduced, pregnant, and abandoned, she begins to sense a third level, one deeper than her folly and ignorance: "She could never be broken while the vein of iron held in her soul" (180). This vein of iron consists chiefly of her Presbyterian conscience, with all that means about fortitude, endurance, work, self-reliance, and success, and about facing facts and fearing dreams (182). It seems her essential self because the ideal her mother holds up for emulation is her great-grandfather, John Calvin Abernethy, a retired Presbyterian missionary of Scotch-Irish descent, a man given to a narrow but deep piety (7–8). This ancestral voice serves to stabilize her personality, and (during the long middle third of the book when in her behavior, as well as in the eyes of others, she resembles a man) it enables her to purify her body, redeem her family's Old Farm, and make a pile of money—all in the name of survival. In the process, the vein of iron works its way up from the depths to become her hardened surface, her own pattern of dreary habitual conduct. Others may believe that she is still "human enough" at the core; but when they tell her so, she smiles at their "flattering ignorance of fact" (473). The narrator hints, however, of activity at a fourth level of Dorinda's psyche, at the supposedly dead core of her being; for something down there undermines her success by preventing the facts of reality from satisfying her. She continues to feel that she has "never known the completeness . . . she had expected of life." She cannot quite put her finger on what she has missed. We are told it is not love or motherhood. Then the narrator adds: "No, the need went deeper than nature. It lay so deep, so far down in her hidden life, that the roots of it were lost in the rich darkness" (345–46). The nearest she can come to identifying what she lacks is the general term *happiness*.

Although not a great deal of help with this last level, the narrator gives us enough information unavailable to Dorinda to suggest that Dorinda's psyche develops through four phases. In each phase, her behavior is dominated by a different one of the four levels of her personality: public, conventional habits; romantic impulses, generally repressed but released by Jason; a vein of iron that starts deep down and rises to the surface; and a core, said to be dead or hollow, but still active. The relationship between the levels proves so precarious that, when Jason triggers her romantic impulses, they take over her personality completely and alienate her from conventionality in herself and others. Similarly, the vein of iron, once developed by adversity, displaces the two more superficial modes of behavior at the surface and thereby forces her romantic passion toward the core. To identify other elements surviving in this core that Dorinda's Abernethy conscience will not permit her to express, we must go beyond the narrator to two complex devices that reveal the deeper levels—symbols and projections.

The novel is rich in symbolism, perhaps the richest Glasgow ever wrote. We must distinguish, however, between objects and persons that seem symbolic to Dorinda in her conscious states because she attaches unusual significance to them, and those objects that arise spontaneously from her unconscious mind. The latter form the deep structure of the novel and permit the author to communicate information to the reader while bypassing the character's understanding.

Central to this structure is a dream Dorinda has in New York. It occurs two years after she aborted her child (in one of the most convenient collisions between a pedestrian and a moving vehicle in modern fiction) and on the eve of her accelerated course in scientific farming, just after she has felt a strong call from the farm to go South and—Science save us!—redeem Old Farm from its fallen state. In her dream she is back home again, trying desperately to plow one of the abandoned fields. Suddenly at the end of the first furrow, her two favorite horses turn and speak to her:

> "You'll never get this done if you plough a hundred years," they said, "because there is nothing here but thistles, and you can't plough thistles under." Then she looked around her and saw that they were right. As far as she could see, on every side, the field was filled with prickly purple thistles, and every thistle was wearing the face of Jason. A million thistles, and every thistle looked up at her with the eyes of Jason! She turned the plough where they grew thickest, trampling them down, uprooting them, plowing them under with all her strength; but always when they went into the soil, they cropped up again. Millions of purple flaunting heads! Millions of faces! They sprang up everywhere; in the deep furrow that the plough had cut; in the dun-coloured clods of the upturned earth; under the feet of the horses; under her own feet, springing back, as if they were set on wire stems, as soon as she had crushed them into the ground. "I am going to plough them under, if it kills me," she said aloud; and then she awoke. . . . It was the first time she had dreamed of Jason. (239–40)

If we feel we should hesitate before plunging into the interpretation this remarkable passage calls for, let it be to point out that Glasgow's copy of Freud's *Interpretation of Dreams* was published in 1913, her copy of *Psychopathology of Everyday Life* in 1914.[7] A Freudian reading of the dream may well be

7 Tutwiler, *A Catalogue of the Library of Ellen Glasgow*, 10–11.

what Glasgow intended. If so, it seems to be the only large passage in her novels that she deliberately constructed around Freudian dream symbols. If a Freudian reading is not intended, the passage has apparently been so contaminated by the author's own psyche that it should be of interest to those readers intent upon biographical criticism. The present analysis, however, takes the dream to have originated in the unconscious mind of the fictional Dorinda and assumes that Glasgow selected the imagery to reveal Dorinda's character—not the author's. At some point, the participation of the author's unconscious image-making powers is, of course, also assumed, although it is not directly relevant to this discussion.

All the motifs of the dream have been prepared for so carefully that they resonate strongly. The horses associate with her fatalistic father, with fallen Presbyterians and sportive epicureans (40,94). Life-everlasting, the scent of which hangs over the field, recalls her mother and "the aroma of countless dead and forgotten Sabbaths." The abandoned field suggests not only Old Farm but Dorinda herself, especially her emotions and her womb (abandoned fields and ground provide perhaps the most effective recurring symbol in the novel). The single furrow plowed calls to mind Dorinda's brief experiment with sex.

Most important, however, the masculine and earthborn nature of the millions of thistles bearing Jason's face reveals the deeper meaning of Dorinda's passion to purify. Working backward, we discover that the ubiquity of the thistles echoes the scene of anxiety on the day she first left the hospital where she was taken after her accident; everywhere she went, everyone she saw looked like Jason (223). The dream thus betrays fear and hatred of people in masses—a misanthropic, perhaps genocidal, impulse. Through their association with Jason and their earth origin, the thistles also pick up the book's recurring snake imagery. Just after she came to in the hospital, still drugged, she began to daydream about thirst; she recalled "a hollow at Whistling Spring, where she had stepped on a snake in the tall weeds." This jars an earlier memory: "Jason had put his hand on a snake, and that was why everything else had happened" (215). Here snakes associate with the evil that stands guard over desired pleasure, an association that justifies the ferocity of her need to purify. The problem arises when we recall that, to Dorinda, Jason embodies both the pleasure and the evil. After he abandoned her, she began to pile her mistakes upon him and to make him the source of all her woe; she then "longed to destroy him and she knew that she was helpless" (166). The twinned nature of pleasure and evil also catches the masculine dimension of the thistle-snake cluster; for to the mind of a woman with a Presbyterian conscience and strong impulses, the male organ might seem the serpent that hovers between herself and the possibility of idealized love. Thus her will to eradicate the Jason thistles hints not only of a homicidal impulse (repeating the Freudian accident in which the gun held by Dorinda misfires at Jason) but suggests once more a genocidal drive, since she would strike—like Medea before her—at Jason's desire for offspring. Of course, she feels her outrage is justified. To her way of thinking Jason has polluted her womb and left her similarly barren. Larger than the prickly thistles is the plow Dorinda employs, a dream act showing that in her depths she is psychologically prepared to turn herself into a super*man* to get her revenge.

The earliest reference to a snake in the book (and the superficial reason she daydreams about Jason putting his hand on a snake) supports the masculine sexual association. Snakes arose first in one of Jason's favorite alibis, the excuse he gives for flunking everything. Warning her indirectly that he will drop her, he describes how a moccasin struck at his hand once when, as a boy, he was gathering dewberries with his mother (64). His other alibi for failure turns out to be that his father "broke [his] spirit . . . when [he] was little," kept him from doing what he wanted with his life, and made him study medicine instead (90). The two alibis are, of course, the same: they describe the intervention of the paternal barrier, the domineering father who robs the son of his will and confidence. The nursery tightness of Jason's early memory, the probability that the desired dewberries associate with mother and the moccasin with father, makes it a neat little paradigm of the Oedipal situation. Because the memory also parallels Dorinda's daydream of intense pleasure guarded by evil, she naturally associates the two. Her manly revenge thus strikes a blow against Jason's brand of fatalism as the cause of human weakness and failure, especially against the fatality that traces its roots to human sexuality, the puritan's deep source of original sin.

In the overdetermined world of dream actions, this need to extirpate evil from the abode of man (or woman) has a further dimension. As Dorinda is slow to realize, this dimension shows that her urge to purify involves other drives as likely to destroy her own femininity as they are to castrate Jason. For where does this recurring emblem of evil guarding pleasure come from? Before she fell in love, Dorinda spent much of her free time reading in the Abernethy library. Even if she did not stumble across stories of Jason and his model Cadmus, frequent parallels show the author clearly intends for the reader to know the legends. In Jason Greylock's mind, reaching for the dewberries proved tantamount to his first try for the golden fleece. Because the moccasin-dragon blocked him, he never really tried again; and his fatalism transformed the golden fleece into his true fate, the Greylocks of death. In Dorinda's mind, the snake at Whistling Spring functions like the huge dragon that kept parched Cadmus and his men from the spring near which he was to found Thebes. Working from either myth, we may infer that the thistles springing up where Dorinda plows carry a significance similar to that of the armed giants who sprang from dragons' teeth sown by Cadmus and later by Jason. Since the Cadmean giants became the original earthborn race of the Western imagination, Dorinda's revenge seems to express a desire to eradicate the tie of mankind to the earth. At one level this is another form of her rebellion against fatalism, especially that of her father, who is as mired in the earth forces as any dark-blooded character of

D. H. Lawrence (40). But there is more: Five of the giants of
Cadmus survived his guile (a rock thrown among them) to become his chief lords and the builders of noble Thebes. Jason's
earthborn giants, by contrast, devoured one another after he
threw dust in their eyes (an episode that foreshadows the fate
of his offspring by Medea). Dorinda's struggle seems closer to
Jason's, defensive and totally destructive, except that she has
no guile (it is to her mind a feminine trait)—only her raging
hatred and the vein of iron.

Because the thistles are masculine, ubiquitous, and earth
rooted, Dorinda's retaliation entails an ultimate assault upon
fertility. At this hidden level of associations, her revenge is
castrating, genocidal, and antichthonic. If this is what she
deeply desires throughout the second half of the novel, there
is no way she can redeem the barren ground. All she can do is
exercise her will and vent her venom.

Fortunately, revenge constitutes only one of the elements that
rise from the deep repressed core of Dorinda after the vein of
iron begins to dominate. If revenge were her only drive, she
might have known greater fulfillment of a sort when she purchased Jason's Five Oaks and left him a helpless pauper. To
understand the other forces working inside her, we must turn
from dream and myth symbols to the way Dorinda sees other
people through masks that her mind has created of previously
unrecognized contents of her own psyche. As with her heroines since Gabriella, Glasgow uses Dorinda's projections
upon other characters to turn her psyche inside out.

The narrator establishes the device at the start when we are
told that, because Dorinda's environment is "bare, starved,
desolate," her nature is also "starved for emotional realities."
"Nourished on the gossamer substance of literature," it
"found its only escape in the fabrication of dreams," which
she generally projects—like many a Eugene Gant to come—
upon the rapidly disappearing faces seen on the train that
runs by the store in Pedlar's Mill where she works. The passing train calls her to an "expected miracle, the *something dif-*

*ferent* in the future, to which she looked ahead over the tedious stretch of the present" (11–12, italics added). This is her phantasy before Jason comes back from New York to take his father's medical practice and to assist the dissipated old man into his grave. Jason, in effect, displaces the train. Suddenly all her vague yearnings become concrete: "Her old dreams had come back . . . infused with the *warm blood of reality*" (27, italics added). Her personality does a flip-flop, and the stern daughter of the Presbyterians turns into a bucolic Juliet taking off across the fields for assignations under the pines. For Jason has opened to her "the secret ecstasy at the heart of experience," which alters the glow of the lamp that shines within her to a "clear golden light" (10, 27). By contrast, the world seems colorless, and her home appears "as unfamiliar as if she had never seen it before" (27, 38). She begins to feel suffocated in the store and to appreciate more than before the way her mother has been trapped by "religious depression" and by the austere ritual of compensatory work; she senses too how her father's life has been swallowed by the farm's unrelenting seasons (17, 37–40). From all this, Jason helps her escape into "the celestial sphere of enchantment," from which she observes the actual environment as from a distance (33). Her love for Jason—and it is obviously *her* love alone from the very start—has created an alternate reality in which everything around her appears "fresh and strange and wonderful, as if she were looking at it clearly for the first time" (35–36).

This new reality flows almost completely from Dorinda's imagination, as Glasgow makes clear all along by stressing Jason's inability to keep his mind on the girl, even when they are together (35). But acknowledging the imaginary source of this experience, are we as readers meant to take Dorinda's cynical view after all her illusions have collapsed—that romantic passion exists as an "importunate necessity . . . in the imagination," one she was "compelled to work . . . out into experience" before she "could settle down to the serious business of life" (230)? We would perhaps do better to suggest that both the blindness of her love and the absoluteness of her rejection offer measures of the emotional poverty of her earlier life. Dorinda's reaction to her father's scent, chiefly of earth and manure, poignantly reveals this early paucity of feeling: "The *first time* Dorinda remembered his taking her on his knee, the strong smell of his blue-jeans overalls had frightened her to tears, and she had struggled and screamed. . . . And after that *he had never tried to lift her again*" (40–41, italics added). In rejecting her father and his tie to the earth, she not only rejected his fatalism (that is her adult view of it), but she also evaded completely the emotions of the Electra phase. She was never feminized. Much of the affectionate side of her nature thus remained unexpressed. These softer emotions no doubt became increasingly importunate until Jason brought them to the surface of her personality, where for the first time she claimed them as her own. Before Jason, she had the sense of a desolate barrenness within. With Jason "her whole body" grows "softer, lighter, more intensely alive" (36).

This is the rhetoric of love fiction, and to our peril, we may not trust it from a woman novelist. But it is also language a psychologist might use to suggest what happens when a patient overcomes a feeling of alienation from the body. If we are to trust anything in a novel, it must be—mustn't it—the language of the basic image pattern of the novel. And the narrator chooses the imagery of the earth to tell us that, with Jason, "her inner life, which had been as bare as a rock, was suddenly rich with bloom" (36). Her love may take an illusory form, but its psychological sources and effects are real. They are so real, in fact, that even after she has dismissed love as an illusion and settled down "to the serious business of life"— revenge through success—debilitating memories of their time together keep flashing in upon her until she feels trapped in memory (273, 359). Indeed, the deep drama of the second half of the novel is not the outward one—whether or not she will succeed in redeeming Old Farm. There is never any question about her success, which proves all upward and onward. The true conflict centers about her inner struggle to wipe out "one of those natural instincts which Presbyterian theology has damned but never wholly exterminated"—her unacceptable desire (9). After the vein of iron and her scarring affair have led her to deny her love for Jason because it is weakening, her pain drives all her affections so deep into the unacknowledged core of her being that she feels separated from them. Her feelings are "dead, turned into stone or wood." Or, as she puts it, "I'm dried up at the core. . . . I'm no better than a dead tree walking" (218, 222). This emptiness comes immediately after the abortion. When her emotions begin to revive, they consist largely of the drive to reclaim Old Farm. As the dream about Jason and the thistles makes plain, redeeming the land masks her true desire to eradicate Jason from her being.

From all of this, we see that revenge does not work alone beneath the vein of iron. Indeed, the hatred itself is but a reaction that formed out of her love at the moment she was wounded by love. Although love and hatred alternate in her memories of Jason, hatred occurs more frequently because it seems less unacceptable to her conscious mind, which strives desperately to bury them both beneath work. But work did not succeed for her mother—whose dream of escape to the Congo kept flashing back on her—and work proves of questionable value for Dorinda.

Moreover, projections on other characters indicate that love and hatred are but two of the many forces in her emotional core. Her original fascination with Jason also betrays her need for a father, a man of ideas and authority able to give her life direction. This aspect of Jason, specifically his superficial interest in scientific farming, recurs in Dr. Burch of New York, who both guides her culturally and steers her study of agriculture. Nathan Pedlar, by practicing what Jason preached, becomes an even more effective authority on sound farming techniques; she listens to his advice so closely that, after his death, his words return to her when she needs them (474). Nathan also answers Dorinda's deep need for a male to pity and help, a need Dorinda had earlier projected upon Jason when she imagined him a creature of "heroic weakness confronting insurmountable obstacles" (30). After she marries Nathan, his clubfooted son, John Abner, provides the perfect screen for her projected pity.

John Abner's deformity seems also to mirror what has become of her capacity for love. Along the same line, because Nathan settles into a handyman role too humble to make sexual demands of his arrogant and overbearing wife (she sometimes thinks bitterly "that if she had married another man, he might not have found her overbearing"), her sexual drive remains in a channel deep beneath her conscious fear and frigidity. It begins to surface only after Nathan's death in her dealings with Bob Ellgood, who repeatedly reminds her of a "sleek, mild-mannered Jersey bull," a comparison surely not lost on a dairy farmer who had once taken a long admiring look at the Ellgoods' Jersey bull, the sire of her own herd (283, 286, 458, 459). But, she tells Ellgood, "I've finished with all that" (459).

Three other characters—Nathan's daughter Lena, Jason's wife Geneva Ellgood, and Jason himself—throw additional light on what has happened to her sexual and romantic potential. It is not difficult to see Dorinda's contempt for her own sexuality in the way she treats Lena. Lena has a face, to Dorinda's mind, "like an infant Aphrodite, vacant but perfect as the inside of a shell. A deplorable waste of any good man's affection" (382). As the girl's stepmother, Dorinda buries her hostility beneath indifference by persuading herself that Lena is "dangerously oversexed" and that it would be futile to try to steer the wildness of one who possesses "the obstinacy peculiar to many weak-minded women" (392). Nor is it difficult to see Geneva Ellgood as a mirror of what Dorinda might have been had she succeeded in snaring Jason. But Geneva's role in the novel proves so dreamlike and freighted with meaning that she seems hardly to exist except as a chimera of Dorinda's imagination mirroring what the Jason-haunted side of Dorinda has become. This holds true especially for Ge-

neva's obsession that Jason has killed her baby but that she
(Geneva) is pregnant again to get even (351). Dorinda's plan
for Old Farm provides her own parallel "pregnancy" of revenge. That Geneva drowns herself, like Ophelia, the day
Dorinda marries Nathan seems more effective if taken to indicate what Dorinda wants to do with the self Jason created in
her, rather than as a sign that Geneva can rest at last now that
Jason can no longer backslide to her rival (373).

The same dream quality adheres to the episode in which
Dorinda prepares a home for pauperized Jason.[8] The episode
goes well beyond revenge, since Dorinda satisfied that dark
urge when she purchased Five Oaks from Jason, wed it to Old
Farm, and redeemed it to new life (358, 468). The reunion
bears more resemblance to classical retribution: here, too, su-
perabundant success eats the heart out of the protagonist's
triumph. The inappropriateness of Dorinda's preparing a
long-postponed nuptial chamber for the only love she has
ever known—one whose features are now "like the face of a
mummy"—establishes the nightmarish atmosphere that turns
this decaying automaton, Jason, into a mirror of what Dorinda has made of her emotional self. Several times she has
tried to disown Jason, but the others in Pedlar's Mill know he
is hers alone. They are right. With Jason, some of her emotions return: the essence of sadness, a sense of the pathos of
life and the futility of revenge. But the image that brings the
only tears to her eyes is a glimpse of Jason's "boots, with
lumps of red clay still clinging to them," both a reminder of
the earthbound fatality of all mankind and a poignant evoca-
tion of her never expressed love for her father, to whose heavy
boots the earth always clung (40, 489–93).

Under Dorinda's care, Jason awaits the slow approach of
death, much like his Medea-broken namesake, who sat beneath the rotting hulk of the *Argo* until a beam fell and killed
him. Ultimately, Jason's puzzled fatalism brings Dorinda the

8 Marion K. Richards suggests interesting parallels to this scene in *Ellen
Glasgow's Development as a Novelist* (The Hague, 1971), 162–73.

most piercing illumination of her life. It breaks upon her when Jason revives long enough to say that he doesn't know why she has been good to him. Among the dimly perceived thoughts that flutter to light from "the penumbra of darkness" must be the hint, for the first time, that Jason can never have known he made Dorinda pregnant (she discovered it the day he came back married to Geneva), nor have known how deeply he affected her life. Therefore he cannot have known the depth of her hatred nor measured the success of her revenge (498). Revenge takes two. Hers has been wasted upon a figment of her own imagination. Even now she cannot consciously acknowledge this deep failure. But, after he is buried, she walks across the field into which she has plowed her passion, and her life crumbles "like a mountain of cinders." It rolls over her: "She was suffocated, she was buried alive beneath an emptiness, a negation of effort. . . . Not pain, not disappointment, but the futility of all things was crushing her spirit." She has learned, she understands, the worst of all knowledge—"the end of expectancy" (506). The rain is over everything, the wind howls like wolves, because "love was the only thing that made life desirable, and love was irrevocably lost to her" (508).

After a perception of such desolation, one which has been growing at the core of her being for over thirty years (and more than 250 pages), can we trust the last three pages of the book when Dorinda and the narrator seem to collaborate in a final paean to optimism, endurance, the land, fortitude, and the vein of iron—all inspired by the passing of a storm and the dawn of a sunny day? If so, then it seems impossible to trust the author.[9] To answer this central question, we must turn to the book's poetic structure embodied in the basic pattern of imagery, the nature imagery. Unfortunately, a conflict seems to exist between the narrator's authority and that of the imagery.

9 Rubin has argued this in *The Teller in the Tale*, 12–13.

Among the many uses of nature in *Barren Ground*, four are especially relevant to this conflict. First, because Dorinda spends much of her life alone, unable to grow through relationships with other people, Glasgow uses the landscape as an alternate screen upon which to project her inner being. Glasgow establishes the device early when Dorinda ascribes to the land a "secret spirit," which traces "an image on the flat surface, glimmering, remote, unapproachable, like the expression of an animal that man has forced into sullen submission"; the girl wonders "if everything has a soul" (10–11). This she does even before she begins to feel that there is a secret being trapped inside herself, since it is easier to see this force outwardly.

Along a similar line, Dorinda sometimes thinks anthropomorphically. From this habit, Glasgow creates the symbols that establish the theme of each of the novel's three parts: "broomsedge," her father's favorite big "pine," and "life-ever-lasting" (12, 98, 125, 233, 239, 268, 461, 482).[10] Also anthropomorphically, Dorinda turns her dogs and horses into various kinds of philosophers and theologians (27, 94). The third use reverses the anthropomorphic process and draws on nature for metaphors and similes, but the effect is much the same: farmers are like trees, and so forth.

Dorinda's habit of turning people into animals or parts of nature, and vice versa, not only enriches the figurative language of the novel, but also closes the gap between character and nature to render less artificial the fourth use of nature as a choral presence. The three uses already described show Dorinda imposing her will upon nature: much as her body transforms it from gall to fertility, so her mind, with greater subtlety, turns it into the mirror of her inner being. But the landscape has an existence of its own, free of coloring by Dorinda's inner lamp. This independence makes it at times a cho-

---

10 For a fuller discussion of the three key symbols, see Richards, *Glasgow's Development*, 173–82.

ral presence commenting upon the action. Its commentary may be trusted more completely than Dorinda's—perhaps even more than the narrator's.

Frederick McDowell has limited the chorus of the novel to old Matthew Fairlamb, a Hardy-like one-man tragic commentator.[11] But in her letters and various prefaces to the book, Glasgow spoke continually about an "added dimension, a universal rhythm more fluent than any material texture . . . the whole movement of life," beneath the scene and the spirit of place.[12] To Allen Tate, she wrote that she had "been afraid of making [herself] too explicit" in her novels and that what she actually meant was expressed through this "added dimension." The universal rhythm thus provides the ultimate point of view regarding the characters and events. In fact, Glasgow had used the rhythm of natural vegetation cycles as a structural principle since she wrote *The Battle-Ground* after reading *War and Peace*.[13] The seasons had long furnished her work with the universal rhythm and movement of life, but never as completely as in *Barren Ground*.

Most of the episodes take place in a season appropriate to the action. Jason appears to Dorinda during a snowy period at the end of winter. With her romance, spring begins—the next day. By Easter she is lost in love, and in May and June the two of them plan a wedding. Dorinda aborts in late October and then spends two winters lying fallow in New York before returning to Virginia to redeem the farm. By October her venture is well underway, and each subsequent October provides a sense of triumph as she contemplates her increasing harvests. During the snowy January of her forty-second year, just as she reaches the peak of her cold and stainless purification, Nathan dies as a hero in a rail accident; his heroism gives her life some of the vicarious adventure she has longed for. Jason

---

11 McDowell, *Glasgow and the Ironic Art of Fiction*, 147.
12 Glasgow, *A Certain Measure*, 153–54. See also the shorter preface to the Old Dominion edition of the novel and Glasgow to Tate, September 22, 1932, in Rouse, *Letters of Ellen Glasgow*, 125.
13 Raper, *Without Shelter*, 171–72.

dies in a November and is buried in raw wintry weather. In the second half of the novel, springs and summers usually pass in the summaries. Autumns and winters—chiefly autumns—become the occasions discriminated with scenic development. With such pervasive congruity of season and event, exceptions call attention to themselves. When Dorinda and Jason do their most fervid lovemaking during a long and scorching August drought, the silent commentary of the landscape indicates that their assignations will prove barren. The seasons, of course, only hint this; they say nothing.

What then is the commentary of the seasons in the troublesome final pages of the book, when Dorinda springs suddenly from her perception of the total desolation of her emotional life to a final affirmation of optimism and the vein of iron? We find much talk here of the seasons, for the dark night of her soul passes only after she is "caught again in the tide of material things." She invests her heart once more in the land and thereby reestablishes "that sympathy which was deeper than all other emotions of her heart." She tells herself: "While the soil endured, while the seasons bloomed and dropped, while the ancient beneficent ritual of *sowing* and *reaping* moved in the fields, she knew that she could never despair of contentment." Or again, she looks forward to other bountiful autumns, glowing winters, coral springs, and profuse summers (509–10). In other words, she throws herself upon the time of the seasons for consolation. This is a perennial ploy in despair; and the poetic structure of the novel, by returning her to the winter weather in which she began, has clearly established the cyclic quality of time.

What the novel does not do is have the narrator hold this consolation out to her, for these last pages are the movements of Dorinda's own mind. Nor does the novel itself lend its structural support to her faith in the eternal return of spring and summer; the discriminated occasions of the second half show that Dorinda's time has become one without seasons—other than autumn and winter. Since the dream of the Jason thistles, she has projected all her fertility into the land (along with her heart). She does the same here, by endowing the landscape with seasons and fertility she should know are no longer hers.

Dorinda's new view of time serves, no doubt, to balance her despair. In this sense, it is an *essential* phantasy, a vision to offset her emotional emptiness, a solid dream upon which to build the next decade or so of her life—just as romantic love, revenge, the redemption of Old Farm, and control of Five Oaks have all been, in turn, her necessary phantasies. When, like the earlier dreams, this one also proves inadequate, Dorinda will certainly create a new vision. This is Dorinda's nature, the quality to be admired despite her hardness. Resilience through perfected phantasies is the nature of most Glasgow heroines after 1916. Whereas earlier heroines had to settle for mere abstractions, Dorinda invests her phantasies in the solid earth.

Even so, seen against the image structure of the novel, the affirmation at the end seems more pathetic than cheering. Its fervor becomes one more measure of Dorinda's barrenness, one more product of her will to power over the feminine, masculine, and earth sources of fertility. There may be more hope for her in the "pensive, ironic, and infinitely wise" way she tells John Abner at the very end, in regard to bull-like Bob Ellgood, that she is through with love, sex, and marriage. For if Dorinda *is* infinitely wise, as the narrator claims, she must recall that she has been telling herself exactly the same thing for over thirty years and that she told Nathan Pedlar something very much like it—just before she married him (224, 355–56).

If *Barren Ground* casts a significant shadow across the southern imagination of the decade after 1925, we should perhaps cease to regard the back-to-the-land impulse of much of that writing as an anachronistic escape from the ills of industrial society. We should come instead to see this longing as a sure measure of the emotional barrenness of the lives of the characters, as another manifestation of a hunger much like the emptiness that drives denizens of Faulkner's hamlet when they lust after the wild energy of Flem's Texas ponies. Dorinda's rejection of the loving, open, and fertile resources of her own femininity, only to find it reflected in the landscape, has itself a long history in the southern imagination. Southern writers have seen the earth as a "fertile womb," the "primary landscape of the Mother," promising wealth, enclosure, and stasis for over three hundred years.[14] The need is as old as slavery—older, in fact. But Glasgow was probably the first in this tradition to recognize that the fertility seen in the land may be a compensating reflection of the world behind the eyes. Perhaps because she understood the source of the agrarian longing in this way, she generally assigned it, in her late novels, to older characters near death.

In acquitting the narrator of responsibility for the jarring note of uplift on which *Barren Ground* ends, we are actually placing more of the blame on the novelist, since the intrinsic force of the ending makes it seem doubtful that Glasgow intended these pages to stand in ironic relation to the major image structure of the novel. Much of the optimism of the ending belongs to Glasgow, not to Dorinda. It was Glasgow who had made contact with a rich inner vein of creativity during the writing of the book, not Dorinda. And it was Glasgow, not Dorinda, who sought psychiatric help to free her creative force.[15] The ending and one or two other passages (see 267) show that she had already transcended Dorinda's frozen world and was entering the Richmond spring of *The Romantic Comedians*. The profoundly comic vision of the ending belongs, not to secular Presbyterians like Dorinda, but to such unapologetic pagans as Glasgow became for a few years after she sloughed Dorinda from the core of her being. However,

14 Annette Kolodny, "The Unchanging Landscape: The Pastoral Impulse in Simms's Revolutionary War Romances," *Southern Literary Journal*, V (Fall, 1972), 46–67. What Kolodny says of William Gilmore Simms is doubly true of a post-Freudian like Glasgow.
15 Godbold, *Ellen Glasgow and the Woman Within*, 133.

this is a problem best left for biographers. The critic who trusts novels more than novelists has to bemoan the fact that, in the final pages of *Barren Ground*, Glasgow could not keep her own affection for Dorinda out of a novel which otherwise rings both strong and true.

# Chapter VI

# Love Among the Gerontocrats: *The Romantic Comedians* (1926)

World War I has ended but the tomfoolery of Prohibition has lived on, much longer than any man with a sense of proportion would have thought possible. In the best-stocked private cellars, the gin gave out last year, and even the most gracious host has begun to keep an eye on the old Bumgardner when friends come to call. To make matters worse, the world war has set the women to "telling the truth about themselves": they have grown forward enough to *ask* for the whiskey. And they haven't told half of the truth yet, for the twenties are still young. Ancient Queenborough has entered one of those epochs of swift change during "which the high tragedy of one generation declines into the low comedy of the next."[1] But before the Victorian gentleman metamorphoses into a dirty old man, there is just enough time to celebrate the resurrection of ancient values through comic ritual and to do so from a perspective as old as Aristophanes.

More than any other book Ellen Glasgow wrote, *The Romantic Comedians* (1926) demonstrates the attributes of classical comedy described by Northrop Frye in *Anatomy of Criticism*. It is the story of the subversion of an established society by youth. It follows the comic plot formula: a young woman and a young man want to be together; but their desire is opposed by an older person, usually a parental figure, until in the end

1 Ellen Glasgow, *The Romantic Comedians* (Garden City, N.Y., 1926), 223, 287–88. This book will hereafter be referred to by page number only.

a twist in the plot enables youth to have its way. Here the blocking character, Judge Gamaliel Bland Honeywell, is a surrogate father, an impostor whose great wealth gives him a fraudulent claim over a far younger girl, Annabel Upchurch. Annabel, Angus Blount, and Dabney Birdsong, the young people of the novel, are relatively undeveloped; eirons, they seem to have far more promise than their characters yet reveal. Annabel's mother, Bella, is a flatterer and parasite, who in the comic role of evil mother collaborates with the possessive father figure, Judge Honeywell. The judge's twin sister, Edmonia Bredalbane, embodies the pure spirit of comedy, the norm achieved by Annabel in the end when she and Dabney triumph over the old judge, the norm to which even he is converted as he gives way to the young man's and the young woman's desires and allows them to run off together. Of the major characters, only Bella the mother remains stuck in the old sentimental moral position; all the others have embraced the "amoral" but ancient values of comedy.

And yet there is a problem with applying Frye's formula to *The Romantic Comedians*: the point of view is not quite right. Although the angle of vision is omniscient, in twenty-three out of the twenty-nine chapters the narrator sticks very close to the mind of the blocking character, Judge Honeywell, placing the emphasis of the book upon the obstructing forces. This focus forces the novel into an ironic phase of comedy, a comedy of manners, in which the romance of the young lovers takes place off-stage. Limited, as it so frequently is, to the judge's point of view, the book contains a good deal of romance and pathos. These sentiments, however, are undercut by a perspective larger than the judge's.

A more accurate approach would modify Frye's formula and regard the entire comic plot as set within Judge Honeywell's soul. He contains his own spirit of youth, his own comic impulse, and his own obstructing forces—the latter driven by the morality of fear and the emotional impotence of age. Seen in this manner, the other characters mirror the antagonistic dimensions of his being; they are screens upon which he projects his phantasies of need and fear.

As in so many psychological stories written since 1926, the key to the situation is delivered at the very end. In this case, the judge, bereft of his young wife, has had to seek consolation from the "inviolable sanctuary of dreams" in the soft cool billows of his bed; this "serene haven," this "deep below the deeps of experience," brings "the changeless beatitude beneath the shifting cycles of birth and death." There in the "dark pulsations of memory,"

> he saw *his mother*, whom he had passionately loved, and whom he remembered as immortally fair and young. From her dissolving image there emerged and dissolved again *all the women he had ever desired or might have desired in his life*. . . . Inchoate impulses which had shuddered out of life even while he resisted them. Though they had died in the flesh, he realized now that they must have lived on in some submerged jungle of consciousness. (342–43, italics added)

Earlier, in the major recognition scene, the judge comes home suddenly to find his young wife "tearfully disengaging herself from the arms of a young man" named Dabney Birdsong. He sees Dabney in a mirror thus: "Fair, strong, well-favoured, the strange young man looked at him from the glass with a pair of singularly living blue eyes, while the fantastic thought sprang in the Judge's mind, 'That is the son I ought to have had!'" (267–68). The two scenes provide strong evidence that the female characters should be considered as projections of the woman within the judge, the memory of aspects of his mother, and that the young males mirror the self he would like to liberate by using certain women as catalysts.

Although the fit of Don Juanism that comes over the judge in his sixty-fifth year sends him in quest of his own lost youth, his quest is ultimately less important than the specific configuration of women who have ruled his whole life. Given the nature of his quest, it is rather sad to realize that, other than the one brief glimpse of Dabney in the mirror, the only males who appear by name in the novel are his doctor, his manservant, and an octogenarian skirt-chaser named Colonel Bletheram. As in the year covered by the story, his life has been dominated by women, all of them his mother in her five masks: Amanda Lightfoot, the ideal and static beauty of his youth; Cordelia Honeywell, the ideal wife and good mother of his two children; Edmonia Honeywell Bredalbane, his twin sister, a realistic and amoral woman; Annabel Upchurch, the youthful and changing ideal of his old age; and Bella Upchurch, a pragmatic woman. Each of the women has a basic, even archetypal, role to play in the judge's emotional life.

The ideal of Victorian virtue, Amanda Lightfoot reigned for twenty years as the belle of Queenborough society. But she meant more to the judge, for she was his first love, the embodiment of all his youthful idealism. After a brief engagement, he grew jealous, and she left for Europe. Now thirty-seven years later, with his first wife dead, the image of his earlier ideals has become a reproach for all he never achieved. When he sees her "framed in her doorway" like Poe's Helen, he can feel only a sense of duty, a guilty obligation to make good on old and impassioned promises (11–14). Although she is to others a well-preserved figure of hypocrisy and fortitude, she is to the judge the image of his guilty conscience (304). His desires have changed, even if Amanda his ideal has remained what she was in the 1880s.

When Amanda ran off to Europe, young Honeywell followed her, though not as promptly as she had expected. On the ship he met Cordelia, and she caught him unawares. If his memory of their thirty-six years of marriage is an indication, Cordelia played on his need for a mothering woman: for all those years she sacrificed her life to protect him, often from his own appetites (6). Sexually discouraging, she was so wonderful a mother that she was scarcely bearable (77, 156). Like her namesake, her love went unappreciated until too late. Dead one year, having ceased to "live" in his memory, she has turned instead into the "impressive marble angel" he placed at her grave (1–2). But the marble comes back to life in his phantasies when the pace of his second honeymoon causes him to wish he had brought Cordelia along, though more "in the capacity of a ministering angel than of a wife" (176). At the end, after Annabel leaves him, Cordelia seems reincarnated in the young mother-nurse his doctor sends to care for him. "There is the woman I ought to have married! " he thinks, not realizing that he has already fulfilled that imperative at least once in his life.

Edmonia Bredalbane, the third of his women, seems to me the most extraordinary character Ellen Glasgow ever created. With four husbands and other company, she echoes the Wife of Bath (as the judge and Annabel do Chaucer's January and May); but since she has the "courage of her appetites," she speaks with a boldness more like that of Shakespeare's Edmund, from whom Glasgow may have taken her name.[2] Like Edmund, and without the self-doubt of the Wife of Bath, Edmonia calls upon nature and experience rather than recognized authorities. The result, of course, unsettles her conventional twin: "One of the most exasperating things about her, considering how wrong she was in principle, was her incurable habit of being right in fact" (52). Much unlike

2 Still playing the name game, we cannot help pointing out that Amanda is both a "one man woman" and "without a man"; that Gamaliel Bland Honeywell was listed in a notebook as Philip *Byrd* Honeywell, which choice would have underlined (perhaps too boldly) his role as the pure distillation of Virginian gentlemen; and that Gamaliel is the name hidden behind the secretive "G." in Warren G. Harding, whose term as president (1921–23) remains a symbol of the most memorable political and sexual high jinks of the twenties. One of Glasgow's favorite romantic comedians, her former fiancé Henry Anderson, had been mentioned for the second position on the ticket Harding eventually headed; Harding later considered Anderson seriously for appointment to the Supreme Court. Finally, the way the names seem to flow into one another (Edmonia/Amanda/Annabel/Bella/Gamaliel/Honeywell) underscores the psychic economy implied if the females are projections of the women within the judge. See Notebook #3 and pamphlets on Anderson in the Ellen Glasgow Collection, Alderman Library, University of Virginia.

her American prototype Hester Prynne, she wears "her scarlet letter less as the badge of shame than as some foreign decoration for distinguished service," presumably the red badge of courage (84). She is, as she well knows, an affront to Gamaliel's sense that the universe is just; she tells him: "You resented the way I wasn't satisfied simply to stay ruined and to stew in a consciousness of sin for the rest of my life. It wasn't my fall, it was my being able to get up again, that you couldn't forgive—" (227). Her ability to cut through the fog of conventions, principles, and morals to come to terms with nature—both human nature and her own—has elevated Edmonia to the position she now holds in Queenborough, that of arbiter of conduct to the inquisitive youth of Annabel's generation (84). In the book she speaks for a realism based on the deep perception of natural forces. Thus she embodies the comic spirit, the comic vision of youth, which always rises with new energy and fertility to throw aside the rubble that previous generations have left behind.

Against his own convictions, the judge can feel the appeal of Edmonia's vision. Whenever he retreats with his twin to a quiet room for a conversation, the scene seems dream haunted like one of Cabell's dialogues between a character and the latter's sprite or double (26–36, 223–35). But the judicial mind of the judge has robbed him of the courage of his appetites, as Edmonia knows. Whenever she advises him with the voice of deep wisdom, he evades her realistic suggestions by deflecting his mind to one or the other of her peccadilloes (36, 234–35). Although Edmonia runs a very real risk of becoming the libidinal grotesque that she is in the mind of her twin, the cyclic structure of the novel, especially the conversions of the ending, supports her in the role of an Aphrodite who is mellowing gracefully into Sophia (51). Because the judge deceives himself too thoroughly to either vanquish or accommodate the shadow side of his being that he projects upon his twin, he is doomed to become the foremost romantic comedian referred to in the title. Whenever he mentions

Annabel in their talks, Edmonia turns the subject to Amanda (32–33). This seems odd given Edmonia's most recent marriage to a much younger, poorer man who is using her great wealth to live extravagantly in Paris (9). The paradox is actually one more indication of her wisdom. She knows that her brother is not like herself—that he is too principled, too sentimental in the Victorian manner, too duty bound to trot about as she does with the very young. Annabel can only burn him out, whereas Amanda could preserve him just as Amanda has preserved herself.

But Judge Honeywell rejects the wisdom of the "criminal" side of himself and reaches out, not only for new life, but for the flown swallow of his youth. The Annabel trouble starts on an Easter Sunday one year after Cordelia's death, when the judge, who in self-pity thinks of himself as "a bird with a broken wing," feels "an odd palpitation within the suave Virginian depths of his being, where his broken wing [is] helplessly trying to flutter" (1). Birds fill the trees of the cemetery in which he stands, "and in his soul as well, beneath the gloom of his sorrow, there [is] this miracle of budding and piping and twittering, as if winter woods had awakened to spring" (2). Before he reaches his home on that Easter Sunday, his "one impulse of vital magic" has obliterated his memory of Cordelia and his long-suspended duty to patient Amanda, both of whom are later to be associated with caged canaries. This same impulse has carried him safely past the temptations of Bella Upchurch with her pigeonlike plumpness and her dove's eyes—when suddenly he finds his longing reflected back at him in the "fresh young voice" and "small heart-shaped face" of Annabel. Her "flying rhythm," "winged eyebrows," "swift gestures," and "small fragile body" are "as light as a swallow, he thought, with poetic imagery, as light and graceful as a swallow in the air" (1–21, 59, 118–20). The sexual nature of that "broken wing . . . helplessly trying to flutter" is lost to a man who lacks the courage even to recognize his appetites, but it is not wasted by a novelist who is shortly to become the confidante of James Branch Cabell. What happens next clearly proves this economy:

> While he looked [at Annabel] a strange, an almost miracu-
> lous thing happened. Suddenly, so suddenly that the vision
> came and went before he had seized it, the playful wind
> blew Annabel's striped green and brown frock like shreds
> of mist from her body, and he saw her white limbs dancing
> against a background of fields and streams. An instant only!
> Then the enchantment vanished in a golden haze . . . and
> he realized that he was trembling. (22)

If he were more like his twin, the judge would be able to deal with Annabel as he does in this forthright scene; but his orthodox mind cannot accept the vital impulse from the depths of his being. He must disguise his sexual itch, even to himself, by finding a moral alibi for devoting his mind to Annabel: not only is she pretty, but she is the poor and helpless niece of his late wife. Therefore, it is his *duty* to lavish gifts upon her. And so his principles become the pander and mask of his lust.

Since his desire must always conceal itself behind his noblesse oblige, his lust, as Edmonia had anticipated, fails to emerge in a healthy, full-bodied manner. All his life he has found himself periodically disturbed by startling dreams and "visions of the glimmering ivory beauty of girls" and "the smooth marble beauty of women" (48). But he has always managed to hold down these phantasies, even after his first marriage when his madness for Amanda threatened him "with a complete nervous breakdown" and the loss of his career (313). Now with Annabel, when he is sixty-five, the combination of desire and chivalric self-deception leads to an exceedingly prurient mode of sexuality. On their honeymoon he discovers that the mask he created for her does not fit: he is "never so distant from her in feeling" as when she stands "close at his side. . . . For the mild caresses he lavished upon her were too fleeting to ease the burden of his overcharged heart" (167). If we read between the lines, this seems to indicate that he has been unable to consummate the marriage. He is reduced to voyeurism and fetishism. He likes to watch her undress, to handle her clothes and put his hands on her body; Annabel complains that he fondles her too much (106, 169, 193, 203). More than any book Glasgow ever wrote, this one toys with the sexual taboos. Beneath the cool metallic surface created by the scintillant style, we can now and then sense a fevered velvet core. The judge's passions often cross the boundary society has imposed upon erotic feelings both between age and youth and between men and daughters. In contrast, Annabel at times seems frigid.

Yet it is unfair to accuse Annabel of frigidity, despite the predisposition she receives from her very cool mother. Indeed, when we consider her situation, Annabel's postmatrimonial fear of sex comes as a sign of health recovered. She seems to be emerging from a serious bout with whatever the classifiers of perversions would call her idea that she can do anything for money. Annabel is a gold digger, not a Lolita—a serious-minded, even philosophic gold digger. After her first lover jilts her, she announces that she is through with romance, silly boys, and all other shams. She proclaims herself a realist of the American variety: "I'd rather have money than anything in the world! " (68–69). But like many realists with an absolute reality, she lives to regret her words; her erstwhile realism quickly becomes her self-deception. After less than a year of marriage to the richest man in town, she has changed her absolute: "I want to be free. I don't want to be married. . . . All I want is my own life. That is all" (299).

This pronouncement has the same flaw of one-dimensionality as the first; but here the dimension seems in content to be a sounder one, for it coincides with several of the more authoritative elements of the novel. It corresponds, for example, with the practices of Edmonia, the "amoral" touchstone of the book's comic vision. Even the judge yields to Annabel's superior force. When he does so, we seem to feel the narrator speaking through his response to his wayward but determined wife: "Her guilty passion enkindled her being. . . . The glow of prophecy and vision was in her face, and he realized that the ancient mysteries of earth were using her ecstasy as a vessel of life" (326). The moment after she proclaims her freedom, the judge feels he has been warmed by divinity. Even the best people in Queenborough, Glasgow hints, commune occasionally with the pagan gods, although they have no name or sense for them other than the dry memory of words they once declined from a Greek or Latin grammar. Inadvertently, Annabel has served as the vessel of these powers, just as she earlier allowed herself for a short while to be filled by the judge's dreams and phantasies. For that is the sort of person she is meant to be—open, malleable, resilient, but with a will, when she knows it, like a vein of iron (136–37, 165). Consequently, for all her innocence, self-deception, and inconstancy, there is hope for her, as even the judge knows.

Only her mother, Bella, completely refuses the comic vision and clings to moral sentimentalism to the end. When she finally realizes that the judge will not exercise the full array of righteous powers which tradition grants a dishonored husband, Bella falls back upon the anticipation of ultimate justice: "After all, unless the precepts of morality, unless the sanctities of virtue and the sacredness of marriage—unless all these consecrated beliefs were merely illusions. . . . Annabel must reap the inevitable whirlwind of her betrayal" (339–40). By way of divine compensation, Bella believes that Amanda will at last get the judge, as she justly deserves. On the last prediction, if not on both, Bella is apparently wrong, for in the final scene the judge has his eye on his young nurse. Bella's moral positions are probably not to be taken with a great deal of seriousness. Like everything else about her, her morality smacks more of pragmatism, if not mere utility, than of deep understanding. Her attitude toward duty gives a fair measure of all her ethical thinking: "You can't hold people in when you take the sense of duty away," she tells herself. "And not only duty, but remorse also, which she had found even more efficacious in unlawful love, appeared to have flown on wings of levity and ridicule." She would prefer the reestablishment of suicide as the sign of remorse obligatory for lovely ladies who stoop to folly (288). No moral measure is too strong that has the practical effect of keeping her access to the Honeywell millions unblocked. All acts are moral or immoral as they apply to a "particular circumstance"—her financial security (257).

In general, Bella mirrors the pragmatic side of the judge. Still plump and pretty at forty-eight and young enough to be the judge's daughter, but not his granddaughter, Bella seems a practical solution to the problem he has with mathematics when he insists on translating his own sixty-five winters into a mere thirty-five springs, while insisting that Amanda's fifty-eight summers make her automatically an "elderly woman" and therefore uninteresting to a man as young in spirit as he feels (26). But Bella is too pragmatic to try to change the sexual double standard as it applies to age. She finds it much simpler to push the judge toward Annabel. She thereby aids the process of self-deception by which his principles become the sanction of his desires. Although there is something admirable about the "tranquil immunity" she achieves by refusing to become one of the romantic comedians, such pragmatism carries a high price (269, 305). There is justice in Annabel's charge that her mother has never experienced the passion and divinity that she and the judge share even as it drives them apart. This lack constitutes a failure in knowledge on Bella's part and indicates that her vision is finally too narrow to embrace or direct her daughter's (284). Indeed, Annabel gives strong evidence that her own mind has subsumed and transcended her mother's when she puts her finger directly upon the major alibi of Bella's life: "You were all afraid of life, and you called your fear virtue" (297). Bella and the judge live by moral and social authorities because they lack the courage of Edmonia and Annabel to live by experience or desire.

Bella's moral alibi belongs to an essential dimension of the novel—one that determines whether ultimately we should regard the judge's ordeal as tragedy or comedy. In his passionate pursuit of Annabel, Honeywell discovers too late that nature has set limits to his power to realize his will. Consequently, he has to accept the sad truth that Amanda is a better match for his limited being, although she cannot satisfy his less limited imagination. This conflict between passionate imagination and the limits imposed by time is the source of man's ultimate tragedy, and the book was reviewed thus by Glasgow's psychologist-friend, Dr. Joseph Collins.[3] But tragedy is often comedy seen from too short a distance: the control of perspective is all-important. The use of alibis to undercut the preachments of the characters ranks among the most important of the devices Glasgow employs to place the "tragedy" of the judge in a comic perspective. Although an isolated alibi may occasionally demand that we take it at face value or as a pathetic aspect of character, there is something inherently humorous, because ironic, about an entire class of persons who fall back upon sanctions outside themselves for every action they take. Such irresponsibility betokens bad faith as a primary trait of the society.

A classifier of such evasions would have a field day working out the types and nuances of alibi in this novel. We have already noted the judge's use of his parental duty to Annabel to disguise his lust, as well as Bella's evasion of desire in the name of virtue—both moral alibis. Closely related is the social alibi Annabel employs to hide her own pleasure in leaving the ailing judge at home by himself: "Mary Percy is giving a dinner dance, and if you're sure you won't be lonely, *I'd rather not disappoint her*" (221, italics added). The judge and Bella make as ample use of history as Karl Marx to explain events, but to opposite effect: the judge excuses his inability to keep up with Annabel by saying that his generation may have been

3 Joseph Collins, "Ellen Glasgow's New Novel: A Tragedy of Old Age," *New York Times Book Review*, September 12, 1926, Sec. III, p. 5.

too strict but "the pendulum is swinging too far in the opposite direction today," and Bella overlooks her own part in Annabel's predicament by using World War I to excuse the girl's capitulation to the divine passion (285, 291). There is more pathos than humor, however, to the view Edmonia takes of Amanda's long career of unrequited love: it has given a purpose to Amanda's life. This is the sentimental or romantic alibi, though Amanda does not use it herself (312).

In other contexts the romantic deceptions occur in close association with biological and sometimes Providential sanctions. Bella uses biology to explain that what is called nymphomania in a woman is only human nature in a man: "It is disgusting," she says, but it is because of the "way they're made" that elderly men get "the maggot of youth" in their head (134). And Annabel falls back on biology and romance to justify all her excesses of the heart with Angus and Dabney (110–11, 282–84, 315, 323). Each time she says, "There's nobody in the world but—," the corners of the reader's mouth start to creep up. At times Annabel's self-pity elevates her weakness before the vicissitudes of passion to the level of almost noble fatalism: "Oh, well, what does anything matter?" she groans before going on to take the judge from Cousin Amanda (155). Similarly, Bella's fatalistic alibi smacks of the universalizing earnestness of philosophy. After the judge abdicates his treasure to young Dabney, Bella sighs, "I ought to have known life! " (278). In this mock serious vein, even Edmonia and the narrator, usually trustworthy commentators, use the rhetoric of alibi. Edmonia asserts that "Heaven intended [Gamaliel] to marry Amanda"—by which she probably means that convention and the judge's conscience so intended, for to him the latter embody heaven (140). And the narrator holds "original sin" rather than the world war "responsible for Annabel's misguided behaviour" (285). But in this book, as in other Glasgow novels, when it comes to large and earnest perspectives like this statement about original sin, it may be better to trust the imagery and the total structure of the work rather than Glasgow's narrators, who are

sometimes given a personalized and therefore limited character. In the total structure of this novel, original sin turns out to
be no more than human freedom and the life force seen from
the point of view of traditional morality, rather than from the
broader perspective of pagan comedy.

By the end, the judge, Edmonia, the imagery, the cyclic
structure, and for a moment even Bella, the unconverted re-
fuser of festivity, all bow to the pagan divinity of Annabel's
new generation. "The earth belongs to the living," Thomas
Jefferson said, and the young have more of the living in them,
Annabel reminds us (301, 322, 326–27). So we smile with relief when in the final scene the judge, an old eagle well-nigh
plucked by recent events, feels his wing once more start to
stir. Youth, spring, and the vital sap will triumph again (345–
46). At some point—probably between the judge's acquies-
cence and Bella's moment of hestitation—the biological alibi
has ceased to be mere excuse and has become a true descrip-
tion of the reality in which Annabel lives (291, 301). The
judge speaks of Annabel's position, in quasi-Nietzschean
terms, as a "revaluation of morals": "Annabel has her point of
view as clearly defined as we have ours. That is why we can't
bring the old pressure of authority to bear on her. It is like the
thunder of the papacy to a Protestant; it thunders as hard as
ever but it fails to strike. The thing that has disturbed me
most is that there seems to be some intellectual basis for the
whole attitude" (291). Just how far we can take this bit of
philosophical earnestness is suggested by the feeling of uncertainty that arises when we think about the judge's throw-
away clause, "as clearly defined as we have ours," or about the
logic implied by the last sentence in the quote. Thus the comic
spirit triumphs once more over sententiousness, and we find
ourselves thrown back upon the imagery and total structure
for guidance. The latter support Annabel, not because her position is modern, but because it is as old as Aphrodite and
spring.

The way Annabel's dreams flow from the book's basic reality stands out against the larger pattern of the novel, which

usually plays intentions, dreams, and alibis off against other realities and dreams to undercut each point of view and keep it in comic perspective.[4] The mere conjunction of events, without interference from the narrator, suffices to take the wind out of any character's sails. For example, Bella's incurably pragmatic commentary and Annabel's self-deceiving gold digging continuously turn the judge's romantic profusions into foolish evasions of reality (114–15, 269). Moreover, the author needs only to give the judge a little rope and he hangs himself. There are too many flaws in his logic; he has too many invalid opinions. He himself recognizes that "his own mental state resembled, at its best, a reservoir of opinions rather than [the] babbling stream of consciousness" he bemoans as the "loose thinking" of the new generation (16, 109, 123). The judge's own process of thought forces the reader out of the judge's reality into a larger perspective, one to which the Olympian and aphoristic style of the novel proves more appropriate than the undistanced streams of consciousness we find in many modern psychological fictions might have been. For the judge's sententiousness seems but the cutting edge of senility.

The handling of time also prepares us for the broader perspective. The judge's view of his own past is that his youth constituted a farcical web of ironies and errors, the worst of which was falling for Cordelia while he thought he was tracking down Amanda. Combined with the weaknesses in his present thinking, his distanced attitude toward the events of his early manhood prepares the reader for the recurring commentary of the narrator, who is usually not only detached, but objective, critical, and nonsycophantic enough to deserve the abused adjective *Olympian*. In a subtle mood, the narrator can control the ironic conjunction of events or use ambiguous phrases to alert the reader to tensions between dreams and realities. For example, the narrator describes Annabel's fare-

4 My comments on point of view build upon the acute observations of C. Hugh Holman, "The Comedies of Manners," in M. Thomas Inge (ed.), *Ellen Glasgow: Centennial Essays* (Charlottesville, 1976), 115, 119.

well gesture the first night she sleeps across from her husband's bedroom as "one of her *light* kisses," a phrase suggesting tenderness to the romantic and coolness to the suspicious (212, italics added). But the narrator obviously finds the judge such a flawed being that there is no real need for subtlety. Now and again the narrator takes time out to remind us of the judge's illusions, his bad faith, his innocence, his fundamentalism (40–41, 53, 180, 235). Elsewhere the narrator emphasizes the gap between his youthful itch and his "inelastic arteries" (112). The narrator (probably she, if not a cosmic androgyne) seems especially fond of judging the judge for his "nimble masculine logic," which persists in "the chivalrous interpretation of biology"—that is, that old men want young women but that old women don't have sexual needs (40, 62). Although central to the ironic perspective, if not to the comic vision, of the novel, this weakness in the judge's logic may be driven home too often and too heavily for such a graceful study of sexuality among the gerontocrats.

This loss of deftness is one of the few flaws in a masterful work. Another may be the absence of felt anguish in the judge's statement that Annabel is revaluating values (291). For a moment his character is lost in the earnestness. But these are mere blinks of the author in a novel of such scintillant wit and penetrating vision.

That the book ranks no higher in American letters than it does may have to do with two literary prejudices. First, many twentieth-century readers prefer dramatized streams of consciousness rather than intruding and aphoristic narrators. Second, the nineteenth-century novel created a prejudice in favor of long, lacerating, ambitious, if flawed, works rather than perfected or comic writing. This last prejudice Glasgow seemed to share when she described *The Romantic Comedians* as meriting "a special, if narrow, niche of its own" among her novels; generally she chose *Barren Ground* and *The Sheltered Life* as her best books.[5] If this valuation seems to condemn *The*

5 Glasgow, *A Certain Measure*, 211.

*Romantic Comedians* with faint praise, we must certainly take exception and—as in all other cases—trust the novel, not the novelist. For this totally enjoyable comic vignette is clearly superior to her more ambitious but uneven novels, such as *They Stooped to Folly* and *Vein of Iron*. It stands with *Barren Ground* and *The Sheltered Life*—a very high niche indeed.

*Chapter VII*

# The Great American Matriarchy: *They Stooped to Folly* (1929)

Winter dominates Ellen Glasgow's *They Stooped to Folly* (1929), as spring had the comedy *The Romantic Comedians* (1926) which preceded it, and as summer and fall would the romantic tragedy *The Sheltered Life* (1932), which would succeed it. Whereas time seems to fly in circles in *The Romantic Comedians* and to flow toward inevitable catastrophe in *The Sheltered Life*, time in *They Stooped to Folly* simply piles up, like dust or snow. In the gloomy world of the latter novel, no possibility exists that the inhabitants might either burst forth into new life or succeed in bringing about the final destruction of their suspended existence. They are frozen forever, the novel suggests, into the frustrating roles dictated by the great American matriarchy, a purgatory they and their ancestors have created. This is the fictive world into which Glasgow, tongue in cheek, invites the reader; but because her narrator here is much closer to her central characters, the ironies are less obvious, the laughter less free, than in *The Romantic Comedians*.

Winter is the season for irony and satire, modes that permit no progress and, in this case, very little movement of any sort. To protect the static quality of *They Stooped to Folly*, Glasgow refused to develop any character with the potential for decisive action. The young members of the cast—Mary Victoria Littlepage, Milly Burden, and Martin Welding—remain mere shadows, characters sketched from the outside with no developed interiority, about whom the reader cares very little—too little perhaps for the novel to succeed. The focus falls instead upon two persons either too old, too timid, or too complacent to move the action forward into comedy or tragedy; these two are Virginius Curle Littlepage and Victoria Brooke Littlepage, the parents of Mary Victoria and, in the world of this novel, the creators of the American matriarchy, which victimizes all the characters, especially Virginius. Not only these characters, but the world at large has fallen prey, the novel implies, to the American influence. The year is 1923–1924, and World War I has just given the nation its first excuse for the wholesale exportation of its way of life under the missionary cover that it is saving the world for democracy. For this deceptive potion there seems to be no antidote— aside from the painful anecdotes of a satirical novel.

Of all the characters, Marmaduke Littlepage, the elder brother of Virginius, comes nearest escaping the traps of the matriarchy. On three occasions one of the two major characters undertakes the arduous ascent to the attic apartment where Marmaduke paints his purple nudes and hoards his forbidden knowledge. The view from that height suggests that, although Marmaduke remains a "caged hawk," he has achieved that beast's superior vision of the world in which he lives, a world in which his brother remains a mere monkey at the end of an organ grinder's tether.[1] Marmaduke blames Virginius' symptoms of chronic dyspepsia upon the "artificial conformity" of "American men": "How can you digest your meals when you live in a protracted panic, and your whole philosophy of life is rooted in the fear of women?" Then Marmaduke paints a picture of the American century:

> "Rabbit souls, you are afraid of a shadow. That is why you are so eager to escape into the stock market or into a war, which is the only complete escape from civilization. Good Lord! But I don't wonder. I'd escape that way myself if I were imprisoned in this woman-ruled society. After making a republic, you men have not had sufficient courage to keep

---

1 Ellen Glasgow, *They Stooped to Folly* (Garden City, N.Y., 1929), 125, 336. This book will hereafter be referred to by page number only.

what you had won from women, who know nothing of freedom because they have embraced sacrifice as an ideal. And
you are still too cowed to realize that you have turned the
American Republic into an *oligarchy of maternal instincts*. For
the belief in *sacrifice* is so firmly embedded in the minds of
women that freedom means little more to them than an extended area of *reform*. Already they have obliterated the distinction between a willing and an unwilling martyrdom. It
is only human, you must admit, that after centuries of suc-
cessful self-sacrifice they should seize with genuine enthusiasm an opportunity *to sacrifice the other half of the world*. So
*complete a reversal* of the situation doesn't often occur in human affairs." (130–31, italics added)

Although Marmaduke's clairvoyance will later be tinted by
irony when another character pursues the etiology of the national malaise deeper than he does, his statement about the
matriarchy very accurately sums up the larger situation in the
book.

But *They Stooped to Folly* presents no sweeping panorama of
an international epidemic of female evasive idealism; it
dramatizes instead a particular culture in which the sources
and pathology of the disease can be studied in detail and for
humorous effect. Marmaduke, operating again as the author's
spokesman, explains how this is to be done, since the method
of the novel parallels his own technique for painting the inside of his subjects (28). When Victoria comes to ascend his
stairs, he tells her as they climb that he is doing a study of her
husband "to catch those jolly purple shadows in Virginius'
face," shadows Victoria has never seen. To Marmaduke (and
Glasgow) "the shadows in a man's face are more significant
than anything that he says." Still climbing, Victoria asks, "Are
you implying that my husband is leading *a double life*?" Marmaduke replies: "No, Victoria. I am implying that, like every
other man, he is leading *a quadruple one*. *Four secret lives* aren't
too many to allow a man when you consider the millions of
predatory cells of which he is composed" (205–206, italics
added). All of Marmaduke's reply is suggestive, but "quad-

ruple" is an unexpected number to find applied to the selves hidden within a realistic character. It is larger than the twinned nature of man we are used to in either moralistic, naturalistic, or "secret-sharing" literature—larger even than the tripartite self of Freudian fiction. The test of Marmaduke's reliability will be to discover whether Virginius has actually developed four secret lives—no more and no less—in response to female control.

Marmaduke does not, of course, explain how Glasgow will dramatize the power of the matriarchy through Virginius' four hidden selves. That is a literary secret, not a visual technique. Although cubism cannot help here, a literary equivalent of cubism can. For more than ten years (since *Life and Gabriella*, 1916) Glasgow had worked with a technique for allowing supporting characters to mirror the hidden dimensions of the protagonists. The method remains essentially the same for Virginius Littlepage, although there are complications.

Virginius is no psychologist, let alone a modern novelist, but he realizes he is leading a "double life" whenever he gets the chance—even though he would not admit this lack of integrity to anyone he knows in Queenborough. To no one, that is, except Amy Dalrymple, the sprightly and festive divorcée and widow who mirrors his own doubleness. Virginius has been happily married for more than half of his fifty-seven years to the perfect wife, Victoria; and this is a long time, he has decided, to try to live with perfection (13). Thirty years before, Virginius chose security over freedom when he combined his fine name with Victoria's splendid fortune in a marriage that lacked nothing his Victorian imagination might have desired (13). Victoria has always cheerfully done her "duty" as a Victorian woman: she has inspired her husband with her optimistic idealism and, by pretending she is satisfied, preserved the sacred institution of marriage. She has had such a "fine influence" upon him that for most of their life together Virginius has seemed to her to be a "man who did not have that other side to his nature"—the side that would pull civilization back to the jungle, they and other Victorians believe, were it not for the saving virtue of women like herself (92). As he tells his wife, "Whatever I am to-day, I may say honestly, is owing to your example more than to anything else" (81). Because his public role and his image of himself are thus mirrored by Victoria, she is one of his "lives," or selves. But she is not one of the "four secret lives" mentioned by Marmaduke.

What Virginius does not dare tell her is that after thirty years even the finest inspiration turns into an impediment (to use the language of Glasgow's later preface to the book).[2] When he looks back over the "creditable years of his life," he feels that he hates them. He has always "respected convention" and "deferred to tradition"; it seems to him that he "learned to bridle his impulses from the hour of his birth." The result is that (like Faust) he cannot pinpoint a time in his life when "he really lived" or actually "reached after happiness" (3). He does not know whether to attribute his November of discontent to "middle age," to "the fatal inadequacy of all human experience," or to his happening to be a "disappointed idealist" (4). (The action of the novel eventually points an accusing finger at all three of these as they are reflected in the American matriarchy.) What he does know is that he feels "his thwarted longings" most intensely whenever he remembers Amy Paget Dalrymple, "one of those fair, fond, clinging women whom men long either to protect or to ruin" (15–16). Because Amy Dalrymple is so frivolous, fascinating, feminine, and gloriously fallen (the alliteration telegraphs the message), she seems the perfect embodiment of Victoria's opposite traits. Whenever Virginius dares "in his hours of leisure" to think of her, there is "a motion, a surge, a buried whirlpool, far below in some primeval flood of his being" (16). That buried whirlpool is the first of his secret lives—one that he almost set free one night before World War I when he

2 It is difficult not to bring in the preface, since Glasgow's analysis there of the force of mythology in dictating sexual roles seems exceedingly accurate. Glasgow, *A Certain Measure*, 228.

took Amy, then his legal client, in his arms. But Virginius was
a slow lover then, a Victorian gentleman, and the major suspense of the novel proves to be whether a dozen years are
adequate time for a woman like Amy to allow a man like Virginius to muster his courage. Alas, Amy (and the reader) are
to be frustrated once more when Virginius' concentration of
his secret impulse is disturbed, this time by the mere tinkle of
a bell that sends him home to find Victoria dead of a heart
attack (303, 314).

Something like Victoria's death had to be the inevitable conclusion of his dalliance with Amy Dalrymple. For this whole
strand of the novel simply shows Virginius reenacting a scenario he learned from his father, a *Georgian* gentleman who
would stumble home late at night and then the next day inevitably bring "tribal offerings of flowers and fruit" to Virginius'
mother, which supplications for forgiveness he would accom-
pany with "the dreary monotone of abject apology" (82). This
ritual of the religion of the matriarchy has seemingly survived
through Virginius and Victoria, but in a sadly etiolated form.
Virginius, the *Victorian*, finds himself incapable of his father's
passion, only of sentiment, and incapable of sin, only of inhibited pleasures (69, 112). As the pale shadow of his Georgian
model, even though he falls short of robust transgression, he
pays double with his remorse and guilt. Like a wayward child
who disobeys to earn the attention of punishment, Virginius
completes his learned pattern of freedom, guilt, and repent-
ance when he confronts his wife's corpse: "I was not worthy,
but I loved her! I was not worthy, but I loved her!" he groans
over and over again (317). When he discovers she has kept her
approaching death a secret for six months, he realizes that "it
was in these last months that he had wronged her in his heart,
that he had betrayed her devotion" (319).

The upshot is that Victoria suddenly undergoes a Victorian
apotheosis in his guilt-ridden imagination. It is as though he
is "worshipping at the shrine of some tutelary divinity.
Crowned, radiant, incomparable, a new Victoria, one whom
he had never even imagined, had flowered there, out of the

throbbing light of his vision. . . . All the beauty of Helen adorned with the meekness of Mary could not have transformed him so utterly as this miraculous visitation of pity and terror" (320). Death is Victoria's ultimate ploy, one she could not have bettered had she chosen it consciously. Louisa Goddard, Victoria's best friend, suspects that Victoria has thus "felt her way," without seeing it, to "everlasting remembrance"—in other words, that she unconsciously fell back upon her own death as the most effective device for returning her straying lamb to the safety of the matriarchal fold (322). And for a short while Virginius himself seems divinely satisfied, as though he and his father had unconsciously created the matriarchy and the tyranny of maternal virtue as the surest institution for keeping them good little boys. But more of this later.

The death of Victoria was not brought about, however, by Virginius' feeble transgressions under Amy's grape leaves; for Victoria always felt that she had made the right wifely sacrifices to keep him a satisfied husband, even if she herself didn't find their marriage completely fulfilling. But the second of Virginius' secret lives might have triggered her final crisis, which effectively ended both his first and second selves. This second life takes us back to Marmaduke. Although Virginius might knowingly yield to the influences of Mrs. Dalrymple, he is less likely to acknowledge his unconscious tie with Marmaduke, who in effect mirrors the shadow side of his younger brother. Virginius has always tried to "trample down these low but vigorous impulses," this "secret pulse of wildness in his heart," which seems to urge him "to an irregular alliance with the obscure and the profligate" and to a "childish admiration for his elder brother" (27). Their mother had translated her own wildness into wild roses painted on French mirrors or into snowy landscapes stitched upon satin sofa pillows while her errant husband groveled for her forgiveness (28, 82). Marmaduke compensated for his proper upbringing by "driving an ambulance under fire" in Europe and by transmuting his "thwarted desire" for Louisa Goddard into phantastic nudes (28, 82). Virginius, however, does no more than sense that the "vagabond impulses" of a "roving buccaneer" are "hidden beneath the cloak of his correct Sabbath attire" and think that "the buccaneer in his blood" is "allied with his brother" before deciding that perhaps his "liver is going against" him (97). Ambivalence dominates his attitude toward his rejected Marmaduke side, however, for he knows that his brother has enjoyed life more than he has and that he "chose wealth, security, steadfast position," while Marmaduke "gave all those things in exchange for liberation of spirit." Marmaduke may be "shabby and untidy and disreputable," but he is free of the fears that have caused Virginius to conform his life "to other people's ideals": "fear of the stock market, fear of public opinion, fear, most of all, of what people would think of me," he moans to himself just before Marmaduke denounces the "oligarchy of maternal instincts" that governs American life (129). Virginius can nod silent agreement with the voice of his shadow—until his brother attacks womanhood and its assorted institutions. Then he recalls that Marmaduke holds "dangerous views" and "disreputable opinions" (28, 133).

In the course of the novel, Virginius grows closer than he realizes to Marmaduke's embittered, antimatriarchal thinking. What moves him in Marmaduke's direction is the conflict that constitutes the central dramatic (as opposed to psychological) plot of the book. This plot consists of the struggle of Virginius' daughter, Mary Victoria, to "save" her husband, Martin Welding, from Virginius' secretary, Milly Burden, by whom Martin had, without knowing it, an illegitimate child (it failed to live) before Martin ever met Mary Victoria. Virginius is directly involved in this triangle because Milly came to him for help in locating Martin after Martin returned to Europe in postwar disillusionment, still without knowing Milly had been pregnant. Virginius passed the task of tracking the drifting father on to his daughter, then a volunteer struggling to save the Balkans from the ravages of war.[3] Virginius possessed absolute confidence in Mary Victoria's idealism and honor, but her idealism proved flexible enough to slip from the reconstruction of the Balkans to the salvation of doom-driven Martin (6, 8, 12, 91–92). Through her blend of "intemperate virtue" and self-deception, which permit her to take another woman's man and call it an act of righteousness, Mary Victoria has fallen from a position of honor in her father's judgment (90–91, 268, 283). His feeling of honest disappointment with his daughter comes out when he discusses the triangle with Victoria, a woman who always looks for the cheerful and favorable side of every subject, especially those involving members of her family. When Victoria claims that their daughter did all in her power to make Martin go back to Milly and Virginius wonders whether she went "so far . . . as paying for his passage," Victoria claims he sounds bitter (90). When Virginius points out that, unlike Mary Victoria, he is "neither an act of God nor an instrument of salvation," Victoria replies, "There are times, Virginius, when you sound almost like Marmaduke" (92).

Marmaduke thinks that Mary Victoria's overpowering "sense of duty" is simply an alibi, a moral sanction for her will to power. He says, "What she craves—though I am not sure that *she herself is aware of it*—is complete *domination* of the world within reach of her influence. The wider her sphere of inspiration becomes, the more flattering it is to her *vanity*. And vanity . . . is the controlling interest in most feminine efforts to improve the nature of man" (132, italics added). Virginius cannot listen to such irreverence when he is with Marmaduke; but when he is alone or with Victoria, the wild buccaneer in him, who rebels against the female hegemony in his life, echoes the heretical opinions of his liberated brother.

3 The frequent snips at the saviors of the Balkans were probably meant for Glasgow's former fiancé Henry Anderson, who had rescued Rumania for the Red Cross and, rumor said, carried on a flirtation with the queen. His dalliance led Glasgow to attempt suicide and damaged their engagement beyond repair.

In his last conversation alone with Victoria before she dies, Virginius finds himself dissenting in silence over and over again from her orthodox views of God, duty, Martin, Milly, nymphomania, and the permanence of the moral law (253–57). The turning point comes when Victoria informs him that Martin has been seeing Milly again. Virginius rebels against the sacredness of marriage and family feeling by pointing out that "the seduction of a woman does constitute some sort of moral claim on a decent man" and that a child makes the claim stronger (258). His final blow against the soft chains in which Victoria has held him for so long follows: "We must not forget," he adds, "that Milly Burden deserves every consideration. Though she has made mistakes, she is at heart a good woman" (259). The words themselves are mild, but the assertions question the axioms of Victoria's moral view of life. If Milly is a good woman, her single stoop to unwed sexuality does not make her a nymphomaniac as Victoria assumes the single folly of Virginius' Aunt Agatha proved her to be; therefore, the moral law must be malleable. This possibility throws into question the existence of a static ideal deity, Victoria's Unseen Absolute, the cornerstone of her world picture and the sanction for matriarchal dominance through marriage. But Victoria does not allow her mind to pass thus over the smooth web of her moral vision. With the withdrawal of Virginius' moral support, she simply sinks "into a windy hollow space" where she discovers that, beneath the genteel mask she wears, she is "as hollow as a drum" (260). If there is a single blow that kills Victoria, it is her husband's rebellion through expressing his Marmaduke-like doubt. This is another of the transgressions for which he must pay, by siding once more with Mary Victoria, although this transgression does not loom as large in his guilty imagination as does his misbehavior with Mrs. Dalrymple (325–29).

Virginius' shadowy tie to Marmaduke also accounts in part for those occasions when he disapproves of Curle, his second son, as well as for those moments when he thinks fondly of Duncan, his elder son, and sympathetically of Martin Welding. Victoria's optimism and Virginius' bland desire to get along with others have simply gone to seed in Curle's healthy vulgarity and boosterism: Curle is too much a mirror of the frustrating day-to-day life Virginius leads for the father to think fondly of him. But Duncan came home from the war demoralized, morose, cynical, inscrutable, like Marmaduke but worse. Though Virginius might call his fondness for Duncan family feeling, it is chiefly the young man's honesty he admires (4, 55–57). Martin articulates a jaundiced view of postwar America much like that of Marmaduke and Duncan (9, 309).

Because no family tie exists to help Virginius overlook Martin's unpleasant attributes, his attitude toward his son-in-law seems even more ambivalent than his feelings about Marmaduke. When he first hears about Martin from Milly, he calls the young man an "unmitigated cad," perhaps because he has never found himself in exactly the same situation with a woman (9). But when he learns how Mary Victoria has taken over Martin's life and has liberated him from his habits, the older man glances at the younger "with a stifled feeling of human—or was it merely of masculine?—solidarity." As he reminds himself, he married Mary Victoria's mother, and the girl "is her mother all over again, only more so" (70). The tie between the two is that they are fellow victims of women for whom neither is good enough (73). It is appropriate then that Mary Victoria should forbid Martin the bourbon and pour him instead a glass of "Father's oldest Amontillado," for that sherry has no doubt been the proper toast to the buried life in Queenborough since the time of Poe (163, 169–70). When Martin says that he is in hell, that he's had enough of women, that he wants "to get away from every woman on earth," Virginius understands all too well; there have been hours when he longed "to escape to some desolate polar region of the mind, where woman, even as an ideal, could not hope to survive" (310). Although Martin acts out Virginius' own phantasies, neither can give the other moral support. Virginius considers his compassion for Martin's hell an instance of his own "weakness" of pitying the failures of life; and Martin feels he is "rotten inside" because he cannot accept the premises, "a single one of" the "fundamental beliefs," upon which Virginius has built his public and family lives (312). In short, the moral ideology of the matriarchy conquers by dividing the rebels from one another. Through most of the novel, Virginius cannot stomach Martin, and his disgust for the man provides a measure of the degree to which he has been separated by conformity from the victim and rebel lurking within himself. Martin mirrors the third of his secret lives, one more cynical than that reflected by his critical brother.

As candidates for the fourth of the secret lives Marmaduke ascribed to Virginius, three important supporting characters remain: Louisa Goddard, Mary Victoria, and Milly Burden. Because Louisa is Victoria's best friend and Mary Victoria's godmother, she seems too much like what Virginius has become to hold any fascination for his unconscious personality; he can only "admire" her, although she has secretly loved him for thirty years (31, 44, 345). Mary Victoria is excluded for much the same reason as Louisa from participation in her father's secret lives. Although Victoria claims that their daughter is the romance of his life, the truth is that Virginius is projecting his own view of the mature Mary Victoria upon others when he thinks that her moral idealism and her willingness to follow the "Stern Daughter of the Voice of God" have made her sexually chilling to "all the romantic satyrs of the Balkans" (12, 45). He has not always felt this way; his heart still dissolves "into a rainbow mist" when he remembers her as "a little girl wearing a short white frock with starched frills and a blue sash"—Mary Victoria, seven years old. "Nothing in his whole life, not Victoria in her bridal veil, not Curle in his soldier's uniform, not Mary Victoria marching in a Red Cross parade, had ever touched him so deeply as the image of *those helpless feet* in white socks and black slippers" (23–24, italics added). Although she has "outgrown his protection," his emotions have remained fixed upon that image of her.

With Mary Victoria away saving the Balkans, Milly Burden has displaced her in Virginius' emotions, for Milly is "as dear . . . as a second and less formidable daughter" (10). He tells Milly that he feels she is related to him because she came to his office the week his own daughter left (22). Milly also appeals to him in the way his daughter did as a seven-year-old: Milly's helplessness stimulates his sense of pity, his manly desire to help and protect (5). Because she accepts this help, Milly is less formidable than his own flesh and blood. There are, of course, complications in his relationship with Milly, and these keep her among his secret lives. First, although Milly remains free of any feminine sense of sin, the Victoria part of Virginius cannot help seeing her as a fallen woman and a threat of some vague sort to the other, unsullied secretary in his office (6). Therefore, he ought to let Milly go. But this side of him overlooks "the fatal indulgence of the paternal heart," which keeps her in the office. Second, although Milly is not as beautiful as Mary Victoria, Virginius is struck by her "eyes, large, deep, radiantly blue . . . burning with life" and by "her indescribable charm"; she has the sort of face that exerts "an improper influence over sober husbands and dignified fathers," her mother believes (24, 223). Therefore Milly also appeals to the same forbidden side of Virginius' personality as Amy Dalrymple. Third, her refusal to accept "the sense of sin that makes the fallen woman" both fascinates and affronts Virginius. It is part of her "youth, her gallantry, and her imprudent passion," which stir him "more deeply than he had ever dared to confess"; but it also makes her one with "all modern youth," who are "too hard, too flippant, too brazen," he feels, "to awaken romantic desire" (5, 7). He prefers his fallen women in the Victorian mode of Mrs. Dalrymple. In the end, the negative modern attributes of Milly's character seem to weigh more heavily for Virginius than the attractive ones. This is especially true when she confesses that she has permitted herself to see Martin again even though he is married to Mary Victoria and, worse still, that she will not accept Martin even after Mary Victoria sacrifices him to her (348). In the same scene, Mary Victoria's helplessness as a deserted wife transforms her once again into "the image of a little girl with auburn curls on her shoulders and bare, sunburned knees above her white socks and black slippers." Thus, as Virginius' "lost adoration and romance" ebb "back into his heart," Mary Victoria reclaims the side of her father he had lavished upon Milly (347–48).

This confused paternal dimension is the only one of Virginius' secret lives to survive the efficient death of Victoria. But far from lending a thrust of progressive motion to the novel, this survival is clearly regressive. It casts Mary Victoria in the part of "helpless little girl," which she outgrew twenty years before, and pushes Virginius into the familiar and quasi-incestuous role of the helpless adoring "big daddy"—clearly a dead end, as even he seems to realize in the final sentence when he lets her hand "slip from his arm" while he stares at "the darkening drift of the twilight" (351).

The ending here is far from the comic vision with which *The Romantic Comedians* concluded; there we saw the nearly destroyed Old Judge Honeywell coming back once more to romantic and sexual life. Nevertheless, in so far as we have yet examined *They Stooped to Folly*, the technique of the two novels seems very much the same: the dynamics of the psychic lives of Honeywell and Littlepage are both revealed by using other characters to mirror their hidden dimensions. But *They Stooped to Folly* happens to be a good deal more complicated than its predecessor. Here Glasgow has taken great pains to assign a compensatory shadow life to each of the supporting characters. Rather than stopping with a portrait of Virginius Littlepage, as the earlier book did with a vignette of Honeywell, the present novel surrounds the major study with a series of medallions, each of which has a secret depth of its own. For example, Aunt Agatha has become a legend for having stooped once then retreating from life to the upper story of her nephew's home, as every proper fallen woman ought. But she compensates for her legendary role by going out for "banana sundaes" (a compulsion we dare not examine too closely) and by running off to the movies with Mrs. Dalrymple to see sensations like *Passion in the Purple* and *A Scarlet Sin*, in which her own transgressions are elevated to phantasy and adventure (85). As another example, war was the only power equal to, and therefore capable of complementing, the moral idealism of Mary Victoria; it alone could provide "all the extravagance and excitement she and so many other women were able to indulge in" (89). The same is true of war and Mrs. Dalrymple, except that, after the stifling morality of Queenborough, the war simply provided her an opportunity to put her ample powers to noble use (100). These three, however, are simple examples among the medallions.

The complications begin to emerge when we examine the intricate interrelationships between the characters. We have already noted that Marmaduke is Virginius' dark side. But Marmaduke in turn has stabilized his own plunge into artistic and intellectual freedom by clinging for thirty years to an unattainable ideal, rocklike and God-hard Louisa (128). To close the circle, Louisa has placed an ultimate check upon her own intellectual probe of "the Morals of Babylon" and other modes of classical human depravity by loving, for the same thirty years, a proper Virginian of Virginius' fine cut (32, 344–45). She does not realize, of course, how close he has come himself to plunging, with Amy Dalrymple, into the moonlight and grape leaves of classical amorality. A similar complexity characterizes the Milly–Martin–Mary Victoria figure. Milly in part fell under Martin's influence to compensate for the education in good, good, good that she received from her mother—who is so righteous that even Victoria finds her too gloomy an influence to serve as matron in a home for unwed mothers (219, 241). But, after Milly has fallen, Martin finds what he thinks he needs to balance his cynicism and guilt in the angelic influence of Mary Victoria. Although she cannot admit it, Mary Victoria must feel similarly complemented by Martin's decadence and powerlessness, since he has nothing else to offer. The ending of their story proves as regressive as that of the

Milly–Virginius–Mary Victoria plot. Martin leaves Mary Victoria with child, just as he had abandoned Milly before the novel began.

To further complicate this triangle, Milly Burden also serves as the mirror of the dark side of Victoria's personality. Although Virginius has sacrificed his own freedom to make Victoria happy within the sacred matriarchal institution of matrimony, she has, it turns out, sacrificed her own dreams to make him happy in the same structure. The amusing result is that neither is content, though each imagines the other to be (4, 144). Victoria has sought to compensate all these years by serving as president of "the Home for Unfortunates," a refuge where the "honey" is extracted "from wingless daughters of joy," a hereditary compensation founded by her mother-in-law (86). But at the unsatisfied core of her being, there still lurks the memory of a silly dream, "which had returned to her often as a girl and once again in her young wifehood": "While it lasted she had imagined herself to be in the midst of an immense level plain, caught up suddenly into the thunder of galloping horses. . . . A liquid fire ran in her veins, and she had asked herself, 'Is it he? Is he coming at last?' " The youthful dream had referred to "the intrepid lover, the young Lochinvar of the mind," for whom in actuality Virginius had finally become the disappointing substitute (151). With this secret life, Victoria cannot help but be fascinated when she meets Milly Burden, the only woman in Queenborough (aside perhaps from Amy Dalrymple) who truly has the courage of her appetites. Rather than accept Milly as the shadow of her own unfulfilled life, she compares her to her daughter: she finds Milly "not so beautiful, not nearly so perfect in feature as Mary Victoria, but more human and certainly far more exciting." Milly seems to her "the kind of woman whose every act, every gesture is instinct with vitality"—so much so that Victoria can "understand the spell" the girl has cast over Virginius. Rather than embrace her opposite and gain some of that vitality, however, Victoria rejects the girl the way she has always repressed the living side of herself: "No really good woman could look so alive," she decides, for the bloom in Milly's face "served definitely to place her in a class with those other women who are not all that they should be" (234–35). A month later Victoria achieves the condition that places her own goodness on a level with all pure ideals: she passes from this world into the mental life of her guilt-ridden but adoring spouse.

The greater complexity *They Stooped to Folly* attains through these overlapping medallions does not make it a superior novel to *The Romantic Comedians*—only a longer one. Nor is the book improved because it first presented itself to Glasgow as "a disembodied *motif,*" which she insisted no book before it had done.[4] This abstract conception leads to a thematic rigidity that may be appropriate enough for a satiric panorama of persons caught between Matthew Arnold's "two worlds, one dead / The other powerless to be born." But this rigidity is finally less convincing than the more fluid treatment of alibis and evasions in the shorter work. Like *The Romantic Comedians*, this novel catalogs a large number of alibis employed by the characters to sanction, or at least to explain, their questionable behavior. Most notably, Europe, World War I, and civilization are used to justify all sorts of cruelty and unusual conduct. But unlike *The Romantic Comedians*, all the excuses here seem to derive from one gigantic and tyrannous evasion of reality—the great American matriarchy, which sent Americans forth to conquer the world in order to save it (131).

What saves the novel from this ludicrous didacticism is the way Glasgow ultimately places the idea of the matriarchy itself in a comic perspective. The women who seem to belong most completely to this power structure—and therefore must be counted among its perpetuators if not its creators—do not, at base, believe in it. For example, in an unguarded moment, Victoria wonders "why poor Aunt Agatha, or any other woman, ever consented to become a superstition"—that is, a fallen woman. Although Victoria checks herself, the unthink-

4 Glasgow, *A Certain Measure*, 224.

able thought has penetrated her mind "that ruined women, like ghosts and goblins and warlocks and witches, vanished into the dark ages of faith as soon as the world ceased to believe in them" (240). The division of women into the fallen and the pure, into nymphomaniacs and angels, is an axiom Victoria has heretofore always accepted. To doubt it is a serious blow to the sacredness of the matriarchy. But the thematic climax comes when Louisa exposes the matriarchy as the creation of men, a myth women actually want no part of: "Nothing," she decides, "was worth all the deceit, all the anguish, all the futile hope and ineffectual endeavour, all the pretense and parade, all the artificial glamour and empty posturing, of the great Victorian tradition. . . . For her heart had cracked and broken as quietly as the hearts of all perfect Southern ladies broke beneath the enamelled surface of beautiful behaviour" (331).

And why have men created their own traps and sealed their own doom? No one in the novel can answer that question, but the pattern Virginius copies from his father shows the reason: so long as there are perfect ladies to inspire, control, and finally forgive them, men can escape from the freedom to which nature has condemned them into the eternal boyishness that the myth of cosmic motherhood makes possible. Glasgow has, in effect, not only exposed one of the preeminent religious dodges of the West, but also laid bare the psychology of the great American predilection for petticoat dominance. As Henry Adams said, Americans may have left Venus and the Virgin in Europe; but we were careful, as Mark Twain showed, to bring Aunt Polly along. Virginius depends on feminine dominance over him. This is the ultimate and secret punch line of the book.

Exquisite wit and trenchant social commentary cannot raise a novel with the flaws this one possesses to the level of Glasgow's finest work—*The Romantic Comedians* and *The Sheltered Life*, which are nearly flawless, and *Barren Ground*, which transcends its faults through its profound powers of characterization. The problems here are varied, especially in the opening chapter, which includes too much past while characters are being mentioned for the first time (7–10). The major themes are also drawn too broadly and too plainly at the beginning (3–4, 20). The management of the time loop that concludes the first chapter is awkward. A loop this early in the story, like an epic simile, needs a solid return; but the first chapter ends with a very fuzzy return to the present time of the story. (Glasgow seems to have written the first two chapters as one and then cut them to fit the rhythm of the subsequent chapters and to give the reader a quicker sense of entering the novel.) The subsequent attacks upon the foibles of the Little-pages seem to use millstones to crush butterflies, unless we accept the premise that Victoria and Virginius represent an entrenched power structure which is the true target of the satire. At times the Littlepages seem mere straw men, set-up pre-Freudians to be run down by a post-Freudian steamroller. They are such solemn pontificators and self-absorbed persons (though their interiors lack any rich potential for sensual imagery) that their musings create a generally slow tempo. This slowness works in passages when Virginius is about to "seduce" Amy Dalrymple, since here there is some action to be suspended. But in general the potential for action, and therefore for suspense, depends upon the decisions of Milly and Martin, who are never adequately presented to make them real to the reader. Consequently, the reader cares little what happens to them, and their fates provide insufficient mystery to compensate for the slowness of the Littlepages. (Glasgow would do better with her wild young types in her last full-length novel, *In This Our Life*, 1941.)

Finally, it does not really redeem *They Stooped to Folly* to call it a wasteland novel and Virginius a Prufrock, as Robert Holland has done.[5] By 1929, *The Great Gatsby* (1925) and *The Sun Also Rises* (1926) had done better work with the wasteland

5 Robert Holland, "Miss Glasgow's Prufrock," *American Quarterly*, IX (Winter, 1957), 435–40.

theme. Indeed, the oldest edition of T. S. Eliot in Glasgow's library was the 1922 edition of *The Waste Land*,[6] and by May of that year she had already published a novel with a character, Stephen Culpeper, who makes a finer Prufrock than does Virginius Littlepage—except that Culpeper is as close to Arnold as he is to Eliot and closer to Glasgow's own postwar life in Virginia than to either. Queenborough suffers from an excess of, not an absence of, the tradition whose demise Eliot bemoans in *The Waste Land*.

No, Glasgow must take the blame for this book—and the credit. For the view it expresses of the American matriarchy she reached the hard way. And she had not yet exhausted the subject. In her next book, she would go further into the reasons that males elevate their women to a ruling ideal and would show in fuller detail why patriarchs will the matriarchy into existence.

6 Tutwiler, *A Catalogue of the Library of Ellen Glasgow*, 87.

# Chapter VIII

# Creatures of Illusion: *The Sheltered Life* (1932)

If *They Stooped to Folly* ends with a whimper, *The Sheltered Life* (1932) builds steadily toward a bang. This is possible, in part, because in *The Sheltered Life* Glasgow returns to a view of reality older for her than that explored in her recent novels. For a decade and a half, she had examined the need for psychically based phantasies to correct imbalances imposed upon modern man by too narrow a belief either in the sufficiency of surface reality or in the illusions of moral idealism. In *The Sheltered Life*, the limit society imposes upon individuals drives them to compensatory phantasies, as it did in her last seven novels; but here the phantasies fail to show the characters the way to new health. Indeed, the phantasies cannot withstand the test of reality; and when they collapse, violence ensues. The dreams fail either because they are inadequately rooted in psychic need or because the world is no match for man's imagination and life is inherently tragic. In either case, the emphasis falls, not upon the compensatory drives of the unconscious, but upon the pernicious use of illusions as a shelter from reality, an evasion that had furnished one of Glasgow's strongest themes in the first half of her career.

Even though the book returns to a situation already mastered in early works like *The Deliverance* (1904) and *Virginia* (1913), *The Sheltered Life* is Glasgow's most intense drama of deceptions, the fulfillment of the theme she had experimented with since her second novel—the way minds sheltered from reality develop habits of self-deception that, in this case, lead to tragedy.[1] Here the novelist exploits the social metaphor (whereby social exchanges of a small community suggest habits of thought and behavior of the world at large) to portray the ironic tragedy of southern womanhood and, by gentle suggestion, the tragedy of the tradition of Western idealism, which culminated in the events of 1914. The heroine of the drama is southern woman, whose facets we see presented with seriousness in Eva Birdsong, the belle of a golden time now grown middle-aged, and mirrored with comedy in Jenny Blair Archbald, the fledgling belle of a fallen age. The order within which and against which these two struggle for self-realization, the order that inevitably deflects their agon in the direction of tragic recognition, we find embodied in aging General Archbald and adulterous George Birdsong, the best and the lovable worst of southern manhood. The trait these four share—and the major theme of the novel—is the habit of deception, chiefly the often amusing but ultimately dangerous self-deception of romantic idealists.

The deceptions of George Birdsong, the all too human villain of the story, require little comment. He is exceedingly handsome, generous to a fault, and imperfectly faithful. Wed to Eva, the greatest beauty of the 1890s, he takes advantage of his wife's faith in his love and of his own charm and looks to seduce any attractive woman who comes his way. Less blind than the other characters, he freely admits that he lacks the strength of character to control his own roving nature and recognizes that at eighteen Jenny Blair's flirtatious innocence is wicked.[2] Yet Birdsong deceives himself when he chooses biology as an alibi, blames his weakness on birth, and uses this to explain if not excuse his various escapes from responsibility through sport, women, and drink (251). His decision to accept weakness as the essence of his character allows him to be trapped by Jenny Blair in their feverish affair.

Birdsong is not alone in permitting a limited view of the self

1 Raper, *Without Shelter*, especially 47–50, 108–18, 190–92, 241–46.
2 Ellen Glasgow, *The Sheltered Life* (Garden City, N.Y., 1932), 64–65, 354. This book will hereafter be referred to by page number only.

to lead him along the path of destruction. Jenny Blair, Eva, and the general are equally given to this form of self-deception, although the pernicious qualities of the roles they have elected to play are less immediately apparent.

In one of the most informative early descriptions of Jenny Blair, Glasgow suggests the theory of personality that she has in mind for all her characters: "From the warm mother-of-pearl vagueness within, a fragment of personality detached itself, wove a faint pattern of thought, and would gradually harden into a shell over her mind" (4). This is a rather poetic way of saying that Jenny's "personality" evolves from a vague impulse which she rationalizes, then allows to harden into a dominant way of viewing herself; as such, it becomes, of course, a major determinant of her behavior. The impulse that drives her when she is nine-and-a-half is very general and libidinal, the simple desire to put down books, leave libraries, and escape into life: "I'm alive, alive, and I'm Jenny Blair Archbald," she sings to the rhythm of life. She moves quickly from this impulse to the view that she is "different" because she has a "hidden self" that her mother does not know. This hidden self provides an excuse when she disobeys her mother and furnishes the alibi for all the little perversities of her rebellion against the world of *Little Women*, a world much like her mother's (43).

Complicating the development of Jenny's libidinal impulse is the fate of her father, who died in a fox hunt when she was five (4). His absence leaves her extremely susceptible to the power of older men and immune to the appeal of boys her own age. Older men, she persuades herself, "are more like her handsome father, who had been simply too wonderful to live in the world" (312). Thus it is to "the look of tender protection" in George Birdsong's face and the comfort of his "arms encircling her shoulders" that she yields her nine-and-a-half-year-old self when Birdsong rescues her after a roller-skate fall before the door of his mistress in the black section of Queenborough (57). From time to time, she is almost conscious that in some dark corner of her mind she is confusing

Birdsong with her father: "'There isn't anything to be afraid of,' she said aloud. . . . The eyes and smile of Mr. Birdsong shone down on her, just as the eyes and smile of her father had shone down on her when she was little and awoke crying from fear in her crib in the old nursery" (52, 90).

Further complicating Jenny's emotional growth are the protective tendencies of the role Birdsong has chosen to play in life, that of the weak but chivalrous lover. Not much of a lawyer, Birdsong is a master of the courteous and solicitous arts of the lover; they not only won the heart of the greatest beauty of his own generation but have kept him interesting to beauties of each generation since. After Jenny's skating accident, Birdsong feels he must turn his power loose on her, since she has discovered him in a potentially embarrassing situation. Using all his charm and flattery, he molds the need of the not very pretty little girl for a father into the need for a lover (59, 63, 80). He is so skillful that eight years later he can with justice accuse her of having been "an incorrigible flirt ever since she was nine years old" (290).

As a flirt, Jenny has channeled all her early rebellious impulse and sense of being different into a role her society created for women but does not publicly accept. When she chooses to think of herself as being in love with George, she must employ patterns of evasion similar to the split mind her society used in creating the coquette. One part of her is fully aware that her feeling for George can hurt Eva Birdsong, whom she at times loves as much as she loves George and almost as much as she does herself. To drive this foreboding of responsibility from her mind, she has to convince herself that she will not ask George to love her in return and indeed that she doesn't "mean anything" at all in feeling the way she does (239).

Pushing Jenny Blair to more powerful modes of self-deception is the gnawing fear that she could suffer a fate similar to that of her spinster Aunt Etta, a lonely, ugly, professional invalid whose lifelong frustration drives her to neurotic behavior, including a compulsion to pinch her best friend black and

blue (88–89). Because Jenny feels that George's affection protects her from Etta's fate, she is eager to find more and more
subtle evasions of guilt (90). In time she perfects the romantic
version of the biological alibi that George uses in his continuing infidelities. "It isn't . . . as if I were to blame. It isn't . . .
as if I had chosen to suffer like this," she tries to persuade
herself as she hurries to meet George, fully aware that her beloved Eva is away convalescing from a serious operation and
the nervous breakdown that followed (326). Earlier Jenny had
convinced herself that "she had not chosen to fall in love with
him. Some winged power over which she had no control had
swept her from the earth to the sky. . . . And, besides, even if
she were to try with all her strength, she could not stop loving
him; she could not destroy this burning essence of life that
saturated her being. 'When you can't help a thing, nobody
can blame you.'" That Glasgow intends Jenny's internal arguments for dramatic irony is made perfectly clear by a moment
of recognition that she allows the girl on the eve of the catastrophe which her will to love is to bring about: "And then,
with a start of surprise, she realized that . . . she was no
longer in love. For an instant only her passion yielded to the
shock of reality. Then the blow passed and was gone; the faint
sting of aversion faded out of her mind" (350). But having
elected to live by the romantic alibi that great passion has a
consecration of its own—even when the passion fades and has
to be willed back into being—she finds herself a moment later
"in his arms, while the sense of security, of ecstacy, of perfect
rightness," floods her being (351). Although Jenny Blair was
"blooded" when she fell from her skates into the world of
adult experience and although George Birdsong has spent
eight years initiating her into that world, it remains for his
wife, Eva, to complete the initiation by *showing* her what it
means to live by the romantic alibi and the other self-decep-
tions she must practice in her chosen role—that of southern
woman.

Eva Birdsong's effort to evade reality is the most poignant
agon in the novel because it is a desperate struggle, against

the combined pressure of society and biology, to preserve her sanity. It was Queenborough society that elevated her at eighteen to the role of its reigning beauty for the first five years of the 1890s, and it is biology, both her own and George's, that twenty years later brings her down from that high position (19). Like the hero of traditional drama, Eva has been forced to embody the ideal of her civilization. To George, the general, the city at large, she means very much what she does to Jenny Blair: "order, beauty, perfection, an unattainable ideal of living" (271, 360, 386). Thus, in significant ways, her tragedy is that of her entire society.

After twenty years of "being somebody else . . . being somebody's ideal," she is "worn out." Like the general, to play this role she has had to put an end to herself. But she recognizes this only after she can no longer, she fears, embody the ideal for George. "Unless I go [out] alone, I can never find myself. When you've never been yourself for forty years, you've forgotten what you are really," she warns the new belle, Jenny, only minutes before she discovers George with their initiate in his arms—and kills him (385).

Eva's use of the figure "forty years" implies that she has been guided toward belledom all her life, but the two decades from 1894 to 1914 have been the critical years. In 1894 she sacrificed a potential operatic career, and all her other possibilities, to the transfiguring joy of unbridled passion and married George Birdsong, "the least eligible of her suitors" (20, 28). Since that choice she has lived with "the necessity to justify her sacrifice to herself—perhaps to the world. To have given up all that," Jenny's mother explains, "for anything less than a great passion would seem inexcusable" (28). To sustain this romantic alibi, she must keep affirming her faith in the "great passion" of her marriage. This, in turn, requires that she always believe that George still loves her completely (81, 190, 194). Vaguely realizing that this illusion keeps their ideal as woman from going mad, the whole of Queenborough society conspires to shelter Eva's willed belief from reality. As Aunt Etta says, "Who could have told her [about George and his women]? Who would be so heartless?" (25). Even the otherwise honorable General Archbald, who loves Eva more than he does his grandchild Jenny, lies to reinforce her faith that she has "had no reason to doubt" George's love for her (191, 224). Surrounded by dissemblers, it is natural that Eva lies to herself. Of course she knows, and has known for at least ten years, since the night she went to retrieve George from the "dreadful place" of "plush furniture, pink shades, and straw-coloured hair" where he lay ill with ptomaine poisoning (192). But the artificial self she has willed into being out of her strong passion and even stronger pride causes her to persuade the general, and herself, that George was at the other woman's house on business (194). For it is her life-lie she defends by deceiving herself (190).

But there is another self within, "something deeper and darker than her eyes, something fugitive, defiant," which mocks her affirmations that she is happy, passionately loved, and in love with life (109). And it is this part of her psyche, which doubts because it cannot keep from knowing, that comes to dominate her personality after a serious operation—apparently a hysterectomy with complications—leaves her, in George's phrase, a "maimed woman," no longer capable, even in her own mind, of holding his love (130, 134). The first effect of this recognition is a nervous breakdown and an extended period of invalidism for which the doctors can find no cause (277, 346). The prolonged illness, Glasgow hints, is Eva's instinctive attempt to hold George through his pity if not his passion, just as eight years before, in the defining episode of the novel, her sudden sickness drew him from the embrace of Delia Barron (120–22). When this regressive behavior fails to keep him from wandering and Eva's willed faith in their great passion collapses completely, a murderous pride replaces it.

In one of the subtler insights of the book, Glasgow seems to intend that we see the collapse of self-deception which has been raised to a life-lie as a cause of paranoia and thereby of certain forms of violence. The shock of losing her reason for

being, false as it was, leaves Eva hostile, vulnerable, driven by
a blind panic (277, 366–67). And through a gentle juxtaposition, which gives the action considerable resonance, Glasgow
parallels Eva's fall from idealism into terror and violence with
events of 1914 in the world at large. If we are to regard Eva's
crime of passion in shooting George as the effect of fear
brought on by disillusioned idealism, are we not meant to
draw similar but broader inferences—whether true or false—
when General Archbald reflects on the actions of Germany,
the cradle of modern idealism, that "fear drove nations, as
well as animals, and the look of driven fear is not . . . unlike
malevolence" (373). This seems to be what Glasgow had in
mind when she wrote in the preface to a later edition of the
novel that "the same tragedy was being repeated in spheres
far wider than Queenborough. The First World War was beginning and men were killing each other from the highest
possible ideals. This is the final scope of the book's theme."[3]
When reality finally breaks through the inner walls of idealism, violence bursts forth.

One function of General Archbald is that the experience
gained from his great age (he is eighty-three through most of
the book) and from his many years abroad (England and Germany are mentioned) allows Glasgow to expand her investi-
gation of evasive idealism in time and space without giving
up the dramatic tightness of the otherwise provincial setting
and characters. But she intended something more for General
Archbald, as C. Hugh Holman reminds us in his fine essay
on the novelist. The general, she wrote Allen Tate, is "the real
protagonist": "I was dealing with the fate of the civilized
mind in a world where even the civilizations we make are un-
civilized."[4]

Although this comment makes it seem as though Glasgow
sentimentalized the general, when he stands by himself in the

---

3 Glasgow, *A Certain Measure*, 205.
4 C. Hugh Holman, *Three Modes of Modern Southern Fiction: Ellen Glasgow, William Faulkner, Thomas Wolfe* (Athens, 1966), 21; Rouse, *Letters of
Ellen Glasgow*, 124.

dramatic context of the novel, we are able to see all the way around him. His attitudes, opinions, and prejudices become not only a commentary upon the action but a dramatized point of view to be judged against the real events of the book.[5] To view Archbald in this manner, we need only cut him loose from Glasgow's statements about him outside the novel. In doing so, we argue with Wimsatt and Beardsley "that the . . . intention of the author is . . . [not] desirable as a standard for judging the success of a work of literary art." External evidence of the author's meaning is "private or idiosyncratic; not a part of the work as a linguistic fact." Glasgow's statements in letters and prefaces are thus to be taken as a mixture of her good wishes for her book and high-toned advertisements.

To be sure, there is a real conflict here between Glasgow's "obligation to seem dispassionate and objective" and what Wayne C. Booth calls the author's "obligation to be as clear about his moral position as he possibly can be." Faced with similar choices in earlier novels, Glasgow often sacrificed her characters to her moral (or emotional) position; Louis D. Rubin has shown this to be true, for example, in *Barren Ground*. The solution she hit upon here, however, is a good deal more graceful. In choosing the general as one of her two angles of vision, she has selected what might be called a "capacitating point of view," a character whose sensibility, spirit, and intelligence are equal to those of the author. As a capacitating character, the general enables Glasgow to project her own thought and feeling into the story without making her presence excessively felt or otherwise taxing the reader's belief in the fictive reality.

If, in addition, the author is willing to undercut the capaci-

---

5 Contrast McDowell, *Glasgow and the Ironic Art of Fiction*, 192. Otherwise, I agree completely with McDowell's high estimate of the book. For the discussion that follows, see: W. K. Wimsatt, Jr., and M. C. Beardsley, "The Intentional Fallacy," in Ray B. West, Jr. (ed.), *Essays in Modern Literary Criticism* (New York, 1961), 174–89; Wayne C. Booth, *The Rhetoric of Fiction* (Chicago, 1961), 389; Rubin, *The Teller in the Tale*, 11–14; C. Hugh Holman, "April in Queenborough: Ellen Glasgow's Comedies of Manners," *Sewanee Review*, LXXXII (Spring, 1974), 267–68.

tating character's oracular tendencies with ironies (as Glasgow does the general's) and to turn him loose as the protagonist in the story so that he lives a life of his own, then weaknesses in his or the author's outlook (the general's idealism, for example) take on a dramatic interest; and the novel becomes a mode of self-discovery for the author as well as the reader. If the author is obliged to make her moral position clear, it surely ought not to be in a statement of principles by the author's spokesman, but instead by showing the total effect of all the characters' principles and opinions, their strengths and weaknesses, in action. The moral position ultimately revealed may be quite different from the author's original abstract position. In the long run, a capacitating character like the general is far more likely to weather changes in moral climate than a transparent authorial spokesman.

But Glasgow's comment about the general being the real protagonist does remind us that the tragedy of Eva and George and Jenny is very much like a Henrik Ibsen play enacted before the eyes of the general and that the interposition of his complex sensibility between the play and the reader makes this a novel capable of probing shadowy corners of the mind. Like that of the other characters, the drama of the general's mind is a story of self-deception. To a large degree many of the characters in this book are his creatures, whom he has either dreamed into being, provided with a model of behavior, or sheltered through life. Even philandering George, were he privy to the deep past, might detect an impulse kindred to his own, not only in the general's sympathy for women, but in young Archbald's affair that April in England in the 1850s with a married English woman—although the general persists in viewing this episode as the lost love of his life, rather than as adultery (153–55). Eva, Jenny, and the women of his family are even more than George his creations.

After a long life the general considers himself an evasive despairer rather than an evasive idealist, for he has sought shelter from pain and disappointment under "the hardened crust of despair" (162). But idealist he remains, and his imperfect despair only renders his idealism ineffectual, without freeing him from the anguish of persisting but impossible dreams. Not only does he retain a "Victorian faith . . . in the rightness of life, the essential goodness of God," and an un-seeable plan and meaning behind the agony of life; but he sincerely affirms the first principle of all evasive idealists, that there is a good which is *above* truth: "It was the way her higher nature lent itself to deceit," he reflects about his daughter-in-law, Jenny's mother, "that amused his intelligence while it exasperated his conscience. . . . Because she was charitable and benign, her dissembling became, in some incredible fashion, the servant of goodness. . . . If it exists at all," he decides, probably without irony of his own, "pure goodness must be superior to truth, superior even to chastity. It must be not a cardinal but an ultimate virtue" (187, 195, 234–35). Separating goodness from the check of truth is, of course, where the trouble begins for anyone who fails to see the danger in his (or her) well-intentioned actions.

Because Archbald has the "sense of something missing" in what he knows to be *true* about life, he wills to cling, "with the tenacity of age, to his last illusion"—the Eva Birdsong he, as the mind of the past, and his descendants have dreamed into being (162–63). Only in this illusory ideal of woman can he recover the lost "part of the whole," happiness, serenity of mood, the courage of dying, acceptance of life—in short, the sense of his own fulfillment (378–79). But in his pursuit of a good that stands above the true, he refuses to see what it costs Eva to be everybody's ideal. Even with the gun that killed Birdsong lying with the bloody ducks at the foot of her gown, Archbald cannot acknowledge the cost to Eva. So strong is his love of Eva as an ideal that he joins automatically with John Welch, the self-styled scientific realist of the book, in proclaiming the shooting "an accident"—to be reported as accidental suicide (394). He thereby restores the false order of their sheltered lives. To do otherwise would be to recognize the murderous guilt of Eva, as well as the responsibility of Jenny Blair. After all, Jenny "didn't mean anything in the world" in surrendering herself to illusion. Neither did General Archbald (for his ideal lives beyond time as well as truth, [171]).

But Eva did. Illusion was all the life she had.

*The Sheltered Life* is the most intense study Glasgow ever made of the themes she handled best throughout her career—those associated with evasive idealism. Despite some garrulousness and boring repetitions in characterization, it is the book in which she most successfully extracts "from the situation every thread of significance, every quiver of vitality, every glimmer of understanding."[6] Compared with *Barren Ground*, sometimes called her best book, it has more unity of action, of setting (the Archbald and Birdsong homes, a house in the black section, a party in a country house, and the hospital), of time (May and June, 1906, April to November, 1914), and of characters (chiefly the Archbalds and Birdsongs). I find it a more serious work than *Barren Ground*, freer from sentimental sincerity and blessed with genuine wit.[7] All in all, it is her finest achievement.[8] And this is all the more remarkable because the book seems, in its double point of view and its critique of phantasies, to ignore the technical and psychological advances the author had made since 1916. A resolution of this paradox may emerge in the conclusions to the present study, when it will be possible to consider this novel within the total sweep of Glasgow's final three decades.

6 Glasgow, *A Certain Measure*, 204.
7 The comic tone of passages does not detract from the final vision of the novel, which is closer to tragedy. We respond to the individual acts of self-deception with amusement but to the cumulative effect of whole lives built upon illusion with the pathos and self-recognition that belong to tragedy, albeit tragedy viewed with some comic detachment. The novel belongs to that phase (described by Northrop Frye in *Anatomy of Criticism*) where irony and tragedy overlap.
8 As Holman points out, starting with Jenny's point of view troubles the reader the first time through the book. But on subsequent readings, this ploy becomes (for me at least) one of the beauties of the novel, for it carries us into the fictive world on a flow of illusions much like those that fill the other characters' minds. This is not to deny, of course, that Jenny's illusions are precocious. Holman, "April in Queenborough" 275–76.

*Chapter IX*

# Stoics and Dreamers: *Vein of Iron* (1935)

The present action of *Vein of Iron* spans from December, 1901, to April, 1933. The novel thus suffers an inevitable loss of intensity compared with its three immediate predecessors, the volumes of the Queenborough trilogy—*The Romantic Comedians* (1926), *They Stooped to Folly* (1929), and *The Sheltered Life* (1932)—since the present action of each of these covers less than a decade. Furthermore, although *Vein of Iron* returns to the time scale and chronicle form of *Barren Ground* (1925), it lacks the intensity that novel achieved by concentrating on the psychic development of a single character. As Frederick P. W. McDowell has demonstrated, *Vein of Iron* reveals an "attenuated artistry" and an exhaustion of Glasgow's energy, which make it "the least vital of the novels" she wrote after 1925.[1] Although her earlier irony degenerates here into a querulousness intended for satire and although there are apparent inconsistencies in the portrayal of the major characters, the work does succeed in one of its aims: to chronicle an age and preserve a people in print. In this, the penultimate novel she would live to publish, Glasgow set out to capture the essence of the descendants of the Scotch-Irish Presbyterians who had first come to the Valley of Virginia in the second half of the eighteenth century.[2] Although painting a picture of a period and capturing the surfaces of a small col-

1 McDowell, *Glasgow and the Ironic Art of Fiction*, 202–203, 214.
2 Glasgow, *A Certain Measure*, 165–69.

lection of minds is not as high an ambition for a novel as probing the deeper recesses of the psyche—whether of an individual or a culture—it is nevertheless an adequate undertaking for a novelist who may yet only sense that her finest work lies in the past.

Among serious American novels, *Vein of Iron* takes a rather unusual approach. In portraying her Scotch-Irish from the valley, Glasgow expresses less malice toward the puritans of the South than she does toward the happiness-hunters of the 1920s and 1930s. This is remarkable because one of the favorite sports of American fiction and criticism happens to have been the baiting of puritans in their various avatars (a pastime that may often be a form of self-exorcism). Beginning with Thomas Morton's *New English Canaan* (1637) and continuing during Glasgow's life in the writings of H. L. Mencken, Sherwood Anderson, Sinclair Lewis, and their imitators, puritanism has often been considered a synonym for what is wrong with American culture. In the South by 1935, Faulkner had already published *Light in August* (1932), which, through its portraits of Doc Hines and Mr. McEachern and of their effect upon Joe Christmas, condemns beyond all hope various forms of southern Calvinism. Thomas Wolfe was preparing, in what eventually became the Joyner sections of *The Web and the Rock* (1939), an equally venomous thank-you for his own Scotch-Irish heritage, after having offered adequate repayment with his earlier portraits of the Pentlands in *Look Homeward, Angel* (1929).[3] Glasgow had, of course, done her part to expose the puritans—for almost forty years. Her first novel, *The Descendant* (1897), opened with a situation much like that of *Light*

3 Glasgow's library included seven volumes by Mencken, four volumes by Anderson including *Poor White*, *Winesburg, Ohio*, and *Dark Laughter*, five novels by Lewis including *Elmer Gantry*, Wolfe's *Look Homeward, Angel* and *The Web and the Rock*, and four works by Faulkner including *The Sound and the Fury* and *Sanctuary* but not *Light in August*. It did not include Morton's *New English Canaan*. Tutwiler, *A Catalogue of the Library of Ellen Glasgow*, 78–122.

*in August*; in both books a community of southern Calvinists, by its intolerance and cruelty, turns a boy born out of wedlock into a potentially violent enemy of society.

But Glasgow seems to have believed that time brings everything around to its opposite. For the first scene in *Vein of Iron*, she went back to the situation that began her first book: a band of children chasing a young outcast of society, hurling garbage and names at him. This time rather than identify with the victim, she puts the reader inside the skin of one of his abusers to explore the nature of puritan culture from within, rather than to condemn it through its outward effects. From within we discover that this once dominant element of American life includes many objectional traits, to be sure; but it also embodies a number of virtues that the nation, Glasgow implies, might do well to salvage. The essential process of winnowing the chaff from the wheat of the national puritanic heritage seems to be the point of this the most didactic of Glasgow's novels, a book she wrote in an effort to rediscover the bedrock of our tradition during a period she called "The Dying Age." Although *Vein of Iron* is not *about* the Great Depression, it attempts to discover a way out of the cultural decay blatantly manifested by the depression.

In this effort we may find evidence, as McDowell does, "that Miss Glasgow in later years became increasingly dominated by her father's moral seriousness"; for her father, from whom she felt alienated during the large part of her life, came of stern Scotch Presbyterian stock from the Valley of Virginia.[4] However, it may be useful to remember that from as early as 1894 Glasgow had in times of personal crisis looked to Stoical philosophers, especially Marcus Aurelius and Epictetus, for fortitude, stability, and consolation. Thus, when in a period of national crisis she searched for a native expression of stoical endurance, it was natural that she should settle upon the descendants of an old Virginia settler like the scholar-pioneer

4 McDowell, *Glasgow and the Ironic Art of Fiction*, 205.

named John Fincastle who had led his congregation from Ulster to Philadelphia and then down the Indian Road into Virginia, a man who in old age had abandoned civilization and
gone alone into the wilderness, carrying with him two Bibles
(probably because he didn't trust one for the more esoteric
mysteries) and "one other book, a copy in his own handwrit-
ing of the Meditations of a heathen Emperor who had not
even been converted and saved."[5] The Bibles were his dream—
the "heaven and Hell within himself," as the husband of one
of his descendants calls it—the "something evermore about to
be" that had driven him from Scotland to Virginia and finally
into the wilderness (460). *The Meditations of Marcus Aurelius*,
however, was the staying power that enabled him to survive
both his dream and the world outside. It is upon these two
elements of America's puritanical tradition—the habit of spin-
ning new worlds into being and the complementary power of
enduring the worlds we create—that Glasgow focuses in *Vein
of Iron*. To carry the nation through the depression, both
dreams and endurance would be needed. But fortitude, Glasgow seems to have felt, was the more immediate need. The
emphasis she places upon the essential Stoic virtue gives the
novel its title and the dominant note of didacticism, or moral
seriousness, that McDowell mentions.

Stoicism also influenced the novel's sense of history. According to the Stoics, time consists of series of cycles, never to
end; at the completion of each, the universe is consumed by
the divine fire; the universe then starts on a fresh course,
which reproduces exactly the preceding cycle. The absolute
time of *Vein of Iron* begins with the fire of war that drove John
Fincastle's people from the great valley of the Clyde in Scotland, to Ulster, and later to Virginia's valley; here they created
a new world. The time of the novel ends with the death of the
civilization old Fincastle (and his like) brought into being and

5 Ellen Glasgow, *Vein of Iron* (New York, 1935), 19–21. This book will
hereafter be referred to by page number only.

with the return of his distant descendants to the place where he had attempted to make his dream flesh, so that they might begin a new cycle of creation and endurance.[6]

In between old Fincastle's coming and his heirs' return, a process has taken place very much like the diffusion that Fincastle's great-great-grandson (also named John Fincastle) describes when he considers the effect marriage and children had upon the singleness of his own young dreams: "It was love, he perceived, that had altered everything, great or small in his life, that had seemed to change the very beat of his heart. Instead of a *single self*, he had become a *double self*, and then, *with each child* that was born to him, he was *divided into other and separate selves* of his being" (110, italics added). A more widespread version of this dissolution and diffusion has apparently occurred to the original vision and strength of character the first John Fincastle brought with him to the valley. If we are to understand all the adumbrations of his dream, we must look at the ways it has manifested itself in the lives, not only of his physical offspring, but of all who dwell in and about the small village of Ironside, Virginia; for each of them is his spiritual heir. The winnowing of the puritan pioneer vision has gone on for at least five generations. But the effect has not been to identify the virtues of the old way of life and to divide them from the weaknesses and vices; the process has instead scattered the virtues and the vices broadside through the community so that they are mixed together in all possible combinations. And the process continues, even in the family of old Fincastle's most direct descendants. With them, however, enough chaff has been blown away that the virtues at times stand visible to the reader's eye.

The first John Fincastle was a pioneer, a builder of churches,

---

6 Judy Smith Murr has described a repetitive pattern of cataclysm, struggle, winding down, and resurgence in the novel; but she focuses upon the individual aspect of the pattern rather than the dynamics of the universal aspect. See her "History in *Barren Ground* and *Vein of Iron*: Theory, Structure, and Symbol," *Southern Literary Journal*, VIII (Fall, 1975), 40–41.

a scholar, a stoic, a protector of the Indians, a dreamer of the
new world, a leader of men, and a man of God (10–11, 19–21).
Although his life was struggle, he thought he "fought not
against men, but against evil passions both within and without the Kirk"—a fight less sectarian than stoical (39). His son
John, by contrast, is remembered only as a rebuilder of the
family's house and as an enlarger of the church (40). His
grandson John is mentioned only for wedding a woman who
had known wealth and who brought a romantic legend of an
aristocratic ancestor into the family (39). Named Adam (as
though someone had already dreamed prematurely of a new
beginning), the old pioneer's great-grandson became a man of
God like all the rest and preached that "life will yield up its
hidden sweetness . . . only when it is being sacrificed to
something more precious than life" (40). But with the Civil
War Adam, like other ministers, "took up arms in defense of
his State" in a struggle less against evil passions than against
other men (233). Adam's son, the present John Fincastle, is an
ex–man of God who has survived as a dreamer, a scholar, a
stoic, a philosopher, and a protector of his family.

The other spiritual survivors of the first John Fincastle include a varied collection of Ironsiders who range from the
present minister, Mr. Black, to the town's chief businessman,
Mr. Rowan; numerous other characters are scattered along the
continuum from the religious to the secular poles of southern
puritanism. In these living individuals, the shadow side of the
old pioneer's vision, a dimension overlooked by the legends
passed down by word of mouth, is often more apparent than
are his virtues and religious theories. Mr. Black appears hu-
mane enough, a saint of the misery Calvinists call salvation.
But when World War I releases him from his inhibitions, the
fire that has burnt within him leaps out (in his war sermons),
disguised as God's wrath against the Germans (6–9, 186). William Rowan, the richest man in town, is a respected and easy-
going family man. He seems to thrive on plain thinking,
good living, family virtues, and an occasional charity; for example, he gives jobs to bright young people like Ralph Mc-

Bride, the man John Fincastle's daughter seems destined to marry. But when Rowan's own daughter, whom he has thoroughly spoiled, claims that Ralph has gotten her pregnant, Rowan sacrifices the truth of the matter to family feeling and marshals "all the forces of society," including "religion, law, morality, influence, even money," to bully Ralph into making an honest woman of a lost cause (32, 98, 148).[7] Despite his own brilliance, Ralph submits to Rowan's pressure, with far less resistance than he might have mustered. Ralph is weak because he has received a thorough education in Calvinistic morality from his mother. Mrs. McBride seems a proud widow who works hard to keep a roof over her son's head and her own. But her resentment about her hard life finds its righteous outlet (complete with alibi) in the curdled Calvinism that she uses to belittle Ralph until his will to mold his own life has been destroyed (27, 93, 240). In her, the religious vision of the first John Fincastle has turned its dark side to the light: like her patriotism, her piety seems "rooted in hatred." She finds such "a thrill of cruelty in the Christian symbols of crucifixion and atonement" that she seems eager to have her son punished by marrying Janet Rowan, eager even to sacrifice him to the national gods of war (238–43).

The pioneer impulse finds a finer expression in another Ironsider, Dr. Updike. Just as old Fincastle had tried to protect the Indians, so the doctor intervenes time and again to guard the welfare of the present generation of Fincastles: by securing a job for John Fincastle as a teacher after he is tried for heresy and deposed, by sending milk for John's sister when she is ill, and by purchasing the Fincastle home and holding it for them after a third party sells it to pay the taxes (45–46, 92, 304, 351). There seems to be no dark side to Updike's personality, unless we see his shadow in his wife, who in her late years "formed the habit of drink—or it may have been drugs"

7 Like the opening scene, this Ralph-Janet-Ada episode echoes earlier works by Glasgow, especially the Nick Burr–Bessie Pollard–Eugenia Battle triangle in *The Voice of the People* (1900) and the Jason-Geneva-Dorinda relation in *Barren Ground* (1925).

after having been, rumor says, "a trial to the flesh" throughout the marriage. If we then recall that Updike may have been
in love with John Fincastle's rather restrained sister before he
married, there is a hint—no more—that the bad faith with
which he married may have caused his wife's problem (59,
84–85). To be sure, Updike's behavior could owe as much to
his medical training as to the milieu. He appears to be more
*in* the community than *of* it. He is not, for example, part of the
herd who pursue Ralph until the poor fellow weds Rowan's
daughter, although a doctor, one would think, might have
been consulted (146–47, 153).

The community at large presents a collection of puritan-
Protestant traits familiar from our literature of New England
and the Midwest, traits which a decade ago were so much the
mainstream of American life that it was scarcely necessary to
enumerate them. The southern version includes most of the
familiar characteristics, plus several intriguing variations.
Descendants of men driven by their own theory of predestina-
tion, the Ironsiders trust in divine goodness—but look ahead
with thrift (41, 45, 386, 460). They so thoroughly accept the
way God disposes of their lives that they see the Great
Depression as divine punishment and steel themselves to endure it, rather than attempt to correct the economic problems
behind it (59–60, 152, 383). Yet they are a bookish people who
place great emphasis upon education—for which they will
struggle against immense obstacles (51, 305). The product of
their learning, however, seems too often to be either casuistry,
sophistry, or unthinking conviction (63–65). The latter causes
them to place moral dogma above the well-being of individuals; it also leads to a mental confusion that considers personal
freedom a dangerous and destructive goal. They habitually
mistake psychological destruction of the individual for his or
her salvation. Bending or breaking the will of the young
seems the chief means of educating them for life (119, 239,
241). They demand conformity perhaps because—as heirs to
men who lived in fear of the Indians, knew no simple com-
forts, and loved life because it was fugitive—the Ironsiders

consider life something they must fight both for and against. They know they are living only when they feel pain—in short, for them life is war (149–50, 260). Unfortunately, they become trapped in the unstated logic of this equation: all too often, war is life. They seem most completely alive when they have an excuse to confuse God and country and thereby enjoy one of their few pleasures: watching others take the punishment of God's justice. Of such justice they feel they have had their own share (186, 189, 240).

Life as war entails resistance to simple pleasures like alcohol, dancing, and cosmetics, as well as an intolerance of change and of people who are different, whether the latter think in a new way or simply paint their lips (74, 293, 306, 311, 377). The Ironsiders' intolerance of outsiders often reveals, at base, their willed separation from ideologically unacceptable parts of themselves. They fear lipstick, for example, because it hints of sexual pleasures their natural side knows but their dogma-bound minds cannot acknowledge. Their theology tells them that sex is to produce children in marriage. It is "God's law . . . that married people, no matter whether they were half wits or not, *must bring all the children they could* into the world *to share in the curse* that was put upon Adam and Eve"—the finest bit of sophistry for turning a pleasure into an imperative one is likely to come across (167, italics added). Their alienation from sex produces the dualistic view that love is a process in which two people strive "to reach each other through the veils of the flesh," seeking "with passionate tenderness the reality within realities" (213). In a vicious circle, their unembodied view of love thus feeds their dualistic ontology with its stress on otherworldliness and its contempt for life.

Although their blind faith in another reality governing this one infuses them with an energy that drives off vertiginous doubt, it leads to a split in the self, a division between the senses and the conscience, a separation of the part that feels from the part that thinks (130–31, 158, 210, 235). Neglect of the senses and emotions produces families who are unhappy although they are strong, individuals who cannot articulate love although they feel it, and a style of life that is built around doctrines but that lacks emotionally satisfying rituals to sustain it (96, 298, 319). Such people value independence above solidarity and practice a charity more prudent than generous (404, 412). Because they refuse to acknowledge whole dimensions of themselves in their preoccupation with what they should be, they fall into a pride that places them above their true status in the world (138, 363, 460). When the unacknowledged self dominates and they fall short of their pride, they swing wildly into guilt. Because the shadow self keeps creeping up on the ideal one and intense guilt and self-contempt are intolerable, the Ironsiders have developed great powers for projecting the ugly side of themselves upon outsiders.

The novel is framed by two episodes that reveal the sort of phantasies and rituals their rejection of the world and of self may lead to. The last of these scenes is a dream that comes to the present John Fincastle as he dies. He imagines that he has been left by his mother to sit on a charred stump before a cabin high in the mountains while she performs one of her medical missions. As he waits, he is seized by "a sudden dread, a panic terror." Then:

> The family flocked from the cabin and began to dance around him, singing and jeering. And as soon as he saw them *he knew what* he had dreaded—for they were all idiots. His mother had brought him to one of the mountain families *that had inbred until it was imbecile.* Two generations of blank, grinning faces and staring eyes and driveling mouths danced and shouted round him as they pressed closer and closer. A world of idiots, he thought in his dream. *To escape from them,* to run away, he must *break through* not only a throng, but a whole world of idiots. (455–56, italics added)

It is an exceedingly misanthropic and paranoid phantasy and an extreme view to take of the world at large. But it is a recurring fear of Fincastle's race. Hushed-up references to a family of idiots (who fell by the sin of sex into the damnation of idiocy) crop up in several family conversations and reveries (17, 167). The fear seems too deep-seated to go back to a single family living at Panther's Gap; it may be an anxiety rooted in the Ironsiders' past in the Highlands of Scotland. At any rate, it suggests a deep psychic source of John Fincastle's lifelong desire to escape through metaphysics into another world, as his ancestors had through theology (49).

But Fincastle's escape from his fear of idiocy is preferable to the means the children of Ironside use in the opening scene of the novel when a band of girls and boys chase Toby Waters, an idiot boy, through the village to beat him and to stuff his cap with cow droppings. When Toby turns to spit at his abusers and we see his face—"His mouth was only a crooked hole in his face; his small dull eyes squinted between inflamed eyelids"—it is as though the scapegoat had turned a mirror to his tormentors in which each might suddenly catch a glance of the uglier part of himself, the self each is cruelly trying to exorcise (3). Even the minister cannot speak to Toby without "a queer distortion of his mouth" (9). The American Highlanders were, it seems, forced to become a "stalwart breed" because the simple dichotomies of their deep mythology left them no alternative to resistance except to fall through sex into the world of idiots and half-wits—where the outsiders live (17).

This very real portrait of the South's puritans, the best dimension of the novel,[8] comes to the reader with so many pastoral virtues that the final effect is very much like filtering *Barren Ground* through the sweet vision of Heidi. This nostalgia blurs the edges of the portrait as long as the setting remains rural. When the Fincastles move to Queenborough, all their pastoral simplicity seems to turn to disgruntlement with the machines of the city (293). Each mode of coloring throws into question the accuracy of the book as a chronicle and reveals that Glas-

8 According to McDowell, *Glasgow and the Ironic Art of Fiction*, 208.

gow was still committed emotionally to writing novels of
character rather than sketching panoramas of periods. The
two clashing intentions weaken the novel both in style and in
characterization.

Stylistically, Glasgow's forte is subjective, the ability to get
into a man's or a woman's consciousness and flow with the
movements of the heart, be those movements ever so romantic
or self-serving: "Life that autumn and winter was drawn out
into a single aching nerve, Ada felt, a slowly gnawing anxiety.
Ralph was walking the streets, and the echo of his wearied
footfalls was like a thudding pain in her heart" (382). But a
chronicle demands an objective style as well: "Now and then,
Ranny earned a little money by running errands after
school. . . . A greengrocer . . . needed an errand boy only for
a week or two in December, when his regular delivery man
was knocked down in the street and had to go to the hospital"
(382). Among the chroniclers of Glasgow's era, Stephen
Crane, Frank Norris, and Theodore Dreiser so weakened the
subjective dimensions of their characters—whether by intent
or default—that cosmic objectivity or indifference dominates
the people; and John Dos Passos reduced the thoughts and ut-
terances of his characters to such predictable needs and
dreams that the overall effect is satire. But Glasgow's subjective passages are so intense that when she switches from the
objective to the personal the latter dominates and the effect of
the contrast too often proves sentimental—especially when
she falls back on gushy triadic structures: "Yet they had loved
life. They had loved it the more, John would tell her, because
it was fugitive; they had loved it for the sake of the surprise,
the danger, the brittleness of the moment" (40). The reader
longs for the slightly awry triads of Glasgow's ironic comedies, such as *They Stooped to Folly*, where we find the following bathotic third: "In all the essentials of the code (including
his respect for women and his antipathy to unwholesome
books, and indeed to books of any character), he was a Southern gentleman of the permanent school." This last example
uses the "language of the mind" that Glasgow rightly avoided

in turning to the chronicle; but in creating, past the age of sixty, the "language of the heart," she seems to have forgotten that enough is plenty and more than enough, a serious flaw.[9]

As for characterization, the process John Fincastle describes, whereby his single self has been divided by love and children into other and separate selves, provides an effective device for chronicling a dying age through portraits of the separate selves. It does not, however, produce the intense probing of character Glasgow achieved in her previous four books (*Barren Ground* and the Queenborough trilogy) by using a limited cast of minor figures to mirror the hidden dimensions of one or two major characters. So many minor characters are marched through *Vein of Iron* and used so inconsistently as mirrors that, compared to their counterparts in the other books, their impact resembles the force of scattered similes in contrast to extended metaphors.

Toby Waters, for example, seems meant to carry a good deal of meaning. At the start when he is pursued by the children, he reflects the hidden side of the community at large. But as Ada Fincastle begins to pity him, he becomes an archetypal victim through whom Ada recovers the victim in herself, a dimension she has tried to ignore by running with the children (4–5). Indeed, Ada will later find herself chased by other children exactly as Toby was (263–65). In a third scene, however, Toby seems to mean something totally different. Ada has just learned that Ralph will submit to Janet Rowan's plot, and her future has fallen in upon her; she had longed for the physical pleasure of loving Ralph openly but proved too much a daughter of conscience to do so. She has come to a barren gully of red clay, which itself reflects her present state of mind. There she calls Ralph's name to the emptiness. After an unspecified period, hearing a voice whine over her head, she turns to see the "idiot's face bending above her. . . . 'Sugar, sugar,' he drooled. . . . 'Toby wants sugar'" (166). The juxtaposition suggests that Toby is here meant to be a grotesque stand-in for Ralph, a male demanding sweets from a reluctant

9 Glasgow, *A Certain Measure*, 178.

woman. But this function becomes blurred if we recall that sugar was introduced earlier as an example of the pleasant things of life that never last long enough to satisfy and if we notice the narrator pushing Ada to an abstract definition of the boy's role: "Never before had she been so close to his filthy clothes and his evil stench. . . . Yet he was a creature like herself, she thought, more repulsive than any animal, but *born*, as she and an animal were born, *to crave joy, to suffer loss, and to know nothing beyond*" (61, 166, italics added). So Toby once again mirrors Ada as victim—not of the community this time, but of the natural order. This is a separate theme of the novel, the major one as we shall see. The closer Ada associates herself with Toby, the less grotesque he grows; in the end he has become a useful member of the agrarian community, a caretaker of the garden to which the surviving Fincastles long to return (459). This shift, of course, does little to clear up his mirror function; and his function is more clouded than that of later figures—Bertie Rawlings, Bertie's mother, Mr. Midkiff, the Bergens, and the Hamblens—only because they appear in fewer scenes.

The mirror value of members of the Fincastle family is diminished for a different reason: they are too much alike to reveal hidden sides of one another. John's sister Meg seems a carbon copy of their mother; the essential features remain the same though a little blurred in the daughter. Meg lacks some of the mother's rocklike fortitude as well as her dogmatic judgment of people, especially of pregnant Ada (31, 245, 247, 274). John himself carries on the otherworldliness and lonely self-reliance of the first of his name, although his journeys are within and his self-reliance too much a family tradition to seem very lonely. John's wife, Mary Evelyn, may be a more effective mirror. She came from the Tidewater; a complete outsider, she lacks both the emotional stamina and moral bigotry of the Ironsiders. That John chose a woman with her beauty and gaiety, her stress on heart and feeling, reveals a side that he could develop only after he left his family. Forced by circumstance to return, he has to protect the Mary Evelyn side of himself from his own people (24, 43, 181).

The novel focuses, however, not upon exceptions like Mary Evelyn, but on the behavior of John and Ada that falls in line with the traditions of Ironside. Father and daughter both combine the old Fincastle ability to dream with the Fincastle power to endure. But each revises the family dream to suit his or her own generation. In this way each manages to transcend the desperate vision of man's existence that Ada saw reflected in Toby's face: that life is always a condition in which we crave joy, suffer loss, and know nothing beyond (166). The dream must change if John and Ada are to sense there is "something evermore about to be." The vein of stoic fortitude, however, must remain very much the way the scholar pioneer—and the other Fincastles, down to grandmother and Aunt Meggie—knew it. Every Fincastle will suffer loss as his dream in turn collapses to make room for the next. So the winnowing of values proceeds, as the wind of time blasts the family.

John began life with the dream his fathers had taken from their Bibles. But after two years of dangerous freedom in the British Museum, he passed from the God of Abraham, superstition, and tribal law to the god of Spinoza, pantheism, and intellect (34, 45, 52, 155). Having given up his church and pulpit to pursue the transcendental, John dreams his way past Baruch Spinoza and the dynamic cosmic idealism of Arthur Schopenhauer to the beatitude of *The Enneads* and the god Plotinus knew as essence rather than energy (49, 51, 111, 292, 427). Here he finds the consolation he expects of philosophy (321).

Glasgow clearly intends John as an American equivalent of F. H. Bradley, and Bradley is probably the "Scottish philosopher at the University of Edinburgh" included among the six readers of John's philosophical work (110).[10] Like Bradley, John is a mystic using the language of post-Kantian idealism. The

10 The "English Metaphysical Poet" might then be T. S. Eliot. Glasgow had purchased Bradley's *Appearance and Reality* in 1906. As she read the work, she marked it heavily and effectively. The book is now in the Rare Book Collection, Alderman Library, University of Virginia.

two of them agree that the pursuit of the deity is the chief reason for caring about metaphysics. They both believe that we have knowledge of the Absolute and that our knowledge is certain and real, even though our comprehension of the Absolute may be miserably incomplete. But, for a practicing philosopher whose mind employs German as its natural language, John turns out to be surprisingly inarticulate about metaphysics, both in conversation and in private reveries. This dimension of his character remains embarrassingly underdeveloped.[11]

It may be just as well. For, as the novel proceeds, Glasgow carries John away from Western philosophy toward categories of Eastern thought. When his wife dies, he confronts for the first time "the universe, where not a gleam, not a flash, lighted the darkness" and recognizes that there is "no return from the abyss that is loss, no stir, no shadow, not so much as a vibration of light"—only "intolerable stillness" (175–76). With his own end near, the world seems to wear so thin that he can see through it: All "appearances were so transparent that he looked into them and beyond. Only beyond there was nothing. Nothing but vapor. Nothing but a universe dissolving into a void" (444). As a truth-enduring stoic, knowing this and knowing that all his dreams are grounded upon that void, he continues to dream his way from Queenborough back to the valley, and the family manse, to die: "Nothing remained but a blind faith in some motive that he could not understand" (454). Is it to reach the manse and his study where he may look upon God's Mountain and so escape from a world running down—to pull together, one last time, the fragments of himself in the only place where "he was wholly himself" (122)? Is this the motive that drives the dying body back to the manse? If so, his final journey proves totally consistent with his lifelong escape from this world to that of the deity manifest in God's Mountain.

---

11 McDowell, *Glasgow and the Ironic Art of Fiction,* 209–10, for the evidence.

But the vision that fills his final moments undercuts the meta-physical quest of his entire life. He has collapsed just inside the fence about the old manse; he can see his goal but must rest before trying again. And there he dreams he has been abandoned by his mother in a world of driveling idiots. He rises to break through, but vertigo sends him crashing down into pain. Lying surrounded by loneliness, he looks at the manse: "The sunset blazed on the broken windowpanes of the house, and the dark face—dark and stern and bright—watching beyond the panes was the face of his mother," who has long been dead (457). Even though he lacks the strength to make it inside, she will not come out to get him. This vision is the image of his life; it is a mirror of all the years he endured by fortitude while he dreamed mistaken phantasies of a divine father. What he really needed was his stern earthly mother to come back and save him from a world of idiots. John's last moments reveal that, although he has transcended the theology of his fathers, their myth of the fallen world has trapped him.

Ada carries John's quest for a transvaluation of family values several steps further, and succeeds against the mythology as her father never did. Through Ada's struggle Glasgow deals once again with what may well have been the underlying theme of her career—the role sex and unwanted offspring play as a check upon the freedom of individuals and of mankind. From the bastard who is the protagonist of her first novel and the orphan hero of her second; through the pregnancy-haunted triangle of her third (*The Voice of the People*), the illegitimate heroine of *The Miller of Old Church*, and the mulatto son in *Virginia* of her middle period; to Dorinda's accidental abortion of a fatherless child in *Barren Ground*, Milly's blighted baby and Mary Victoria's unborn child, both without fathers, in *They Stooped to Folly*; to Ada Fincastle of the present novel; with Roy Timberlake of *Beyond Defeat* yet to come—the preoccupation is startling. Yet when we consider Glasgow as the daughter of a Scotch-Irish father whose thinking owed much to John Calvin, or as a young intellectual educated on Thomas Malthus and Charles Darwin, or as an unmarried woman working her way through two engagements plus a number of lovers (at least one of whom was already married), the obsession becomes less irrational. To the Calvinist, illicit sex would be confused with original sin and a fallen world; to Malthus, sex, illicit or not, is the cause of human suffering; to Darwin, sex is the key to all survival and evolution; and to the unmarried woman, sex might be either the cause of an affair, the bait, or the hidden trap. In any case sex was a matter of such pressing concern for a woman that it could neither be transcended through metaphysics nor evaded by gentility, even in the age of late Victorianism.

Before Ada, all Glasgow's heroines who confront the problem manage to sidestep the true consequences of their actions through accidental abortions or an early death for either the child or the mother. Ada proves to be too much a Fincastle to sidestep any misfortune knowingly. Early in life when her father brings her a china doll rather than one with real hair, she learns to accept disappointment of her dreams by making adjustments and continuing to dream (15, 28–31). Like her great-great-grandmother Martha, she also happens to be too much a woman to find satisfaction in the seemingly sexless patriarchy of Ironside. By the time she reaches twenty, she has replaced the phantasy of the doll that has real hair with a more womanly dream—her desire for the young man Ralph McBride, who carved the bed her china doll sleeps in (31–32, 73). After Ada learns that Ralph, like the doll, will be denied her—at least within the community sanction of marriage—she recognizes exactly how deep her desire for him goes when she sees it mirrored in Toby's drooling hunger. Unlike her father, who yearned for his mother to save him from the world of idiots, Ada accepts her essential identity with Toby (166). Rather than deny her desire, or try like her father to transcend it through metaphysics, she musters the courage of her appetites. When Ralph returns six years later in uniform, he is still married but waiting for his divorce. She goes with him up Thunder Mountain, where for three nights—in a cabin higher no doubt than the one with idiots who drove her father back—they take pleasure in their dreams and draw the punishment of the tribal gods in whom Ada no longer believes (198, 205–207). Although the inevitable baby comes while Ralph is still in France, Ada refuses to be broken by family pressures and shows remorse only because her sin of freedom hurries the death of her grandmother, whose moral vision proves too brittle for the shock of sexual reality (247, 257, 267). When—an unwed mother and outsider—she is mobbed by the children of Ironside, she finds shelter with Toby's mother, Mrs. Waters—the village "witch" who generally practices the black magic of sex with tall Ironsiders who visit her late at night. Although Ada's reaction to the woman is ambivalent, she is both civil to and appreciative of her rescuer.

Her presence at Mrs. Waters' hovel is in itself significant. Like her namesake in *Tom Jones* (Glasgow's favorite among all English novels), Mrs. Waters is the symbol in Ironside of one who bears the responsibility for illicit sex (84, 264–65). The Ironsiders' mythic threats against sexual freedom have failed to deter Ada. And as probability (unlike puritans) would have it, Ada escapes the terrible responsibility that Mrs. Waters has been forced to accept: she is spared the punishment of idiocy. Ada continues for the rest of the book to adjust her dreams to suit a world plagued by war, mass culture, and depression. She also learns to accommodate a husband who turns out to be a mixed bag, like most of mankind. At his worst, his mother-instilled conscience leads to a psychosomatic paralysis of the legs (341, 346). In general, because he is heavily influenced by Ada's father, he resembles Ada too much for the two to complement one another (113, 215, 462). But her old-fashioned Fincastle stoicism stands her in good stead as she creates increasingly less impossible phantasies: dreams of a normal life with Ralph and of a way to help friends caught in the thick of the depression (221, 403–405). As each dream collapses, she spins another. At the close she yearns to return to the manse, her heritage, her tradition, the tranquil poverty of the land rather than the desperation of the city (459–61). Like the first Fincastle, she will come to the valley a rock and a dreamer, one who creates and endures. She carries with her the finest values the puritan past has to offer.

Although the valley remains the emotional center throughout the book, the city and the depression furnish the crucible in which the values from the valley are tested and found worthy. The city section may, in addition, be the part of the novel that most succeeds as a chronicle. Here the faraway and long-ago quality of the present action—the instant nostalgia of the valley scenes—gives way to a reasonably convincing portrait of a southern city passing through the Great Depression. The southern response included the constant but evasive faith that "this year the market has finally bottomed out" and the resort to alcohol (for a surcease of sorrows) that we associate with the thirties throughout the land. But in the South, as Glasgow's portrait captures it, there were more family heirlooms and relics to sacrifice, more control against self-pity and suicide, more resistance to charity, stronger traditions for uniting whole neighborhoods in a familylike network of mututal aid, and therefore less clamor for sweeping economic changes, than might be found in northern cities.

Unfortunately, the strength of this picture of the depression in the South bleeds away in passages Glasgow devotes to the querulousness of her transplanted country people. Their petty irritation with the world at large probably provides an indirect outlet for a deeper dissatisfaction with their personal lives, a discontent their stoicism will not permit them to express directly. Here cultural decay becomes so largely a matter of noise from gossips, radios, radicals, and Ford automobiles; of gambling, corn whiskey, and chicken fights; and of permanents and painted faces that the modern reader begins to suspect that what the thirties needed was not the economics of John Keynes but a course in transcendental meditation and the invention of more natural cosmetics. The modern reader has too many preconceptions about the depression, however, to be easily swayed to this extreme position and consequently, as he reads, grows all too aware that Glasgow viewed the dying age, not from the breadlines like John Fincastle, but out of the high windows of One West Main Street, where she lived.

It is unfortunate that *Vein of Iron* should be one of the few novels by Glasgow readily available to large numbers of contemporary readers.[12] Although it includes a valuable record of rural life in Virginia during the first thirty-three years of the century, *Barren Ground*, which covers much the same period without the nostalgia, offers greater realism and deeper penetration of character. That these two solemn books, so much alike in some ways (though not in quality), are likely to be the first by Glasgow the casual reader comes across creates a prevailing and misleading impression of a novelist who is at least as accurately—and far more amusingly—represented by the wit of the Queenborough trilogy. The appeal of *Vein of Iron* is far too sentimental and didactic to do Glasgow justice. The same weaknesses occur in *In This Our Life*, although the latter novel employs the tighter structure of the four books that preceded *Vein of Iron*.

---

12 Harcourt, Brace and Company has taken care that both Glasgow novels it published appear in paperback editions; Doubleday has none of the fifteen novels it published out in its paperback series, although at least five of its books are superior to either of the Harcourt titles.

# Chapter X

# Basic Family Plot: *In This Our Life* and *Beyond Defeat* (1941–1945)

It is unfortunate that the second of Ellen Glasgow's heart attacks in 1940 prevented her from taking *In This Our Life* (1941) through her usual third draft, in which she would have given greater attention to the style of the last novel she lived to publish. This work, which won the Pulitzer Prize for fiction in 1942, reveals a sureness of structure equal to *The Romantic Comedians* (1926) and *The Sheltered Life* (1932), a vitality of characterization that matches *Barren Ground* (1925) and *The Sheltered Life*, and a grasp of atmosphere that often seems superior to all her works—at least to present readers whose memories go no further back than the life people led in the shabby cities and towns of the upper South during the depression and early war years, the milieu described by *In This Our Life* and its sequel, *Beyond Defeat* (1966). Despite these triumphs, the serious stylistic weaknesses of the novel (chiefly repetitions of sentiment) deny it the front rank of Glasgow's works. Even so, it achieves within the limits of style the chief goals she set for it: to recapitulate the major themes of all her books and to embrace "the interior life of a community" in 1938–1939, during "one of those perpetually returning epochs, which fall between an age that is slipping out and an age that is hastening in."[1] This combined effort makes *In This Our Life* one of her most ambitious works.

The novel can accommodate "all the varied yet closely related themes" of Glasgow's earlier books "in a single figura-

---

1 Glasgow, *A Certain Measure*, 249, 262–63.

tive pattern" because it is an elemental family story, with
hatreds and conflicts that go as far back as the age in which
Clytemnestra imposed upon a primitive society of military
heroes the domestic forms of a matriarchy. Every unhappy
family may be "unhappy in its own way," but the underlying
tensions between mothers and daughters and the attractions
between fathers and daughters seem to have remained the
same through the three millennia that separate Clytemnestra's
Argos from Lavinia Fitzroy Timberlake's Queenborough.
There is probably no hatred like the hidden side of family
love, whether in Argos or Queenborough, and there is no
better way to reveal "the interior life of a community" that has
left military barbarism behind it than by studying "the play
and interplay of attraction and repulsion in [the] human ties"
that make a family.[2] At the end of her career, Glasgow turned
back to the situation that had produced her best work: the
struggle of individuals to free themselves from the tyranny of
the family and of the society it supports. Whether this
struggle goes on within the individual, between individuals,
or between the individual and institutions, it remains the
same.

At its most intimate, the basic conflict here lies within Asa
Timberlake, between his family-instilled conscience and his
will to freedom. In its more general form, the struggle is that
of Asa's type and generation—of Americans born about 1880,
heirs to noble values and vanished fortunes—to free themselves from the Victorian matriarchy without embracing the
purposelessness of the young who, the novel shows, dominate
the 1920s and the 1930s. Both levels, the inwardly invisible
and the socially abstract, are focused for dramatic presentation
through the pull Asa feels between the part of him loyal to his
wife, Lavinia, and the part reflected in his rebellious daughter Roy. So that this conflict may resonate through the inner
life of the community, Lavinia's drives and values are made to

2 *Ibid.*, 252, 263.

echo in the actions of her uncle William Fitzroy and in the behavior of her favorite daughter Stanley. On the other hand, Roy's need to rebel against the social order that her mother, great-uncle, and younger sister embody finds itself mirrored in three forms: in the theories of Craig Fleming, her sister's fiancé; in the intellectual ambition of Parry Clay, a young man of mixed blood; and in the independence of Kate Oliver, her father's platonic mistress.

Asa's struggle between freedom of the spirit and fear of social reprisal is much like the struggle in *They Stooped to Folly* (1929). The method of mirroring characters used to present the conflict likewise suggests the earlier novel. The difference is that there is nothing at all humorous either about Asa's submission to matriarchal tyranny or about the wife who keeps him under her camphoric thumb, and humor was the essence of Glasgow's earlier study of the matriarchy. There, Victoria Littlepage wore her crown unwillingly, or at least unwittingly. Here, Lavinia Timberlake's ability to establish a tyranny of tears and hypochondria may be an instinctive gift, but it is also an act of revenge. She torments the one man in her power for the unhappiness she suffered in childhood and early youth as "a strikingly plain girl," from "a neglectful father and a morbidly malicious younger brother."[3] She is the most pernicious and conspicuous example of sheltered invalidism Glasgow had created since *The Deliverance* (1904), in which the son and daughter of the blind Mrs. Blake sacrificed their lives to support their mother's antebellum habits although the family's wealth had been wiped out by the war. Like Mrs. Blake's son, Asa must come home from his work—earning fifty dollars a week in the tobacco factory his father once owned—to wait on his invalid with trays of food and medicine (46–47).

Behind Lavinia stands the great wealth of William Fitzroy, a type familiar from earlier novels. He combines the stolid eco-

3 Ellen Glasgow, *In This Our Life* (New York, 1941), 11, 46. This book will hereafter be referred to by page number only.

nomic practices of Cyrus Treadwell in *Virginia* (1913) with the
sexual proclivities of Judge Honeywell of *The Romantic Comedians* (even though he is fifteen years older than the judge).
The foremost robber baron of the South, Fitzroy displays the
sort of monopolistic tendencies that forty years earlier drove
Asa's father, Daniel Timberlake, to shoot himself after he had
been forced to sell the family factory to the giant Standard Tobacco Company (9). Asa's father had fought to the end against
the force of impersonality that makes Fitzroy "the biggest man
in the South" (4, 8, 11). Despite his criminal business tactics,
Fitzroy remains a "pious humbug" and a "pillar . . . of a respectable world" (202–204, 242).

Both he and Lavinia compensate for their inadequate lives
through Stanley, an irresponsible innocent like Jenny Blair
Archbald of *The Sheltered Life* but one whose power for destruction has been compounded by the tendencies to self-in-
dulgence generally associated with the 1920s and the 1930s.
Upon Stanley, Lavinia projects the romantic phantasies of her
own frustrated youth: "All the beauty she had been denied in
youth, all the emotional ecstasy she had craved and missed,
had been miraculously fulfilled through the simple extension
of her maternal ego. In Stanley, she could live more intensely
and more abundantly than she had ever lived in herself" (46).
To realize the full potential of this extension of herself, however, Lavinia must keep Stanley's emotional development in
an arrested state. When Stanley runs off with Roy's husband,
Peter Kingsmill, Lavinia says of her self-seeking daughter: "I
shall always feel that she is my baby. I can still feel her in my
arms" (157). Stanley also gives her a hold on Fitzroy's millions, much as Annabel Upchurch had provided her mother
with a claim to Judge Honeywell's wealth in *The Romantic Comedians*, since Fitzroy—childless, ugly, over eighty, and fighting time and cancer—clings to Stanley with his expensive
gifts and large checks. Through her he feels he may be able to
buy youth and to possess a beauty he can no longer claim and
may have never known, not even in the string of blond mis-
tresses he is rumored to keep in New York (11, 55–56, 114,

179, 200). Like Lavinia, he finds Stanley's babyish weakness attractive, for it fuels his male vanity and feeds his hunger for power (194, 353). Between them, Lavinia and Fitzroy have utterly spoiled the girl, and in the process they have given her power to destroy almost everyone in the family.

Asa finds himself a victim to the combined social force of Lavinia, Fitzroy, and Stanley largely because of events that occurred when he was very young. The nearest person he has ever known was his mother. For her he sacrificed his education and his ambition. After his father's suicide, he helped his mother run a boardinghouse in the Georgian mansion that had once been their family home but was now owned by William Fitzroy (9, 35). Asa thus learned early to sacrifice himself for women. Although Lavinia lacks his mother's laughter and her roselike beauty, she is elderly and maternal and uses her feminine weakness to make demands on his deep instinct to serve (12, 66, 150). His obsequiousness bears an outward resemblance to the willed devotion of chivalry. But it is instead a habitual expression of the diminished self-esteem instilled in him by his elder sister, who drummed it into his head that he was average, mediocre, and destined for failure (6). His constant fear as a boy that his service might offend "his mother's indispensable lodgers" sustained his sense of inadequacy (9). And William Fitzroy further diminished his sense of personal worth. When Asa was twelve and tried to get a better job than the one he had in the factory, Fitzroy told him he would never succeed because he had "no bowels" or guts; and the words stuck with him (303). Fitzroy has continued for forty-eight years to remind him of his inadequacy. Although the old man opposed Asa's marriage to Lavinia, Fitzroy has begrudgingly provided his only niece with a base of economic support, including the commonplace house where Asa and she moved after the neighborhood around his father's Georgian home deteriorated into commercial property (11, 23). The fear that the gerontocrat owns him, his wife, his two daughters, and everyone in their circle—body and soul—continually humiliates Asa (11, 199).

In contrast to her father, Stanley thrives on Fitzroy's financial assistance. In her, Asa can see magnified the worst qualities of the traditional order to which he has sacrificed the fifty-nine years of his life. Nevertheless, he shares Fitzroy's susceptibility to the softness of her nature, her charm, her lack of conviction, and her innocence of moral judgment (177). When Peter Kingsmill, the husband she stole from Roy, commits suicide because he can neither live with his guilt nor satisfy Stanley's need for excitement and sensation, Asa cannot help but feel pity for his crushed younger daughter and want to shelter her, as everyone else does, from the world she has created. Like the others, he is a product of the matriarchy, an heir to its automatic emotions and evasions (283, 292). But even as he protects her, he feels shame for his weakness, for the "savage and irrational instinct of parenthood" that draws him to a creature so deserving of her fate, one so "vain, selfish, unscrupulous in her motives" (283). He knows that "she was born to make trouble" and that her look of "injured innocence" only augments "the most destructive force in life": the power of her "insatiable youth, of youth that has never known wisdom, of innocence that devours" by playing upon sentimentality, maternal hysteria, and the fatherly instinct to protect. He sees her destructiveness as an unconscious power, one that springs "from some secret malice of instinct," not from what she has done but from what she is (243, 291, 297). Even more than Lavinia, she is for him the inevitable product of a society that has transformed an underlying fear of reality into evasive idealism and has made that illusion a way of life. She combines Lavinia's use of feminine weakness with William Fitzroy's ruthless will to power. Longing to dominate men or to be dominated by them, she knows that helplessness is often the most forceful tool a woman can use to take power over men, even men like her father and her great-uncle (142, 208, 370, 411–12). Asa's conscience remains so completely a part of the tradition which created Stanley that he finds it exceedingly difficult to oppose the combined rule of William, Lavinia, Stanley, and the community mind when, at the climax of the novel, they seek to use Parry Clay, Stanley's distant cousin (he combines both Timberlake and Fitzroy blood with black and Indian), as a scapegoat so that Stanley can escape responsibility for killing a small girl with her car (317, 407). Asa thus seems as weak as General Archbald in *The Sheltered Life*.

But there are other voices echoing within him that protect him from his debilitating conscience. We have thus far considered only that side of Asa which the majority of reviewers saw when the novel first appeared: his weakness, his failure to live up to the values of individuals like Fitzroy, Lavinia, and Stanley.[4] But Glasgow created Asa as an *eiron*, a character who appears to be less than he is, one who has inner resources to call upon in emergencies. In one way, it is odd that reviewers did not perceive this aspect of his character. The man who walks softly but carries a big stick and the cowboy who seldom speaks yet proves to be the fastest draw in town are among the dream selves Americans cherish most, and they are both eirons. On the other hand, big sticks and fast guns are forms of power that William Fitzroy might respect; they are not the inner resources that Asa draws upon. The inability of reviewers to detect the ironies of her characterization forced Glasgow to write the far more transparent sequel, *Beyond Defeat*, which spells out her respect for the man. She apparently felt that if the best readers could not grasp her method of characterization with Asa, where the buried strength is relatively obvious, there was no chance that they would understand the secret lives of characters in earlier novels (Dorinda Oakley, Gamaliel Honeywell, Virginius Littlepage, and John Fincastle), where the same method is used but less clearly underlined.

The narrator of *In This Our Life* points boldly to the contrast between Asa's outward appearance, "an inconspicuous figure in shabby clothes," and his inner self: "On the surface there

---

4 Ellen Glasgow, *Beyond Defeat*, ed. Luther Y. Gore (Charlottesville, 1966), ix–xiii.

was no shadow of that *strong man, the sleeping giant, who so often turned and struggled* below the waking stream of thoughts and events" (7, italics added). The sleeping giant is Asa's particular form of the internal "buccaneer" who tied Virginius Littlepage to his rebellious brother Marmaduke (*They Stooped to Folly*). If we see less of Asa's giant than Virginius' buccaneer, it may be because Asa has more completely repressed it beneath the waking stream of thoughts; he is more a victim of Lavinia than Virginius was of Victoria, and his humiliation is far more visible.

But there are numerous and varied reminders of the invisible dimensions. Although these are more subtle than the narrator's initial statement, they resemble devices that Glasgow had been using for more than two decades. First, there is the recurring phantasy that sustains Asa when the demands of family seem least reasonable: his memories of Hunter's Fare, the farm where he runs free one or two Sundays each month with Kate Oliver, her two large pointers, the river, and the wind (14, 54). This side is his true self, his liberty, the elemental happiness that he has pursued for twenty years but will never possess for more than a few hours at the time, unless Fitzroy's will some day takes financial responsibility for Lavinia out of his hands—so that he may ask Kate to marry him (69). In contrast to Lavinia's ceaseless soliloquies empty of all except self-pity, Kate's quiet presence fills (and satisfies) "some vacancy in his mind and heart"—probably an emptiness left by his mother. Kate is "the only human being" who has "ever given him the sense of completeness" (375). After thirty years with a supine and ladylike woman, Kate's erect feminine strength has "a kind of rightness" for Asa. Although Kate is real, she exists for the reader primarily in Asa's daydreams; she seems a phantasy creature, a Gaea whose earthy touch gives Asa, like Antaeus, the strength to withstand his adversities, especially the courage to resist William Fitzroy (181). Largely because the thought of Hunter's Fare stabilizes Asa's inner life, he escapes the fate of earlier Glasgow protagonists similarly belittled in their youth: he neither strikes back in violence as did the protagonist of her first book, nor does he sink into phantasies of total impotence and a state of paralysis as did Ralph McBride in *Vein of Iron*.

Asa seems at times, however, barely to elude the despondence of McBride, a dimension of his character we find reflected in Parry Clay. Parry not only parallels Roy and Stanley (he is young and combines Fitzroy and Timberlake blood) but also mirrors Asa as a young man. Had Asa's father not failed in life, Asa would likely have made a scholar or a scholarly businessman of himself; he was "a bookish chap" who found "learning from books . . . easier than learning from life," and "at twelve, he had won honors in an expensive Queenborough school" (6). After the family's collapse, he attempted to follow the Abe Lincoln–Horatio Alger pattern, but a long day's work caring for his mother's boarders left him too tired for night school and homework (7–8). Parry is another bookish chap, whose family life has proved more stable than Asa's. He has prepared himself for college in part by borrowing books from the old Timberlake family library—through Asa since Lavinia opposes the practice. Like young Asa, "discontented with his lot," he is "trying desperately to pick up an education and rise in the world" (26). Because his family resources are limited (his mother takes in washing and his father works for the post office), he will need a benefactor if he is to go North to law school.

Because he is tied by his family past and his blood to the Timberlakes, he asks Asa for help. Asa's affection for the young man goes deep—although it finds expression chiefly in appreciation of Jasper, a dog he gave Parry (26). Asa agrees to help the young man get away, but within himself Asa knows that he can do nothing, that there is no hope. For he has himself "been through it all in his time" (29–31). It is one more "raw deal" in "an unfinished world," and "there was nothing, that he could see, to be done about it" (31). The scene offers a solid echo of Glasgow's first novel about Virginia, *The Voice of the People* (1900), in which a young poor white, Nick Burr, asks an aristocratic judge to help him get an education and later goes on to become governor of the state. The contrast is stark: in forty years, Glasgow's aristocrats have lost their hope as well as their unwitting power for good; the prospects for a man like Parry, who is visibly white but legally black, seem much less sanguine than those confronting the poor white. Parry has less hope because the forces that oppose him from without penetrate his inner world. There he experiences a confusion between his white and black visions, a conflict between what he wills to be and what society tells him he will be (28). Burr faced a parallel bewilderment, but Burr received encouragement from those around him, especially from his stepmother. In contrast, Parry's mother, Minerva, believes that learning will only mean more trouble for him (76); and Asa's external hope conceals a despair almost as dismal as Minerva's.

The youthful rebel in Asa, the side that wants a better world for Parry, finds its reflection in Craig Fleming. In his own way, Craig is as much a rebel as Parry or as the inner self of Asa, but unlike them his rebellion lives chiefly in words and theories rather than in any expression of the core of his being; it comes from his head rather than his viscera. Because words are less stable than a lifetime of day-to-day commitment, there is something both pathetic and amusing about the way Craig has "identified himself with an external world in confusion" and stuffed himself "full of entangled ideologies." Although his communism is no longer in the late depression a very radical position, he constantly pays a radical's price for turning aside from his promising career as an attorney "to defend forlorn causes in the law courts." To some he seems a "flabby liberal," to others "an embittered idealist," to Asa "a weathercock" of the confused mind of the young (17). Yet Asa prefers him, as Stanley's fiancé, to Roy's husband, Peter Kingsmill, largely no doubt because Craig has tried to define himself apart from his wealthy father, apart from his education at the University of Virginia and Harvard, and apart from his moribund tradition (226). Beneath his theories, somewhere, there lives a true rebel, a creature of good instincts, who commits his money to put Parry Clay through college when Asa proves unable, and Fitzroy unwilling, to help (254, 407).

But Craig has another side: like Asa, he drags his left foot slightly. In each character the flaw may hint that one half of the personality has been thwarted. Probably the impulsive, feminine part of each has failed to develop, since the left side is affected (17, 98). Whereas Asa's development has been distorted by his tie to Lavinia, Craig is so preoccupied with theory that his neglected emotions have a way of slipping up on him to undermine his intellectual positions: "His beliefs were rooted in emotion, and assumed the urgent nature of impulse, as they do when a man begins to think with his heart and to feel with his head" (17). So, while Asa gives Parry only faint encouragement, Craig can with all sincerity pledge himself as the young man's benefactor. However, his sincere commitments keep changing. His promise to Parry parallels his pledge to marry Roy after both he and she have been jilted by the absconding pair, Stanley and Peter. But Stanley continues to have a hold on the impulsive side of Craig, one that rational Roy cannot break. When Stanley returns after Peter's suicide and runs down the child with her car, Craig allows his emotions once more to destroy his commitments of theory, of fact, and of affection. With the worst sort of pity and evasive idealism, he joins the family plot to shelter "powerless" Stanley by sacrificing Parry to the all too willing law (418–19). In the end, Parry is served far less well by Craig's youthful radicalism than by Asa's quiet commitment to the simple truth no matter where the interests of family lie.

Roy provides the clearest mirror of the part of Asa which uses truth to resist the family lies. Upon her, more even than upon Kate, he projects his need for compensation from Lavinia: Roy is "the core of his heart," "his own favorite" daughter, his happiness, his rebellion, his release, escape, and courage (11, 20–21, 41, 134). Of all living persons, she comes nearest displacing his deep affection for his mother. Roy's features seem to contain all the bravery and honesty of Asa's mother, for he has "never seen a face . . . that he liked better" (47, 66, 266). Only Minerva, the family washerwoman, has more of his mother's noble movements; but Roy, in addition, has something of the unforced gaiety of her laughter. In Roy as in Asa, the laughter generally surfaces as a mocking defense against disappointment. Although in Asa's deep phantasies Kate and Roy sometimes fill similar needs (Kate, of course, is a more realistic solution than his daughter), Roy seems to go deeper: "For, with Roy estranged from him, he could see only that the bottom had dropped out of his universe. Kate was still there; but even Kate could not fill the place Roy had left empty" (206). Just as Stanley is the "simple extension of [Lavinia's] maternal ego," so is Roy the finest expression of Asa's buried life, of the silent strong man, the scholar and the youthful rebel bonding him to Parry and Craig.

Roy escapes the parental smothering that spoiled her younger sister chiefly because she has been neglected by Lavinia and William Fitzroy and because Asa has encouraged those qualities in her of independence and self-reliance that, although stifled, have continued to live within himself. But avoiding the southern belle's traditional role has cost Roy greatly. Her "hard grain of integrity" appeals only to the conscious idealism of men: "She possessed all the qualities," Asa tells himself, "that men have missed and wanted in women: courage, truthfulness, a tolerant sense of humor, loyalty to impersonal ends" (21). Even a father's pride, however, does not blind Asa to the perennial bad faith of men who do lip service to these virtues in a woman and yet clearly prefer flattery to truthfulness, and loyalty that is personal rather than impersonal. In short, there is little in Roy to attract the unconscious side of desirable males, since she repeats rather than complements their values. As with Ada Fincastle and Ralph McBride in *Vein of Iron*, both of whom were molded by Ada's father, it is very much like trying to join like poles of magnets. First her husband, Peter, then her fiancé, Craig, follows the pull of his need, rather than the guidance of his ideals, in abandoning strong, self-reliant, and unyielding Roy for her weak, dependent, and yielding sister. The novel makes each desertion seem understandable without making it, in any sense, seem just. Even when Craig takes an interest in Roy, it is as much because her stamina balances the self-pity in which he wallows (after Stanley has left him) as because he and Roy share the same misery (179, 222–25). Unfortunately, when he has regained his strength, Stanley returns, bringing with her his weakness, which again balances his day-to-day existence better than does Roy. His conduct is inevitable; Roy cannot win at love.

Even with Asa, who loves her most, her strength creates her unhappiness. When her own life is secure enough for her to pity Asa's second-rate existence under Lavinia, he, in his pride, responds with a "familiar note of whimsical chaffing," the sort of irony that has long been his chief defense (35). On the other hand, when Asa shows his sympathy after each of her lovers drops her for Stanley, the same Timberlake self-reli-ance puts "a bright edge of steel" in her response: "She did not want pity. She wanted sternness, inflexibility, even that lost sardonic humor. What she needed most . . . was . . . to be convinced . . . that in the midst of a world toppling over in ruins, desire for a single human being had become not merely unimportant but wasteful" (139, 162). She cannot con-vince herself of this, and Asa does not wish to try. Craig's theories of solidarity seem for almost a year to pull her, as she wishes, from the personal to the impersonal—until his choice of Stanley over Parry belies his message (157, 162, 211, 220, 233).

Only one character offers what she wants—"something larger and deeper than self in which one might plunge and sink, and so become a part of the whole" (233). After she re-jects Craig's vacillations, refuses Asa's effort to help, and scorns the "firm hypocrisy" of the family that tried to railroad Parry, she decides her freedom demands escape to New York. In her flight, she pauses during a shower in a pavillion to gather her wits before leaving Queenborough (439, 445). She feels driven by a desperate need to strike back at her family, to smash her "tradition or institutions or convention—or—or love" to revenge herself (and Asa, although she doesn't know it) upon all that she "has loved and hated and valued" in a world she has already left (448–49). In this violent state, she allows herself to be picked up by a young man from Canterbury, an expatriate who, after several years at the University of North Carolina, is returning to England eager to fight Hitler (446). They spend the night together in the apartment of one of his friends, where Roy changes her rain-soaked clothes for the blue pajamas of a woman named Mary (450). At first glance, her lover for the night reminds her of Peter, but she meets him in a park as she had Craig just before their romance began (219, 442). As they talk, his childhood affection for his mother recalls Asa (456). As he continues, he speaks of his need for a real fear "to drive false fear away," of his desire to fight "something solid," "what others are fighting," not alone but with "other poor devils worse off" than he is, to fight where he can feel needed and feel that he belongs with the living. In other words, like Roy, he wants "to find something bigger than life . . . bigger than death" (457). But his "grotesque purple scar," a burn he hides under his hat, mirrors the emotional state of both: their "something bigger," whether Roy's revenge or her nameless lover's war, is the force of destruction—blind destruction of others or of self. They walk thus together in the modern nightmare (449).

Roy can leave this nightmare (unlike her lover, who is surely doomed), purged by him of her will to die or to destroy. She must face the real fear that most people know: the "inner emptiness," the street that leads "toward something or nothing," the banality of a "new age" in an always "new world" (459–61).[5] After her dark night of storm, her new quest is as

5 Glasgow has Henry David Thoreau's "lives of quiet desperation" in mind here, but she firmly opposes transcendental solutions and offers instead the "instinctive fortitude of the average man." See Glasgow, *A Certain Measure*, 253. *Beyond Defeat* moves this fortitude into a setting that affords some of Thoreau's ecstatic naturalism, but the transcendental is expressly denied.

banal as the world in which she will seek to accomplish it: "I
want something to hold by! I want something good! " she
cries to her father when she goes home to get her clothes. Asa
has tried to found his life in *truth* so that the finest part of
him, his daughter, might know a modicum of the *good*. He
tells her, "You will find it, my child. You will find what you
are looking for. It is there, and you—if not I—will find it"
(466–67). His own solitary victory over the false "goods"
founded upon family lies came "for one miracle of psychological time," the moment the "strong man" in him dominated
Fitzroy and Lavinia sufficiently to force them to free Parry and
to make Stanley take responsibility for manslaughter (418–19,
438). His life has been a holding action against the tyranny of
Lavinia's tradition. But he has prepared Roy for freedom; and
her night with the stranger, fraught as it was with the danger
of self-destruction, seems a more decisive rebellion against
family feeling than any Asa has staged.

All of this was far from clear—or perhaps far from acceptable—to the book's early reviewers, who found Asa an
utter failure and did not understand Roy's role as an extension
of his inner strong man.[6] The evidence for the positive view of
Asa exists in the novel, for a careful reader. However, from the
novel alone, it is difficult to know what to make of Roy. She
seems some imperfectly realized cross between an Athena-
like daughter of truth and an Io-like victim of fate—always
abused, always in pain. Worse yet, the chapters devoted to
her suffering too often distract the reader from the chief interest, Asa. The problem is that Roy's story has scarcely begun
in this novel. It is as though *Barren Ground* had ended with
Dorinda Oakley and Jason Greylock making love in the August drought, or as if *Vein of Iron* had closed with Ada Fincastle and Ralph McBride coming back from their three nights
on Thunder Mountain. The extent of Roy's rebellion cannot become clear until we pick up *Beyond Defeat*—unless we recall

6 Glasgow, *Beyond Defeat*, xii–xiii.

that in Glasgow's fiction illicit lovemaking inevitably leads to conception.

As we saw in the previous chapter, the problem of illegitimacy is perhaps the underlying theme of Glasgow's career. Although for her males unsanctioned sex is generally an act of vanity and exploitation, for her women it is an act of freedom. The inevitable child results, not because her men are excessively potent or because their birth control is poor, but because freedom for Glasgow carries responsibility. The line between youth and maturity, between destructive innocence and intelligence, is the line between freedom pursued without contingency and the acceptance of the totally responsible freedom to which all are condemned who do not seek the shelter of evasive idealism and other alibis of environment, biology, and transcendentals. Asa succinctly expresses the difference early in the novel, after a still immature Roy has told him that she would let Peter go because both she and Peter are "perfectly free to change" if they wish. Asa thinks:

> Free! Free! There were moments, and this threatened to be one of them, when the eternal patter of inexperience wore on his nerves. After all, what was freedom, and who was ever free, in a world which entangled you at the instant of birth? The social web, he thought, was worse than unyielding; it was inescapable. For fifty-nine years . . . he had hungered for freedom. And he had never even known what freedom was like. . . . And yet if Lavinia had said to him, as Roy said to Peter, "You are free," what difference would it have made? Freedom, he knew, was not a thing that could be packed into a phrase or a word. The intangible web was still there. It was stronger than impulse, because it was woven not of a single strand, but of an intricate multitude. Like every other unsatisfied and continuously thwarted human being, he had struggled against a conspiracy of tradition and of custom, of reason and of economics. (41–42)

The dialectic of Asa's mind rejects the easy freedom of words and theories and emphasizes social restrictions; but underlying his recognition of limits remains the ceaseless struggle against them. He knows the struggle must be ceaseless rather than impulsive because he married Lavinia as an impulsive act of freedom, an act perversely against the will of his mother and William Fitzroy (15).

Building upon the foundation Asa provides, Roy acts upon her impulse to free herself from tradition by spending the night with the death-bound boy from Canterbury. During the three years that separate her rebellion in *In This Our Life* from its fulfillment in *Beyond Defeat*, she crosses the essential line between innocence and maturity. The responsibility which pushes her over that invisible boundary takes the form of the boy Timothy, who results from her night with the Englishman, a son so named no doubt because at first his birth put the "fear of God" into her (although she denies this) and because, as the fear passes, Timothy both ties her to the *Tim*berlake heritage of responsible freedom and embodies her hard-earned knowledge of the nature of *Time*—her understanding of how she must shape the future, as she endures the present, by taking responsibility for her actions in the past.[7]

Just as *In This Our Life* is Asa's story, so *Beyond Defeat* belongs to Roy and documents her quest for a vision that will enable her to accept responsibility for both her past and Timothy's future—an effort to bind freedom and responsibility together. As a quest the book's structure seems ritualistic: in late October of 1942, Roy returns to Queenborough with twenty-nine-month-old Timothy. She has communicated with no one there since August, 1939. Yet she must find someone to care for Timothy while she turns herself over to a doctor who thinks he can cure her pneumonia, contracted during three years of trying to survive as an unwed mother working the damp, cold basements of New York department stores. She is desperate: she has no money, no health, no friends, no

7 *Ibid.*, 75, for Roy's denial that "Timothy" meant "God fearing" to her or has a family source.

hope—other than Timothy, who is her rebellion, her revenge, her mistake "worth paying for."[8] Having learned that there is a limit to the Timberlake pride in self-reliance, she goes in turn to each member of the family to ask for temporary assistance.

With each there is a problem. Charlotte Fitzroy, William's wife, feels that after fifty years of enduring her husband, now dead, she has earned the ritual peace of old age: "At my age it is too much to ask of me" (28–29). Well set up by Fitzroy's provision for her, Lavinia complains of poor health, inflation, taxes, war, the cost of nurses. Worse, Timothy is not a member of her "decent" family; he belongs in an orphanage. Lavinia has just suffered another of her heart attacks and will accept the boy only if Roy can force Asa to come back to her from Hunter's Fare, where he is living—in sin, she says—with Kate Oliver (44–46, 50–52). When Roy goes to the farm to see her father, she finds Craig, happier and much steadier now that he is a member of Kate's agrarian commune, part of "something bigger than one person—or than two persons." He offers to marry her and to accept Timothy, but he can provide no practical help since he must shortly leave for the navy (77, 108). Asa too has found his long-deferred liberty with Kate; in the process he has transcended the weakness of his conscience that once drove him to sacrifice himself for family members he pitied. A changed man, he firmly refuses to go back to Lavinia but promises, "Somehow, in some way, Timothy shall be looked after." His promise loses its force, however, when he adds, "I can't ask Kate to take on anything else" (101–103).

Roy has exhausted all her options when she talks with Kate, the Gaea-Rhea-Demeter figure of the two novels, a "tall upright figure" who moves as if she obeys "some natural harmony in earth or air"; she seems to Roy "a part of the autumn" itself (82–83). When Roy admits she is pleased that her father will not go back, Kate replies, "You will give [Timothy] to us, dear. You will give him to us until you come back

8 *Ibid.*, 95. This book will hereafter be referred to by page number only.

to live here. Do you think Asa's grandchild could go to a stranger?" Asa knew without asking what Kate's generous response would be (113).

Kate is better realized here as a woman than in the previous novel, but she remains for Asa and Roy very much a personification of Hunter's Fare and of the circumambient universe that sustains Asa and the other characters who gain a proper perception of their relation to it. She (or it) is the something bigger that Asa, Craig, and eventually Roy achieve. By the end of the book, however, Roy has not yet reached Asa's understanding of the important role that perception plays in creating a proper relation to Hunter's Fare. For Asa, the farm is simply the place where he sees the total circumambience of time, where he is "caught and held in some slow drift of time":

> Barred with a pattern of light and shade, the terraces appeared to rise and fall, and to settle back, silently, under the blown grass. Within this stillness, the wind moved, the grass bent and straightened, the fall of leaves broke and scattered. All these separate motions were imprisoned here, now, in the crystal globe of this instant. But, beyond this sphere of eternity, above, below, around the encircled moment, he felt that changeless, perpetual rhythm of time passing. Clouds and light, air and water, tree and flower, all were drifting. . . . For it was the closing season of an abundant earth, when nature, serene and effortless, was drifting into the long pause of winter. (119)

Eternity, in short, is born of the mind perfectly attuned; all around it the cycle of time persists. The repose of eternity is a property of vision—that, and nothing more.

Nonetheless, Asa's vision gives him the power to triumph over Lavinia's final ploy, the full force of family feeling she activates by finally dying. Unlike his predecessor Virginius Littlepage in *They Stooped to Folly*, who broke in guilt and remorse when he found himself in a similar position, Asa gives Lavinia her due as a dying tradition when he stands by her corpse; but he does not break. He is truly free—free enough to guide Roy along the path to the unknown that he has always traveled.

Roy feels that her freedom and strength have their root in Asa and his, in the earth of Hunter's Fare: "I must believe," she tells him, "in something outside myself. I want to hold by something good, not only for myself, but for Timothy. That is why I am holding to you, Daddy" (126). She ought to let go, however, the novel suggests. During her three years away, she has learned that the pulse of tragedy she used to feel beating through the walls of the family's house was actually "within herself; the vibrations flowed out from her own heart into the cast-off shapes of inanimate objects" (31). Her father tries to tell her that the same holds true for her freedom and strength: "You are holding not to me, dear, but to your own inner strength. It was always there." Asa's reply is succinct; but in light of his career in the two novels, there is a great deal we can see in his words: You *are* your father, Roy, he might have added, and I am only the image of the strength you had to create—just as Kate and Hunter's Fare are the mirror of my need and repose. We create the family we need, his words imply, out of ourselves. There is no distinct line between the world in us and the world we are in; our dream starts within and colors all we know. To Asa's suggestion, we may draw on Glasgow's recent novels, especially *Vein of Iron*, to add that the dream must change because our need changes. The dream will remain adequate only as long as it is free to evolve. What Asa means, Roy must learn as she lives. For Asa speaks for the Glasgow of seventy years addressing herself to Roy, who resembles a far younger Glasgow and mirrors the generation that the impulsive 1920s and 1930s had created. The mature author knew that Roy would only hear the truth she had already experienced; time alone would enable her to hear the rest.

Although this emphasis on vision, the ritualistic structure, and the liturgical or Eliotian cadence of the prose make *Beyond Defeat* a suitable coda to the recapitulation of themes in

*In This Our Life*, these same qualities set it apart from that work. In structure, style, and vision, it drops completely the commonplace surface of twentieth-century realism and takes us from the sleazy soap opera interiors of the modern imagination out to the classical and sensuous space of Hunter's Fare. This change frees the book of many of the flaws of its predecessor: the natural imagery allows a more sensuous presentation of themes and thus lessens the dependence upon abstractions and upon repetition of banal sentiments. This economy, in turn, reduces the need for the narrator to guide us through often strained connections between the actions and abstractions, a strain that weakens the internal monologues of *In This Our Life*. For communicating such perceptions as Asa's meditation on time and eternity, natural imagery affords a far more effective medium than did the furnishings of bedrooms, dining rooms, and pantries of *In This Our Life*.

It is a jarring experience to pick up a book like *Beyond Defeat* when we expect the sequel to a novel of commonplace modern life, for *Beyond Defeat* cannot be enjoyed by the same standards as realistic fiction. Indeed, the effect is so startling that Edgar E. MacDonald, a commentator generally sympathetic to Glasgow's work, has suggested that publication of the sequel was a mistake.[9] Yet we need Roy's story, for in a sense she is the fulfillment of a theme raised both by Dorinda Oakley and by Ada Fincastle. Roy takes her freedom with both hands, without the trumped-up deliverance of Dorinda's abortion or the hope of Ada that Ralph will come back and give their son a father. Roy is thus more responsible than either. In addition, *Beyond Defeat* solves a mystery that perplexed Asa in *In This Our Life* when Asa decided that "though family feeling may be at the base of all our difficulties, there is nothing to put in its place."[10] The sequel shows, in a brief scene with Roy, Craig, and Timothy, that the false families which

9 Edgar E. MacDonald, "An Essay in Bibliography," in M. Thomas Inge (ed.), *Ellen Glasgow: Centennial Essays* (Charlottesville, 1976), 194.
10 McDowell, *Glasgow and the Ironic Art of Fiction*, 217.

our past and our facile emotions have imposed upon us may be replaced by *better* families, families to be created out of the core of our being: "Before she could turn away, he put his free arm around her, and drew her into a circle, locked together with the child on his shoulder. . . . This is peace, she thought: I have suffered enough. This is the end of strain and violence, and of wanting that is not ever satisfied" (109). Each of these two contributions seems to justify the initial publication of the sequel and to recommend the automatic inclusion of this short work in future editions of *In This Our Life*.

But *Beyond Defeat* should not be read with the same expectations as its predecessor. Far from realistic fiction, it is a form of "wisdom literature"—one of Glasgow's favorite genres, to judge by her library. Its liturgical cadence and stress on vision give it a thrust similar to her lifelong companions of the mind—*The Meditations of Marcus Aurelius*, the *Bhagavad-Gita*, and *The Enneads*. Its ritual structure ties it to forms in which high vision passes into the drama of the world: the tragedy of Aeschylus or the quests of the Middle Ages, for example. Like these works, it should be judged upon its style and vision. If adequate, its wisdom ought to afford an antidote to the banal reality of *In This Our Life*.

The degree to which *Beyond Defeat* falls short of these models measures the distance Glasgow fell short of her ultimate ambition. And this book must inevitably fail to reach its mark; for it is impossible to match the authority of Zeus, Vishnu, and the mystic's God with the discoveries of an individual and naked spirit, as Glasgow tried to do. But the reader who has sometimes found his own mind similarly stripped of transcendental trappings can begin to value the heroism of Glasgow's attempt.

# Chapter XI

# Essential
# Phantasies
*In This Our Life* and, even more so, *Beyond Defeat* return us to the basic argument of this study: Glasgow was able to develop a more intensely psychological novel after 1916 because she began to use phantasies as an essential test of the reality within which her protagonists find themselves, and these phantasies generally emerge as projections upon other characters who possess an inordinate fascination or antipathy for the protagonist. Asa Timberlake expresses the concept beautifully when he tells Roy that, although she seems to be holding to him, she is in fact drawing upon her "own inner strength." These final novels return to the technique that had made *Barren Ground*, *The Romantic Comedians*, and *They Stooped to Folly* penetrating works (Glasgow had seemingly deviated from this technique in *The Sheltered Life* and *Vein of Iron*). However, the last two novels of her career cannot match *The Sheltered Life* for intensity and beauty. Because *The Sheltered Life* itself looks back to Glasgow's earlier realistic mode by exposing the danger of the phantastical psychology she had long called evasive idealism, the book offers itself as the strongest possible test of the value of the technique under consideration. The novels that use phantasies in a positive manner are at base novels of personality development, whereas *The Sheltered Life* takes a tragic turn because it is a novel about the way one culture distorts emotional growth by controlling the dream life of its members. In other words, *The Sheltered Life* places the essentially

comic thrust of growth within a tragic order. To appreciate this deviation, we first need to consider the recurring pattern.

With the apparent exception of *The Sheltered Life*, all nine novels considered here describe patterns of emotional evolution or at least attempts to grow. This is the conclusion we reach by keeping our eyes on the phantasies that the protagonist of each projects on other characters. The chief differences lie between the patterns followed by female characters and those followed by males.

Gabriella Carr establishes the basic structure of feminine evolution when she rejects the static security promised by Arthur Peyton to pursue the romantic difference of George Fowler, then grows disillusioned, and pragmatically courts Judge Crowborough for his money and advice until in Ben O'Hara she finds romance and masculine authority combined with a number of other abstract virtues, including democracy and cleanliness. The abstractions that conclude the novel suggest a collection of essential phantasies which Gabriella has embodied imperfectly in O'Hara but which nonetheless point the way to future growth. In *The Builders*, Caroline Meade sees David Blackburn initially as a figure of wealth and mystery; but later he too turns into a man of abstract authority like Ben O'Hara, a sort of ideal father to guide Caroline past the hole in reality. In *One Man in His Time*, Corinna Page finds herself in a phase much like Gabriella's growth when she reached out to a man of democratic energy; to Corinna, Gideon Vetch speaks with the voice of collective mankind. The most complexly rounded female character that Glasgow ever created, Dorinda Oakley of *Barren Ground*, reveals all of Gabriella's drives, plus several that give Dorinda her added depth. Upon Jason she initially projects her need for romance, sex, and a new life. Nathan becomes her image of authority and success. But Nathan also, inasmuch as he allows Dorinda to use him as a handyman, becomes an object, along with Jason, through which she works out her hatred for men. In John Abner she finds a recipient for her advice and her stored-up pity. In ad-

dition to her men, the earth mirrors her unused fertility and
unacknowledged desire for revenge.

In *The Romantic Comedians*, Annabel Upchurch grows first
by seeking freedom in wealth and later by turning, like Edmonia Bredalbane, from the slavery of wealth and age to the
healthy freedom of youth. In *They Stooped to Folly*, Victoria's
development fails on two occasions: first, when she settles for
Virginius rather than the Lochinvar of her wildest dreams
and, second, when she rejects the wild freedom she sees in
Milly Burden for the fear that governs her role as southern
lady. She longs to grow, but she attempts nothing. If we omit
*The Sheltered Life* and move to *Vein of Iron*, we find that Ada
Fincastle originally seeks in Ralph romance, freedom, and an
even more ecstatic joy than that Dorinda sought in Jason. But
she comes to regard Ralph as the mirror of her sexual freedom
and settles in time for the simpler phantasies of a normal
family life, solidarity with friends in adversity, and an opportunity to start life again in the home of her fathers. Finally,
Roy Timberlake of the last two novels begins with romantic
illusions, passes through disillusionment with men, moves to
pity for individuals and collectives, then in an act of rebellious freedom attempts to sacrifice herself for something
larger than herself, and ends holding to the strength and
goodness she projects upon her father. The recurring situa-
tions in these novels make Glasgow's answer to Freud's fa-
mous query, "But what do women want?" quite clear: in their
youth they want romance with a handsome man and sexual
freedom; in maturity they want authority, a fatherly man to
mirror their own strength and to support their wisdom. At all
times they want strength to live and freedom to grow.

Because these novels usually center around women, the pattern of growth found in the males appears far simpler. Since
the men are generally weaker than the women, their development often seems distorted. Gabriella's first love interest, Arthur Peyton, reveals the basic male distortion when he seeks
in Gabriella an ideal wife to substitute for his ideal mother.
He thus looks back to Harry Treadwell, the mother-trapped

son of Virginia Treadwell in *Virginia*, and forward to a number of characters who impose a static feminine ideal upon the women they know. Gabriella's second lover, George Fowler, marries her as a substitute for his mother and sister, less because she is an ideal than because he needs a woman to mother him in his selfish hedonism. Compared to Peyton and Fowler, Gabriella's final interest, Ben O'Hara, seems an embodiment of simple health. He sees in her an expression of feminine fortitude and, at the same time, a woman to protect as one might a daughter. In *The Builders*, David Blackburn grows from his wife Angelica, the sick ideal he protects, to Caroline Meade, a strong daughter-disciple he can steer toward the light. In *One Man in His Time*, Stephen Culpeper turns his back on Margaret Blair, the old-fashioned ideal of the perfect lady, and seeks health in the youth, beauty, and wild freedom of Patty Vetch. Jason Greylock, Dorinda Oakley's incubus, has long before resigned himself to failure. At first he seems to regard Dorinda as a disciple; but instead he takes the path of many Glasgow males in using Dorinda, like Geneva Ellgood, as a comfort for his body and a mirror of his remaining male vanity. Both the male body and vanity are made to seem aspects of the fatality in which Jason has been nurtured; he ends as Dorinda's helpless dependent.

For all his humorous excess, Judge Gamaliel Honeywell of *The Romantic Comedians* probably remains the most complexly rounded of Glasgow's male characters. He moves from the static beauty of Amanda Lightfoot to Cordelia Honeywell, the ideal wife and mother, before returning, with help from the pragmatism of Bella Upchurch, to the youthful energy of his daughter-wife, Annabel Upchurch. He evolves despite keeping only one ear open to the comic advice of his realistic sister, Edmonia. In the end he discovers that all his women wear the masks of his mother, whom he passionately loved. With far more timidity than Honeywell, Virginius Littlepage in *They Stooped to Folly* pulls against his safe mooring beside the ideal Victoria and nudges the sister ship of his vanity and sexual desire (Amy Dalrymple) at the same time that he reaches out to protect the daughterly beauty of Milly Burden; ultimately he returns to the safety of Victoria.

Skipping once more over *The Sheltered Life*, we find that Ralph McBride of *Vein of Iron* has been so thoroughly trapped by his mother that he experiences freedom only in the sort of perverse rebellion that proves self-destructive. He follows his instincts, including vanity and sexual desire, to abuse the conscience he received from his mother. Unfortunately, the strength and goodness of Ada Fincastle cause him to associate her with his conscience, while beauties like Janet Rowan and Minna Bergen continue to mirror his ego and sexual needs. Ada's father, John Fincastle, spends his life in pursuit—first of a divine father, then of a transcendental absolute that leads him to the void. The moment he dies, he discovers that what he wanted all the time was his stern mother to come take him out of the world of idiots; and in that moment he achieves the consummation of every puritan's deepest desire—to die. In the final two novels, Asa Timberlake emerges as perhaps the psychologically strongest of all Glasgow's male characters. He has grown from early dominance by a loved mother, through a freedom of perverse rebellion against his mother, and through a long life supporting Lavinia, the sick ideal of his rebellion. He has earned the right to live with Kate Oliver, a strong erect woman who personifies the benevolent and feminine aspects of Hunter's Fare. At the same time, despite his debilitating love for Stanley, he has given Roy a model of strength and integrity as well as a good father's support, a support gentle enough to force upon her the growth that is freedom. From all these examples, we may conclude that what Glasgow's men want generally costs women a good deal. At their worst, men seek comfort for their bodies and a mirror for their egos; at their best, they want a good earthy woman like Kate to hold to and a daughter like Roy to guide. Otherwise, Glasgow's men seek the static ideal of beauty and motherly chastity. And this proves perhaps the most pernicious need of all, for it denies the women in whom they invest their ideal the freedom to grow.

With this summary of the basic female and male patterns of development in the novels, we stand ready to reconsider *The Sheltered Life*. We can now appreciate the pressure that exists between the need of Jenny Blair, George, and Eva to grow and the antithetical need of General Archbald for women to embody his ideal of a good that is beyond the truth of this world. Archbald's need may be a key to his fulfillment as a moral idealist, but it nonetheless has tragic consequences in the lives of Eva, George, and Jenny Blair. As the mind of the past, Archbald bears more responsibility than anyone else in the book for creating the social ideal that perverted Eva's natural growth by making her play her static role, the belle of Queenborough. Because Eva allows Archbald's ideal to put an end to her natural self, the reader understands why George finds himself longing for the energy, vivacity, and sexuality of younger women like Memoria, Delia Barron, and Jenny Blair. Again it is tragic that George's desire should pervert Jenny Blair's elemental needs—to be alive, to experience her peculiarities of self, and to discover a protecting father—tragic that he should so twist her phantasies that she dreams the banal dreams of the flirt. Although the flirt plays a socially acceptable part, she can only metamorphose into the belle or the mistress, and neither of these represents growth. All Jenny Blair's growth Archbald finally turns backward toward childish irresponsibility when he restores the shelter of innocence after she has caused Eva to shoot George.

The great pressure created by this profound need for growth in the other characters works against Archbald's absolute order, a shelter without visible walls, to generate the tension essential for tragedy. *The Sheltered Life* thus contrasts significantly with *They Stooped to Folly*, in which Virginius' timid rebellion against the unwitting matriarchy of Victoria—an order he has willed into being—can only generate the feeble tension of satire. In *They Stooped to Folly*, Glasgow avoided increasing the pressure by keeping the young people, who have a strong need to grow, shadowy and at a distance. But in *The Sheltered Life*, she brought the two most forceful currents of her life into the most effective configuration possible. Earlier, in *The Builders*, she had identified the conservative spirit with realism: it sees "things as they are" and stresses race, tradition, philosophy, and age; it is, in short, the vision of the late nineteenth century. In the same book she equated the progressive spirit of the early twentieth century with romance: it sees things "as they ought to be" and stresses the individual, adventure, experience, and youth. In *The Sheltered Life*, she embodied the conservative order in Archbald and the progressive drive in Jenny Blair and then forced them to collide. The approach (if not the result) was much like the tension Herman Melville achieved when he confronted the democratic individualism of his youth with the limits of his Calvinistic ancestors; or Nathaniel Hawthorne, when he checked the romantic individualism of Hester with the Calvinistic fatalism of Dimmesdale; or Eugene O'Neill, when he crossed the Freudian drives of Christine Mannon with the puritan disgust of Ezra Mannon (*Mourning Becomes Electra*); or, for that matter, Shakespeare, when he blocked Iago's Renaissance defense of self and Edmund's appeal to nature with the medieval world order. Both the pressure for change and the unyielding order must be embodied convincingly if tragedy is to result. In Glasgow's early novels, the spirit of determinism proved too strong to permit a tragic force to develop. In *The Romantic Comedians*, the spirit of comedy is too insidious and the narrator too Olympian to yield either pity or terror—only delight. In *Barren Ground* and *Vein of Iron*, the heroines prove too resilient to confront their tragedy squarely. In Glasgow's last two novels, although the lives are tragic or at least pathetic, the stress falls upon the consolation of philosophy. But in *The Sheltered Life*, everything is right for tragedy. And there remains a good deal to be said for the pure forms, comedy and tragedy. The dramatic objectivity of tragedy enables the male part of the reader both to pity the bind of Archbald living in a world that does not match his ideals and to feel terror at the way he sacrifices his women to fulfill himself. At the same time, the female part of the reader pities the sacrificial women and feels terror both at the way Jenny Blair pursues her vain, romantic goals and at the way Eva takes her revenge.

Thus, although *The Sheltered Life* tests our case for essential phantasies, it is less a refutation of the argument than a challenge to refine distinctions between phantasies and illusions, between psychological growth through imagination and the malignity of evasive idealism. In the year after Glasgow published *The Sheltered Life*, another acute student of dreams, Nathaniel West, working independently, wrote as follows in *Miss Lonelyhearts* (1933): "Men have always fought their misery with dreams. Although dreams were once powerful, they have been made puerile by the movies, radio and newspapers. Among many betrayals, this one is the worst." West then went on to detail in *The Day of the Locust* (1939) the way Hollywood, the dream factory, has turned the American collective imagination into a Sargasso Sea of wasted phantasies impossible to reconnect with life. There is then a difference, for West and for Glasgow, between essential phantasies, on the one hand, that arise spontaneously from the shadow side of the mind to guide individuals in their growth, and dreams, on the other, that have been perverted and rendered useless by the mass mind. For West, the media render our dreams puerile. For Glasgow, it is the mass mind in any form, but especially the group mind working through tradition, that perverts essential phantasies of individuals into a culture's static ideals or into an outsider's banal dreams of despair. Because the chief tradition of her region was that strange cult of the lady that southern males willed into being, her strongest theme is the male perversion of female growth phantasies into the lifeless evasive idealism of an Eva Birdsong or into the revengeful rage of a Dorinda Oakley. All her life Glasgow fought against her culture to dream a better dream so she would not be caught either, like Eva, in the static role of lady or, like Dorinda, in the sterile illusion of revenge. Her fiction was, it seems, the essential phantasy that grew, almost a volunteer, in the garden of her mind—essential, because as long as the phantasy continued to thrive, she was free to unfold. And it grew until the end—although less strongly after *The Sheltered Life*. In this sense, her life and her approach to fiction were one.

Glasgow's habit of revealing characters through the phantasies they project upon others is a technique she probably developed through introspection of processes that occurred during two of the major experiences of her life: her countless hours spent as a writer and those spent as a reader (the critics and psychologists, by contrast, simply supported her introspections). If this is so, we ought to consider briefly whether her technique throws any light upon the processes of writing and reading fiction in general. Perhaps we can arrive thereby at a sharpened awareness of why some of her novels succeed better than others.

If conditions exist when a novelist gets to know a character similar to those that pertain, as this study shows, when two Glasgow characters know each other, then we ought to be able to identify four types of characters: first, those whose appeal for the author is like Ralph's adult interest in Ada Fincastle or Craig Fleming's interest in Roy Timberlake, a very limited emotional appeal because the two characters are too much alike in their conscious values; second, those who hold the sort of irresistible fascination for the author that Jason Greylock held for Dorinda Oakley because he mirrored the unconscious hemisphere of her life; third, those who combine the above types in an intuitively controlled manner; and finally, those who, to one degree or another, combine the first two types in an uncontrolled fashion. The first three types describe kinetic or dramatically realized characters. The fourth type consists of emergent or inchoate characters.

In the literary tradition, we find the first type in the way John Milton apparently viewed his God in *Paradise Lost*, William Shakespeare his Cassio in *Othello*, and Ernest Hemingway his Jake Barnes in the *The Sun Also Rises*. In Glasgow, her exemplary female characters—especially Gabriella Carr, Ada

Fincastle, Roy Timberlake—fall into this first group. For critics who view *Barren Ground* as a female success story, Dorinda Oakley seems to be the same sort.

In the literary tradition, we often find the author's ego-ideal balanced by a type-two character, mirroring an unacknowledged side of the author. These figures generally possess an inordinate fascination, even in their forbidden aspects and seemingly for the author as well as the reader. Thus Milton's Satan appears a stronger character than his God, Iago fascinates far more than Cassio, and Robert Cohn seems a far healthier and saner character, for all his weakness, than Barnes. In her novels of exemplary females, Glasgow seldom creates a character of the second type in whom she invests the imaginative force necessary to balance the heroines. The possible exception may be Jason Greylock; but with Jason she takes at the start of the story the same precautions to make him weak and unappealing that Milton took only after he had first given Satan the force of Prometheus. Glasgow's novels are far stronger, on the other hand, when she gives a freer rein to the characters who speak for the shadow side of her personality, as she does with Edmonia Bredalbane in *The Romantic Comedians*, Amy Dalrymple and Marmaduke Littlepage in *They Stooped to Folly*, and George Birdsong in *The Sheltered Life*. Frequently, however, her approach is too critical and didactic to permit her to cut these characters loose from her moral judgment of them. When didacticism dominates, her people become types rather than rounded characters. *They Stooped to Folly*, for example, remains essentially a satire of types since she never sets Amy and Marmaduke free to live out their potential.

Occasionally Glasgow creates a remarkable character who balances the author's conscious values with an equal but controlled force from her buried life. In the literary tradition, such characters seem the rarest of all and are to be distinguished most easily by wild swings of personality, as when noble Othello plunges madly from the idealism of Cassio into the jealous woman-hatred of Iago (and ends by joining all the parts of himself in suicide), or when Gilgamesh swings from the innocence of a demigod into the existential despair of a mortal, or when Dimitri and Fyodor Karamazov dive from their socially decreed roles into cruel buffoonery or baseness. Glasgow's rounded characters do not swing nearly as wildly, but they nonetheless betray important opposites of her own personality. Glasgow may have consciously shared many of Gamaliel Honeywell's civilized tastes, for example; but one doubts that she was conscious of how much of her own vanity she exorcised by pushing the judge's sexual follies far beyond the limits of her own courage. Or better still, because he is not undercut by the narrator, General Archbald clearly expresses, as a capacitating character, the opinions of his creator when he reflects on history, the past, and civilization; but one doubts that Glasgow would have acknowledged her own tendency to sacrifice her relatives and friends to the fulfillment of her ideals, although this trait is powerfully dramatized in what Archbald does to Eva Birdsong. Again, Glasgow clearly admired Jenny Blair's vital force and her rebellion, but the author probably would not have accepted the girl's sacrifice of Eva as a mirror of her own selfishness. Yet all these negative traits are presented with convincing force at the same time that they are controlled intuitively and dramatically. As a reverse of the pattern, in Glasgow's final two novels, Asa Timberlake embodies so much of Glasgow's conscious weakness (brought on by the depression, the coming of World War II, and her ill health) that she dreams into being a series of positive characteristics through him: his gentleness, his freedom-encouraging love for Roy, his respect for others, his humility, his largely unrecognized reservoir of inner strength. Some of these are traits that Glasgow seldom showed she possessed, either in the conscious or unconscious dimensions of her people; but they all emerge here. Dorinda Oakley might be considered a final candidate for this group of rounded and controlled characters inasmuch as her exemplary nature finds its necessary counterpart in the unconscious sexual desire and hatred that Glasgow has her project upon the

landscape. But in the final three pages, Glasgow tips the portrait toward the exemplary side by having Dorinda triumph
over her despair. This change is not dramatically justified and
thus forces Dorinda into the fourth group of characters.

Emergent or inchoate characters, though out of control,
probably fascinate their creators as much as the fully rounded
and controlled figures—and, in at least one way, probably in-
trigue them more. For these figures signify that the creative
force still runs strong and will tomorrow throw up new materials to be worked into shape. Inchoate characters simply fall
short of an aware artist's aesthetic judgment. They have not
been set free to live separately from their inventor. They seem
unfinished. In the American tradition, Wolfe's Eugene Gant
and George Webber provide the most conspicuous examples.
Wolfe could control Eugene's behavior as a student, but he
had not mastered the Gant weakness for motherly women and
self-destruction. Similarly, Webber as voyager and reporter
works beautifully, but in *The Web and the Rock*, Wolfe cannot
handle Webber's swings of mania and depression. It may be
the verisimilitude of the student and voyager ("Was it ever
otherwise for any man?") that satisfies the author's conscious
mind, but it is the exceptional nature of the mother-lover and
madman ("Yes, it usually is different! ") that holds the unconscious of the author and the reader in thrall. In Glasgow, the
inchoate characters may be the dominant group—especially
in her transitional or growth periods, as opposed to her periods of fulfillment. In addition to Dorinda, we have the para-
digmatic case of Virginia Pendleton, whom Glasgow first
satirized and then, half without knowing it, lavished with
love. This love probably provides a clue that Glasgow was
(around 1913) entering one of the phases in which great personal needs would surface and would emerge projected upon
characters who are out of control. She continued to have
trouble managing her distance from major characters (with
the possible exception of exemplary Gabriella Carr) through
Caroline Meade, Corinna Page, and Dorinda Oakley, until she
reached Gamaliel Honeywell, a man whose vanity she ob-

viously knew she could satirize, even if much of it was her own. By the time she wrote *Vein of Iron* and the last two novels, her power of characterization had begun to wane, although Asa Timberlake is a remarkably controlled invention and John Fincastle only less so. Because they are phantasies of their creator's emotional confusion, all of these characters, except Asa, prove psychologically intriguing even while they remain aesthetically disappointing—intriguing, no doubt, for their author as well as for the reader.

As our argument unfolds, it appears more and more likely that a response occurs in both the creator and the reader which parallels the force that pulls characters together in Glasgow's novels. If this is indeed the case, it is unlikely that Glasgow's generally exemplary females—Gabriella, Ada, and Roy—can hold any deep fascination for a mature reader, although they may attract young readers who have neither established their own independence nor put together a set of personal values. We know these women too well already—much as Ralph knows Ada or Craig knows Roy too well in himself—to be held by their mystery. The women are generally banal, like soap opera figures, because they mirror only the already familiar surfaces of life. By contrast, the characters that Glasgow created out of the shadow of her personality—especially Edmonia Bredalbane, Amy Dalrymple, Marmaduke, George Birdsong, and Lavinia Timberlake—are far more compelling. For the reader, the latter figures succeed especially when they complement dramatically rounded characters like Honeywell, Archbald, Jenny Blair, and Asa. When they merely mirror an otherwise unportrayed side of a thin major character, the way Amy and Marmaduke do Virginius Littlepage, they exert less power, probably because Glasgow has done too much of the reader's work for him by dramatically thinning all the characters into abstract types. The appeal becomes the intellectual interest of satire rather than the emotional force of comedy and tragedy. Not after her first protagonist, Michael Akershem of *The Descendant*—a character who at once attracts and frightens—did Glasgow embrace the shadow side of her personality directly to build an entire book around one of her inner devils, the way the Marquis de Sade generally did, or Herman Melville with Ahab, or Mark Twain with the Satan of *The Mysterious Stranger*, or more recently Robert Stone with the drug demons who drive his *Dog Soldiers*.

Glasgow was not on intimate terms with her demons. They turn up chiefly in the deeply repressed hatred and sexuality of Dorinda, in Archbald's selfishness effectively disguised as moral idealism, in the philosophical idealism with which John Fincastle disguises his disgust for the whole world of idiots, and as the longing so many of her heroines betray for the authority of a fatherly lover. Because Glasgow did not know her devils well, when they appear, they generally speak with the vital voice of her unconscious. The buried life of such characters lends them an intense psychological appeal even when their hidden dimensions evade the author's dramatic control. But, because Glasgow failed to use her ironic art to cut herself loose emotionally from John Fincastle, Dorinda Oakley, and the other females, the reader ultimately does not know exactly what to do with the passions they generate. He is robbed of his emotional catharsis.

The case proves otherwise with Gamaliel Honeywell, Jenny Blair, General Archbald, and Asa Timberlake. The Olympian narrator cuts us loose from Honeywell. We may have projected our (male) vanity upon the judge and, in turn, introjected the spirit of his eternal youth, but the narrator shows us that we are free to laugh until it hurts. With Jenny Blair and Archbald, the violence to which they push Eva tells us at some point—perhaps when Jenny must *will* her love into being or when Archbald puts idealism *above* truth—that we must break the bond of phantasy which blurs the distinction between us and them. We may share their pity and terror, but we will pursue neither our desire nor our idealism far enough to become as heroic or as tragic as they. They may continue to live, and walk about, inside our heads until the shot ceases to echo, but we know the essential limit that separates us from them. Finally, Asa Timberlake breaks the bond between himself and the reader, as well as that between himself and Roy, when he tells his daughter that she is her own father—that we too are the creators of our own essential phantasies, that the powers we discover through characters in a book are our own.

Such is the often forgotten language of fiction, this simple magic by which we see ourselves in a mirror of words that at some point cease to be words and become people—people who are, at first, someone else walking around inside our head—and, finally, only our selves. But it is a human magic—subjective and easily betrayed by abstractions, by the mass mind, and especially by the objectivity of a criticism that models itself on the physical sciences. The power is lost whenever the observer—reader, critic, or protagonist—attempts to divorce himself systematically from the observed, whether the text or the supporting characters. The phantasies of fiction have less in common with the quantifiable phenomena of modern chemistry, physics, and biology than they have with the auditory and visual hallucinations that, according to Julian Jaynes, first made human societies possible—or than they have with the animism that enabled Ellen Glasgow in her childhood to endow "every tree" near her family's house in the country with "a name of its own and a special identity."[1]

1 Glasgow, *The Woman Within*, 27, 51; Julian Jaynes, *The Origin of Consciousness in the Breakdown of the Bicameral Mind* (Boston, 1977), especially, 138–45, 361–78. Jaynes's work appeared after the present study was written; but his argument, which draws like this one upon the ideas of E. R. Dodds, suggests a physiological explanation for the hypnotic power of fiction: fiction works (like the voice of the gods) through the primitive right hemisphere of the brain.

# Selected Bibliography

The titles listed below include only those sources cited in the preceding study and those that have exerted a significant influence on the ideas put forth. Fuller bibliographies can be found in William W. Kelly's *Ellen Glasgow: A Bibliography* and my *Without Shelter: The Early Career of Ellen Glasgow*.

SPECIAL COLLECTIONS

Alderman Library, University of Virginia, Charlottesville.
  Cabell, James Branch. Papers.
  Glasgow, Ellen. Special Collections.
Christ Church, Indianapolis. Archives.

Indianapolis *News*. Morgue.
Indianapolis Public Library. Biographical Collection.
Indiana State Library, Indianapolis. Biographical and Manuscript Collections.
Lilly Library, Indiana University, Bloomington. Bobbs-Merrill Collection.
Marion County Clerk, Indianapolis. Archives.
Presbyterian Hospital, Columbia-Presbyterian Medical Center, New York. Archives.

INTERVIEW

Baumgart, Lois Stuart, December, 1975, Indianapolis, Indiana.

BOOKS AND ARTICLES

Adams, J. Donald. "The Novels of Ellen Glasgow." *New York Times Book Review*, December 18, 1938, p. 1.

Aurelius, Marcus. *The Thoughts of the Emperor Marcus Aurelius Antoninus*. Translated by George Long. Philadelphia: Altemus, n.d.

*Bhagavad Gita; or, The Lord's Song*. Translated by Annie Besant. London: Theosophical Society, 1896.

Booth, Wayne C. *The Rhetoric of Fiction*. Chicago: University of Chicago Press, 1961.

Bradley, F. H. *Appearance and Reality*. London: Sonnenschein, 1906.

Campbell, Joseph. *The Hero with a Thousand Faces*. New York: Meridian, 1956.

Carpenter, Edward. *The Art of Creation: Essays on the Self and Its Powers*. New York: Macmillan, 1904.

Collins, Joseph. "Ellen Glasgow's New Novel: A Tragedy of Old Age." *New York Times Book Review*, September 12, 1926, p. 5.

De Voto, Bernard. *The World of Fiction*. Cambridge: Riverside Press, 1950.

Dodds, E. R. *The Greeks and the Irrational*. Berkeley: University of California Press, 1968.

Epictetus. *The Teaching of Epictetus*. Translated by T. W. Rolleston. New York: Alden, 1889.

Frazee, Monique Parent. "Ellen Glasgow as Feminist." *Ellen Glasgow: Centennial Essays*. Edited by M. Thomas Inge. Charlottesville: University Press of Virginia, 1976.

Freud, Sigmund. *The Collected Papers of Sigmund Freud*. Edited by Ernest Jones. New York: Basic Books, 1959.

———. *A General Introduction to Psychoanalysis*. New York: Permabooks, 1953.

Frye, Northrop. *Anatomy of Criticism*. Princeton: Princeton University Press, 1957.

Glasgow, Ellen. *The Ancient Law*. New York: Doubleday, Page, 1908.

———. *Barren Ground*. New York: Grosset & Dunlap, 1925.

———. *The Battle-Ground*. New York: Doubleday, Page, 1902.

———. *Beyond Defeat: An Epilogue to an Era*. Edited by Luther Y. Gore. Charlottesville: University Press of Virginia, 1966.

———. *The Builders*. Garden City, N.Y.: Doubleday, Page, 1919.

———. *A Certain Measure*. New York: Kraus Reprint Co., 1969.

———. *The Collected Stories of Ellen Glasgow*. Edited by Richard K. Meeker. Baton Rouge: Louisiana State University Press, 1963.

———. *The Deliverance*. New York: Doubleday, Page, 1904.

———. *The Descendant*. New York: Harper, 1897.

————. *In This Our Life*. New York: Harcourt, Brace, 1941.

————. *Letters of Ellen Glasgow*. Edited by Blair Rouse. New York: Harcourt, Brace, 1958.

————. *Life and Gabriella: The Story of a Woman's Courage*. New York: Grosset & Dunlap, 1916.

————. *The Miller of Old Church*. Garden City, N.Y.: Doubleday, Page, 1911.

————. *One Man in His Time*. Garden City, N.Y.: Doubleday, Page, 1922.

————. *Phases of an Inferior Planet*. New York: Harper, 1898.

————. *The Romance of a Plain Man*. New York: Macmillan, 1909.

————. *The Romantic Comedians*. Garden City, N.Y.: Doubleday, Page, 1926.

————. *The Sheltered Life*. Garden City, N.Y.: Doubleday, Doran, 1932.

————. *They Stooped to Folly*. Garden City, N.Y.: Doubleday, Doran, 1929.

————. *Vein of Iron*. New York: Harcourt, Brace, 1935.

————. *Virginia*. Garden City, N.Y.: Doubleday, Page, 1913.

————. *The Voice of the People*. New York: Doubleday, Page, 1900.

————. *The Woman Within*. New York: Harcourt, Brace, 1954.

————. *The Wheel of Life*. New York: Doubleday, Page, 1906.

Godbold, E. Stanly, Jr. *Ellen Glasgow and the Woman Within*. Baton Rouge: Louisiana State University Press, 1972.

Gore, Luther Y., ed. *Beyond Defeat*. Charlottesville: University Press of Virginia, 1966.

Halperin, John, ed. *The Theory of the Novel*. New York: Oxford University Press, 1974.

"Henry Anderson Tells of Work in Roumania." Richmond *Times-Dispatch*, July 12, 1918, p. 4.

Hillman, James. *The Myth of Analysis: Three Essays in Archetypal Psychology*. Evanston, Ill.: Northwestern University Press, 1972.

Holland, Robert. "Miss Glasgow's Prufrock." *American Quarterly*, IX (Winter, 1957), 435–40.

Holman, C. Hugh. "April in Queenborough: Ellen Glasgow's Comedies of Manners." *Sewanee Review*, LXXXII (Spring, 1974), 264–83.

————. "The Comedies of Manners." *Ellen Glasgow: Centennial Essays*, edited by M. Thomas Inge. Charlottesville: University Press of Virginia, 1976.

————. *Three Modes of Modern Southern Fiction: Ellen Glasgow, William Faulkner, Thomas Wolfe.* Athens: University of Georgia Press, 1966.

Inge, M. Thomas, ed. *Ellen Glasgow: Centennial Essays.* Charlottesville: University Press of Virginia, 1976.

James, Henry. *The Portrait of a Lady.* Cambridge, Mass.: Riverside Press, 1956.

Jaynes, Julian. *The Origin of Consciousness in the Breakdown of the Bicameral Mind.* Boston: Houghton Mifflin, 1977.

Jung, C. G. *Four Archetypes: Mother, Rebirth, Spirit, Trickster.* Translated by R. F. C. Hull. London: Routledge & Kegan Paul, 1972.

————. *Two Essays on Analytical Psychology.* Translated by R. F. C. Hull. New York: World Publishing Co., 1956.

Jung, C. G., et al., eds. *Man and His Symbols.* Garden City, N.Y.: Doubleday, 1964.

Kelly, William W. *Ellen Glasgow: A Bibliography.* Charlottesville: Bibliographical Society of Virginia, 1964.

Kolodny, Annette. *The Lay of the Land: Metaphor as Experience and History in American Life and Letters.* Chapel Hill: University of North Carolina Press, 1975.

————. "The Unchanging Landscape: The Pastoral Impulse in Simms's Revolutionary War Romances." *Southern Literary Journal,* V (Fall, 1972), 46–67.

Kristiansen, Marianne. "Work and Love, or How the Fittest Survive: A Study of Ellen Glasgow's *Life and Gabriella.*" *Language and Literature,* II (1973), 105–25.

Lecky, W. E. H. *The History of the Rise and Influence of the Spirit of Rationalism in Europe.* 2 vols. New York: Appleton, 1892.

MacDonald, Edgar E., ed. *The Ellen Glasgow Newsletter.* Nos. 1–6 (1974–77).

———— "An Essay in Bibliography." *Ellen Glasgow: Centennial Essays,* edited by M. Thomas Inge. Charlottesville: University Press of Virginia, 1976.

Maeterlinck, Maurice. *Wisdom and Destiny.* Translated by Alfred Sutro. New York: Dodd, Mead, 1903.

McDowell, Frederick P. W. *Ellen Glasgow and the Ironic Art of Fiction.* Madison: University of Wisconsin Press, 1963.

Meeker, Richard K., ed. *The Collected Stories of Ellen Glasgow.* Baton Rouge: Louisiana State University Press, 1963.

Miller, David L. *The New Polytheism.* New York: Harper & Row, 1974.

Murr, Judy Smith. "History in *Barren Ground* and *Vein of Iron*: Theory, Structure, and Symbol." *Southern Literary Journal*, VIII (Fall, 1975), 40–41.

Parent, Monique. *Ellen Glasgow, Romancière*. Paris: A. G. Nizet, 1962.

Raper, J. R. "Ambivalence Toward Authority: A Look at Glasgow's Library, 1890–1906." *Mississippi Quarterly*, XXXI (Winter, 1977–78), 5–16.

———. *Without Shelter: The Early Career of Ellen Glasgow*. Baton Rouge: Louisiana State University Press, 1971.

Richards, Marion K. *Ellen Glasgow's Development as a Novelist*. The Hague: Mouton, 1971.

Rouse, Blair. *Ellen Glasgow*. New York: Twain, 1962.

Rouse, Blair, ed. *Letters of Ellen Glasgow*. New York: Harcourt, Brace, 1958.

Rubin, Louis D., Jr. *The Teller in the Tale*. Seattle: University of Washington Press, 1967.

Todorov, Tzvetan. *The Fantastic: A Structural Approach to a Literary Genre*. Translated by Richard Howard. Ithaca, N.Y.: Cornell University Press, 1975.

Tutwiler, Carrington C., Jr. *A Catalogue of the Library of Ellen Glasgow*. Charlottesville: Bibliographical Society of the University of Virginia, 1969.

West, Ray B., ed. *Essays in Modern Literary Criticism*. New York: Holt, Rinehart, & Winston, 1961.

# Index

103, 104, 156, 175, 182, 195, 196,
197; as economically powerful,
19, 25, 39, 173, 174, 194, 195; as
intellectually dominating, 37, 39,
91, 173, 179, 182; pattern of development, 44, 45, 195–97; female
side of, 55, 61, 103, 105*n*, 181; as
"good little boys," 64, 124, 135;
as father figures, 102, 129–131,
140, 141, 174–77; and sexuality,
108–109, 111, 113, 116, 186, 196–
97; and matriarchy, 118–29 *passim*, 133–35, 137, 172, 173, 178,
198; and guilt, 123, 134, 189; and
weakness, 132, 139, 141, 156, 195,
203; as unfaithful husbands, 139,
144, 147; as southern males, 139,
200; and sacrifice, 175, 196–99,
203; and their needs, 182, 183,
196, 197; as authority figures, 28,
39, 194; as protagonists, 195–96,
197; different types, 201–207. *See
also*, Projection; Sex; Women;
and names of specific characters
Mencken, H. L., 79, 151
Metaphysics, 41, 160, 164–65
Mill, John Stuart, 4
*Miller of Old Church, The*, 10, 166
Milton, John, 201, 202
Morton, Thomas, 151
Mulhern, 34, 37
Mysticism, 2, 8, 9–10, 11, 165
Mythology, 83–88

Norris, Frank, 15, 161

Oakley, Dorinda, 66–82 *passim*, 166,
177, 185, 191, 194–96, 200–204, 206
O'Hara, Ben, 29–34, 37, 194, 196
*One Man in His Time*, 36, 40–52, 53,
194, 196. *See also* Culpeper, Ste-
phen; Page, Corinna; Vetch,
Gideon; Vetch, Patty
O'Neill, Eugene, 199

Page, Corinna, 42, 46–51, 194, 204
Page, Walter Hines, 8, 14
Paradise, Frank Isley, 9
"Past, The," 54, 70–71

Pedlar, Nathan, 91–93, 96, 98, 194
Peyton, Arthur, 19, 22–26, 32, 194–96
Phantasy: and projection, xiii, 103,
128, 193; versus fantasy, 12; and
the supernatural, 12; and reality,
21, 61, 65, 168, 193; romantic, 26,
29, 108, 174; Glasgow's attitude toward, 35, 57, 64–65, 138, 149, 200;
and Jungian psychology, 57; positive use of, 57, 68, 77, 78, 88, 89,
98, 178, 179, 193, 195, 200; and illusion, 57, 200; essential, 98(def.),
193, 194, 200, 207; male and female, 194, 200; Glasgow's, 200–201,
205; reader's 206, 207. *See
also* Dreams
*Phases of an Inferior Planet*, 5, 6
Plato, 11, 12, 13
Plotinus, 11, 164
Poe, Edgar Allan, 75, 78
Politics, 39, 41, 44, 48–49, 50, 51
Presbyterianism, 3, 80, 82, 85, 86, 89,
91, 99, 150, 152
"Professional Instinct, The," 54, 59,
63. *See also* Estbridge, John

Projection: and phantasy, xiii, 103,
128, 193; women upon men, 22–35
*passim*, 91, 92, 194, 195; as literary
technique, 30, 77, 80, 81, 83, 88,
102, 103, 201; stages of, 44, 45, 51;
men upon women, 55, 60, 61, 103–
105, 105*n*, 197; and Jungian psychology, 57; and supernatural, 66,
70, 73; upon landscapes, 79, 81, 95,
97, 98, 99, 204; men upon younger
men, 103; and puritanism, 159; by
Glasgow, 204; by readers, 206
Protestantism. *See* Calvinism; Presbyterianism; Puritanism
Proust, Marcel, 19
Psychology. *See* Freud, Sigmund;
Jung, Carl; Projection
Puritanism, 80, 151–60, 167, 169, 197.
*See also* Calvinism

Realism, literary, 1, 7, 14–19 *passim*,
35, 57, 63, 64, 77, 191–93, 199
Reality: surface vs. core, xi, 5, 19, 20,
35, 42, 61, 62, 63, 82, 138, 177–78;